MEDICAL ASTROLOGY

MEDICAL ASTROLOGY

Dr. Onkarlal Sharma "Prmad"

GYAN PUBLISHING HOUSE

NEW DELHI-2

MEDICAL ASTROLOGY
(Astrology)

ISBN : 81-212-0618-9

Published in 1999 in India by
Gyan Publishing House
5, Ansari Road
New Delhi-110002

Laser Type Setting at : K Computer Services,
Printed at : Mehra Offset Press, New Delhi

Dedicated to my beloved mother Laxmi Bai who left me on 23-9-1938 to serve the world

Medical Astrology *is written for those who want to live believe in astrology. Not for those who want to live only for taste and enjoyment*

Contents

Preface

The book *Medical Astrology* was intended only to be submitted in the form of thesis for degree of Doctor of Philosophy (Astrology) by the author to the Open International University, Colombo (Sri Lanka). The thesis was accepted and the Ph.D. (Astrology) degree was conferred on the author in November, 1997, awarded gold medal on merit basis.

In this book the emphasis is given to the relation between astrology and Ayurveda for the last thousands of years in India and eastern countries. As remedial measures *Yogasan, Pranayam, Yantra, Mantra, Tantra,* urine therapy, herbal therapy, gems therapy, colour therapy, acupressure, palmistry, numerology, horary astrology, *Swara Vigyan,* etc. are dealt in short as a guidance to those who desire of good health and long easygoing life. Some other remedial measures such as Homoeopathy, Allopathy and other modern scientific methods are not included in this volume. However, Homoeopathy is a cheap and reliable method of treatment.

To what extent the book is useful to general readers and to those who are interested in medical astrology only time will show. If readers are benefited and guided to some extent, I think my labour and study of predictive astrology for last 36-37 years has been proved successful. I am obliged to Shri Amit Garg, Director Publication, Gyan Publishing House, New Delhi to bring out the book promptly in world market for readers' welfare.

Ashok Nagar (Guna) M.P. **Dr. Onkarlal Sharma "Prmad"**

1.1.1999

PART I

RELATION BETWEEN ASTROLOGY AND MEDICAL SCIENCE

1

Astrology and Medical Science

What is Astrology?

Astrology is a great and wonderful science. It is the divine knowledge of nature which consists of the study of the positions of the stars and the movements of the planets which affect all the events of the world. It is the store of knowledge based on truth felt by our great *rishis* and *munis* like Bhrigu, Parashar, Narad, Garg, Jaimini, Satyacharya, Varahamihir, Kalyan Verma, Mantreshwar, Vaidya Nath, Kalidasa, etc. It is said about astrology

अप्रत्यक्षाणि शास्त्राणि विवादस्तेषु केवलं

प्रत्यक्षं ज्योतिष शास्त्रं चन्द्रार्कौ यस्य साक्षिणौ

This means other sciences are indirect and there is dispute among them but astrology is a direct perfect science whose witnesses are the Sun and the Moon. Astrology studies our past, present and future. It gives thc knowledge of our previous life's actions which brings fruition in our present life. It lightens our paths of progress and guides our future so that we can make time more useful.

Varaha Mihir, one of the greatest of Indian, astrologers says in the *Brihata Jataka*—

कर्मार्जितं पूर्वभवे सदादि यत्तस्य पक्तिं समाभिव्यनक्ति

which means astrology speaks of the results of good and bad deeds of men's previous births.

Kalyan Verma says in *Saravali*

यदुपचित मन्य जन्मनि शुभाशुभं कर्मणः पक्तिम्

व्यञ्जयति शास्त्रमेतत् तमसि द्रव्याणि दीप इव

This means whatever good or bad deed is done by man in previous life astrology reveals it like a lamp in the darkness. It gives us light in our way of life so it is called *Jyotish Shastra* or Knowledge of Light.

Close Relationship between Medical Science and Astrology

Medical science deals with our bodily defects, diseases, deficiencies and prescribes suitable medicines to recover health. As we all know good health is the first happiness of our life. Some classes of wisemen say that astrology is superstition but they cannot prove "how astrology is superstition". Astrology in the wide sense is connected with every branch of knowledge. So it is nearly connected with medical science too.

Hippocrates of cos (c. 430 B.C.), Greek physician, called the father of Allopathy said : "A physician without the knowledge of astrology has no right to call himself a physician." Through the position of planets in horoscope astrology helps in finding out the causes of diseases, time (of occurrence and duration of diseases). It also helps to foretell in which particular *Nakshatra* and what time medicine should be taken. There is arrangement for selection of auspicious time calling *Muhurtas*.

Dr Kallman of the Psychiatric Institute of New York (USA) said, "Every being has a clock set at the moment of his birth which predetermines particularly illnesses and accidents."

In ancient times astrology and medicine were intimately connected. An Ayurvedic Vaidya (medical doctor) was required to be an astrologer too. Dr B.V. Raman said, "An experienced astrologer could indicate the predisposition of a person towards heart disease, high blood pressure, cancer, etc. with considerable accuracy."

Ayurveda is an upveda which has its roots in Atharvaveda. Ayurveda means the knowledge of longevity. How can we live long happily? For long happy living Ayurveda prescribes us herbal medicines too.

According to Charak, "Life is nothing but the union of the physical body, senses, mind and soul." Lord Dhanvantari is regarded as the propounder of Ayurveda. According to Ayurveda, the disease is known through the pulse near the root of thumbs.

Purpose of Medical Astrology

The fundamental purpose of medical astrology is to define planetary combinations which indicate various diseases, the duration of diseases and whether or not they would prove fatal, can all be known through the horoscope. To fulfil this purpose of medical astrology, Ayurveda has detailed scope for knowing the causes of diseases. The three *Skandhas* (parts) of Ayurveda known as *Hethu* (हेतु), *Linga* (लिंग) and *Aushadha* (औषध) deal with the three pillars of Ayurveda—*vata, pitta* and *kuf* (वात, पित्त, कफ), i.e., wind, bile and phlegm.

These three *dosha's* (दोष), residence in the human body the lower, middle and upper parts of the body. Thus through centuries, medicine had close relation with astrology. In olden days, an Ayurvedic Vaidya had to be well-versed in astrology but nowadays medical astrology has been quietly ignored by the medical practitioners.

Medical astrology deals with diseases like consumption, blindness, hysteria, menstrual disorders, leprosy, rheumatism, gastric troubles, cardiac troubles and many other diseases. Its practitioners predict probable diseases through the study of horoscope and altogether remedial measures were recommended but nowadays doctors treat the patient without knowing the astrological causes of diseases. Palmistry also helps in curing the diseases as the world famous palmist, astrologer and numerologist Cheiro insisted on the study of these sciences in diagnosis of diseases.

The Planets and Parts of Body

According to astrology the Sun and Mars represent bile (*pitta*), Venus and Moon wind (*vata*) and phlegm (cough), Saturn and Rahu wind, Mercury nerves and three *doshas* (*vata, pitta* and *kuf*). Human body is the symbol of *Kalapurusha*. Each *rasi* or sign corresponds with certain human parts.

Sign	*Body's Part Represented*
Aries	Head
Taurus	Face
Gemini	Throat, bronchial region
Cancer	Lungs and upper part of heart
Leo	Lower part of heart, belly (stomach)
Virgo	Navel
Libra	Intestines

Sign	*Body's Part Represented*
Scorpio	Sex organs
Sagittarius	Thighs
Capricorn	Knees
Aquarius	Calves
Pisces	Feet

The planets also represent as follows :

Sun	Soul
Moon	Mind
Mars	Vitality
Mercury	Nerves
Jupiter	Heart
Venus	Sex organs
Saturn	Feet
Rahu	Bones
Ketu	Secret parts

Nakshatras, abode in the parts of body of *Kalpurusha* are as follows:

Nakshatra	*Part of the Body*
Kritika	Head
Rohini	Forehead
Mrigsira	Eyebrows
Arirdra	Eyes
Punarvasu	Nose
Pushya	Face
Ashlesha	Ears
Magha	Lips
Poorva Phalguna	Right hand
Uttra Phalguna	Left hand
Hasta	Fingers
Chitra	Neck
Swati	Chest
Vishakha	Breast
Anuradha	Upper stomach
Jyeshtha	Lower stomach
Mool	*Kukshi* (Womb)

Poorvashada	Back
Uttrashada	Backbone
Sravana	Waist
Dhanishtha	Anus
Shatbhisha	Right thigh
Poorva Bhadra Pada	Left thigh
Uttra Bhadra Pada	*Pindlees* (Calves)
Revti	*Takhne* (Knees)
Ashwini	Upper part of feet
Bharni	Lower part of feet

Diseases known through Astrology

When there are malefics in different signs and *Nakshatras* they cause various diseases in human body. The parts of body of human beings when affected by malefics in transition on the particular sign and *nakshatra* give rise to different kinds of diseases that attack and weaken the body or in *mahadasa* or *antardasa* of that planet the diseases attack that part of body which is represented by that malefic in particular *nakshatra* and sign. In planets Sun, Mars, Saturn, Rahu, Ketu are known as malefics, Moon and Mercury also behave as malefics when they are combust or weak in position. Only two planets are known as benefics, i.e., Jupiter and Venus.

Sometimes benefics behave as malefics and vice versa according to their relations and position in the particular horoscopes as there is friendship and enmity among planets.

Diseases are generally of three kinds: (a) natural, (b) seasonal, and (c) external.

Natural diseases are caused by the change or accidental events influenced by natural powers such as fire, water, air, flood, storm, bus, train and aeroplane accidents.

Seasonal diseases are those which are due to cold, heat, rain, e.g., malaria, cholera, pneumonia, dysentery, sunstroke etc.

External diseases are those which are due to acitics, spirits, planets, persons, firing, wounds, etc. These are mainly based on different external environment in different countries.

Besides, there are other kinds of diseases too: (a) physical, (b) psychological, and (c) based on circumstances. Generally, mental troubles are due to love, hate, anger, happiness, etc. So Ayurveda has given importance to three things : (a) food, (b) sleep, and (c) mental control. If we do not take proper food it will produce deficiency or weakness in the body. Sleeping is necessary depending on age factor. If we do not sleep properly, avoid rest and work in fatigue new diseases are born. Thirdly, mental control is necessary as it is said that there is a "sound mind in a sound body" and that is why it has been said "health is wealth." Hence, study of medical science and curing diseases with the knowledge of astrology is extremely useful and essential.

The Planets and Diseases

Generally, all diseases are caused by interruption in blood circulation and this is mainly due to indigestion. Planets play an important role when they are weak, combust, debilitated, retrograde, in inimical houses with or aspected by malefics, e.g.

Sun: When the Sun is weak, debilitated, in inimical house, unaspected by benefics it causes trouble in heart, eye, lungs, fractures in bones. Sun is bilious by nature so becomes the cause of indigestion. Sun is the embodiment of soul in the human body. Hence its strength plays an important role in our life as it is the master of the solar system.

Moon: Moon represents the mind. Hence when the moon is weak the mind becomes malefic. The waning Moon causes diseases connected with blood, colds, cough, venereal diseases, nasal inflammation, mental depression, etc. Moon is cool by nature. Hence its equilibrium should be maintained properly.

Mars: Diseases due to marrow are the results of weak Mars. Fever, small-pox, swelling, boils, jaundice, blood diseases, menstrual disorder, etc. are some of its effects. Mars is hot by nature like the Sun.

Mercury: All diseases caused to nerves, skin, itches, eczema, etc. occur due to a weak Mercury. Mercury controls the nervous system, speech, ups and downs in business, etc. So when Mercury is combust, retrograded, in inimical house, debilitated, the above-mentioned diseases attack on the human body.

Jupiter: Diseases of flabiness and diabetes are caused by weak Jupiter. When his sign Sagittarius and Pisces are occupied by malefics or Jupiter is with malefics, in debilitation, combust, unaspected by benefics then it causes harm to the body.

Venus: Diseases of semen, sore throat, venereal diseases, eye diseases when the Sun, Saturn are in two, twelve houses from ascendant or moon.

Saturn: Muscular pain, colds, melancholy, epilepsy, fistula, deafness, troubles in feet, paralysis, rheumatic troubles, gastric troubles, disappointment, sorrow, etc., are caused due to different positions of Saturn in horoscope. Saturn is the biggest disease-producing planet among all the planets.

Rahu: It is a cheating planet. It attacks at random and accidentally. Epilepsy, pox, worms, suicide, leprosy, pain in the body where *Rahu* is seated or in which *Nakshatra* is posited, that part of the body represented by *Rahu* are affected. External spirits, etc., are caused by *Rahu*.

Ketu : It is virtually the hidden and malefic among planets. Mysterious pain in part of the body, diseases the cause of which cannot be known, diseases by curse of deities, by unknown sins of previous lives are the handiwork of *Ketu*. All secret diseases are caused by *Ketu* which are not easily identifiable or curable.

The Twelve Signs, Relation with Twelve Tissue Salts

Sea water contains sodium chloride, magnesium, calcium, potassium and other salts. These salts are in our blood in the same ratio and proportion as in the sea water. When this proportion is imbalanced diseases caused by Moon as colds, cough, mental imbalance, epilepsy are the result. So while studying the horoscope observe the nature of sign *(Rasi)* 6th cusp, planets in the 6th house, position of lord of 6th house, aspect on the 6th house and its lord, the relation between lord of ascendant and 6th house and its lord. The 6th house is the house of diseases both from birth ascendant and Moon. In fixed signs Taurus, Leo, Scorpio, Aquarius circulatory and glandular systems are disturbed. In dual signs like Gemini, Virgo, Sagittarius and Pisces the liver is disturbed and there is also disorder of nerves. In cardinal signs like Aries, Cancer, Libra, Capricorn disturbances in renal circulation, stomach, kidney, skin, etc. are effected.

Hindu sages or *rishis* centuries earlier declared that the human body is in short the copy of the solar system. They said, यत् पिंडे तत् ब्रह्मांडे means whatever is found in our body is shortest form of the matter found elsewhere in the world at large, both outer and inner in the earth and sky, in all the universe. Hindu philosophy says that this world is made of five elements, i.e., earth, water, fire, sky and wind. These five elements are present in the human body too.

In the Zodiac there are twelve signs which are seen in the heavens. The seven planets Sun, Moon, Mars, Mercury, Jupiter, and Venus govern the twelve signs. Dragon's head *(Rahu)* and tail *(Ketu)* are called shadow planets which also help in understanding the Zodiac. All these are studied in astrology.

According to medical science there are millions of tiny cells live in our body. Whatever food we take that nourishment forms these tiny cells or tissues. These tissues or tiny cells form in our body the bones, skin, nerves, blood, etc.

As we have said earlier there are salts found in our body. The treatment through salts is called biochemic treatment of diseases in medical terminology. Dr W.H. Schuessler (1821-98) of Germany learned from Dr Samuel Hannemann how to prevent damage and to render a remedy capable of absorption in the body of deficiency. This method is called deficiency therapy.

According to deficiency therapy, the deficiency of inorganic salts in our body causes disequilibrium in the harmonious functioning of organic constituents of our body cell which can be offset by supplying the necessary proportion of inorganic salts. Biochemic treatment consists mainly in the use of the twelve tissue salts for the cure of all curable diseases.

Later, Dr G.W. Carey and Dr I.E. Perry found that there was a definite relation between the twelve tissue salts and the twelve signs of the Zodiac. These twelve signs are Aries, Taurus, Gemini, Cancer, Leo, Virgo, Libra, Scorpio, Sagittarius, Capricorn, Aquarius and Pisces. These signs are related with our birth Sun sign. Hence each Sun sign has its own salt. If proper food is not taken, deficiency of these salts arises. So biochemic tissue salts are taken as preventive measures rather than cure.

The Zodiac signs seen in the heavens are the twelve months of the year. Each sign is connected with the Sun e.g.

According to CHEIRO

Aries Sun remains in Aries from March 21 to April 20

Taurus	Sun remains in Taurus from April 21 to May 20
Gemini	Sun remains in Gemini from May 21 to June 20
Cancer	Sun remains in Cancer from June 21 to July 20
Leo	Sun remains in Leo from July 21 to August 20
Virgo	Sun remains in Virgo from August 21 to September 20
Libra	Sun remains in Libra from September 21 to October 20
Scorpio	Sun remains in Scorpio from October 21 to November 20
Sagittarius	Sun remains in Sagittarius from November 21 to December 20
Capricorn	Sun remains in Capricorn from December 20 to January 20
Aquarius	Sun remains in Aquarius from January 21 to February 19
Pisces	Sun remains in Pisces from February 20 to March 20.

These are the twelve transit periods of somya? Sun.

Now we shall elaborate the twelve signs in detail:

Aries. This is the first sign of the Zodiac whose lord is Mars. Potassium phosphate is the tissue salt found in the bodies of persons born in the period of sign Aries (when Sun transits in Aries, i.e. from March 21 to April 20). The deficiency or lack of potassium phosphate salt causes jaundice, feeling of revenge, speaking lies, headaches, hating tendency, irritability, insomnia, problems of brain, loss of memory and concentration, depression, nervous tension, dizziness, etc. When any planet transits this sign the chemical ground of understanding and material expression is badly affected and the behaviour of man is changed by adverse aspect on Aries. The Arian has more feelings of hate, revenge, speaks lies and suffers heavily from headaches. The best cure is proper food, i.e. lettuce, cauliflower, spinach, olives, potatoes, onions, cucumber, cabbage, etc., which have this salt that should be taken in daily food.

Taurus. Venus is the lord of the Zodiac sign Taurus. Venus is an emotional planet so whenever another planet transits through this sign, the mind of the person whose zodiac sign is Taurus remains in equilibrium position. The tissue salt of this sign is sodium sulphate. Whenever this salt is lacking in the Taurean body the regular water supply is disturbed and balance of lower brain, liver, pancreas, spleen, inner tissues get disturbed and emotional jealousy takes place in behaviour of the person born under the sign of, Taurus (when Sun transits in Taurus, i.e. from April 21 to May

20). The problems of bile and water rise, jaundice, blindness, vomiting, bitter taste, etc., are the resultant maladies. Hence to fulfil deficiency of tissue salt sodium sulphate celery, sprouts, carrots, spinach, figs, peaches, beets, oatmeal, almonds, coconut should be taken to maintain equilibrium position of mind.

Gemini. Potassium chloride is the tissue salt for this sign. The weight of the body is maintained by the salt. When you come across a thin body then understand that there is lack of this salt. Geminians are generally less affected by sex problems. When this salt is in inadequate proportion in the body then constipation, gangreto, pyorrhea are generally found in the patient and his behaviour becomes full of fear, hatred, nervous, etc. So to control this deficiency of salt proper food should be taken such as celery, carrot, spinach, lettuce, tomatoes, strawberries, watermelon, etc. Otherwise problems in throat, tongue, catarrah, asthma, cough, skin diseases may arise. The lord of this sign is Mercury and Mercury is very soon affected by environment. This planet is called "Somya" too which means affect on the mind is generally seen in every action.

Cancer. Calcium fluoride or fluoride of lime is the tissue salt medically prescribed for this sign whose lord is Moon. Cancerians are oversensitive and sometimes they are highly mentally disturbed and non-elasticity to tissues results in negligence of dear ones. The person suffers from tumours, cancer, insomnia, fear, suspicion bone and teeth pains, etc. The proper food for Cancerians should contain milk, cabbage, lettuce, pumpkin, watercress, etc.

Cancer also represents the heart so care should be taken in case of heart and lung ailments. When malefic affect is greater on the Cancer sign then lungs and heart are very soon affected.

Leo. As Cancer is concerned with the upper part of heart so Leo too is concerned with the lower part of the heart. Leo is mostly concerned with the heart as the centre of the circulatory system. Strength, courage and vitality are the exceptional qualities which are found in persons when Leo is not badly affected by malefics either by occupation or aspect. Phosphate of magnesium is the cell tissue salt of this sign whose lord is the Sun. It helps in flexibility of bones and elasticity to muscles and tissues. Overexertion, overexcitement should be checked for security of heart. Besides weakness of bones, problem of nerves, all types of pain, neuralgic pain, spasm of muscles of heart and other organs, etc are the main afflictions. Spinach, lettuce, almonds, cucumber, barley, fig, wheat should be taken in food. When heart is weakened fever, liver trouble, kidney, spleen and spinal problems, etc. are generally seen.

Virgo. The lord of Virgo is Mercury and tissue salt is potassium sulphate. This salt helps in excretion of the poisonous waste matter in the body and if this salt is deficient then constipation, dandruff, eczema, catarrah, pleurisy, pneumonia, diarrhoea, leucorrhoea, measles, menstrual disorder, lack of perspiration, clogging of pores of skin, etc. are found.

Spinach, cauliflower, cucumber, lettuce, cabbage, tomatoes, celery, onions, raw vegetables, fruits should be taken in food. Virgo people are generally happy intellectuals. Though Mercury is a calm planet but when it is affected by malefics or weak in transit the results are not beneficial.

Libra. Sodium phosphate is the tissue salt for this sign. Any planet transiting this sign and if the lord of this sign Venus aspects Libra, then the body is unable to absorb this salt and the kidney gets troubled and disturbed. Rivalry in business, envy, jealousy, fluids of nerves, liver, brain trouble, excessive acid in the body, sugar and digestion problems, vomitting, colic, diarrahoea and yellow creamy discharge from the eyes are the results. Sometimes operation becomes necessary. So to remove obstacles and disturbances rice, peas, cauliflower, cucumber, onions, carrots, spinach, celery, prunes, blueberries, strawberries, black figs, walnuts, wheat bread, almonds, coconut should be taken in food.

Scorpio. Calcium sulphate is the tissue salt for persons born in the period of Scorpio. The action of this salt is to excretion of impurities of the body either through kidneys, skin, bowels or any other means. Scorpions are generally too much fond of sexual delights, so being engaged much in sexual intercourse secret diseases are usual as internal cancer. Precaution is necessary in food taking and there should be some control over excessive sexual activities. Ulcers and blood disorders too are common. Red cabbage, onions, asparagus, gooseberries, blueberries, strawberries, coconut etc., should be taken with or after food. Excitement should be controlled as the lord of the sign is Mars who is ever-ready planet to be excited. The above-mentioned sufferings are due to lack of calcium sulphate hence the position of Scorpio and the lord Mars should be strong.

Sagittarius. Silica or silicon oxide is the tissue cell salt of this sign. Its deficiency in blood makes the person overly pessimistic. Broken nails, early baldness, irregular and broken teeth, tuberculosis, cancer, skin covering of bones are some other diseases. It promotes discharge of pus, tonsil, gout and nose, nails problems. Spinach, carrots, peas, cucumber, almonds, walnuts, wheat, barley and rye should essentially be taken in food. Jupiters position should be strong and topaz should worn in gold on first finger to remove the bad effects due to lack of this salt.

Capricorn. Calcium phosphate is the tissue cell salt of this sign which helps in building new bones. Lack of this salt causes constipation formation of stones, gravel, boils, pimples, teething trouble, weakness of bones, and problems in blood corpuscles. Nose and eye diseases too trouble capricornians. Saturn is the lord of this sign who aspects adversely in transit planets in this sign. Red cabbage, onion, lemon, spinach, turnips, lettuce, asparagus, cauliflower, upper part of potatoes, prunes, dates, pears, raisins, walnuts, almonds, wheat bread are the main foods to be taken to remove the deficiency of this salt. Proper care should be taken in regulating the routine of sleep.

Aquarius. The tissue salt of this sign is sodium chloride. It distributes water in the body. When lacking this salt dryness results in, nerve ends being unable to function, hence bloodstream is affected. Intense nervousness and desire for salty food arises. This salt regulates water in the body and acts on blood, liver, spleen to regulate water. If water is in excess in the body swelling arises in the body. Hence, to check the excess of water celery, sprouts, asparagus, cucumber, strawberries, turnips, oatmeal, almonds, and coconut should be taken in food. Aquarians are generally suspicious by nature. Fault-finding behaviour should be checked.

Pisces. Phosphate of iron or ferrum phosphate is the cell salt of this sign which helps in building nerve cells. Its deficiency leads to anaemia. Open air is very necessary for persons born in this sign. Iron needs oxygen as a carrier. Inflammation or swelling in any part of the body, colds, cough, fever occur in the body as this salt increases red cell in the blood which gives strength to circular walls of blood vessels especially the arteries. Food ripened in sunlight should be taken as they are filled with iron. Lettuce, spinach, raisins, carrots, loger berries, red cabbage, strawberries, onions, ripe olives, beans, etc. should be taken more in foods.

To sum up the twelve signs are correlated with twelve salts as follows :

	Sign	*Salt*
1.	*Aries*	Potassium phosphate
2.	*Taurus*	Sodium sulphate or sulphate of sodium
3.	*Gemini*	Potassium chloride
4.	*Cancer*	Calcium fluoride or fluoride of lime
5.	*Leo*	Magnesium of phosphate or phosphate of magnesia
6.	*Virgo*	Potassium sulphate
7.	*Libra*	Sodium phosphate
8.	*Scorpio*	Calcium sulphate or sulphate of lime
9.	*Sagittarius*	Silica or silicon oxide
10.	*Capricorn*	Calcium phosphate
11.	*Aquarius*	Sodium chloride
12.	*Pisces*	Ferrum phosphate or phosphate of iron

2

Utility of Horoscope in Diagnosis of Diseases

Diseases known through Horoscope

Our great seers found after many years of experience the combinations of planets and houses in the twelve signs in the horoscope. The defects in the body are visible in horoscope. It is also known through horoscope what disease will take place at what time in our lives. This great store of knowledge scattered in olden Sanskrit astrological texts is very valuable and should be applied to our lives.

Eye Disease

धनस्थिते क्रूरयुते सिते चेत्काणोऽथवा मंद विलोचनेन

Means when Venus is with malefic or malefics in second house the person is *Kana* or one-eyed or he has small eyes.

Dumb. If Venus is in second *nāvamsa* with malefic or malefics is in second house then the person is dumb.

Hesitating Speech. If Venus is in third house in third *Navamsa* the person's speech is not clear and he speaks by gaps or hesitantly.

The second house in horoscope is the right eye of *Kalpurusha* and twelfth house in horoscope is the left eye. So when Sun, Saturn, *Rahu* are in second house and lord of second house is combust or with malefics or does not aspect the second house then the person's right eye is defective. In the same way when there are Sun and *Rahu* in the twelfth house, lord of twelfth house is combust or with Saturn, has no aspect on twelfth house then left eye is defective.

Blindness. Natives born in Leo *lagna* and Sun and Moon are there aspected by Saturn and Mars then the person born thus is blind. But if benefics as Jupiter, Venus, Mercury aspect the *lagna* then the person has small eyes.

Blind by Left Eye. If there are Sun and Moon in the twelfth house then the person loses his left eye.

Totally Blindness:(a) When there are Sun, Mars, Saturn and Moon in second, sixth, eighth and twelfth houses respectively they make the person blind according to their strengths.

(b) When Sun and Moon are in third house or in quadrant, i.e., in first, fourth, seventh and tenth houses and Mars is posited in quadrant in the sign of malefics aspected by malefics and benefics are in sixth, eighth and twelfth houses, Sun is in tenth house then the person is blind.

(c) Malefics are in fourth and fifth houses and Moon is in sixth, eighth and twelfth houses the man is blind. But if benefics aspect with less strength then there is some relief from blindness or short-sightedness.

Night Blindness. If Mercury and Venus are in evil houses, i.e., in sixth, eighth or twelfth houses, the person is unable to see at night.

Birth Blindness. When Venus, Sun and lord of *lagna* or ascendant are in evil houses, i.e., 6, 8, 12 then the person born with this combination in his horoscope is blind by birth.

Eye Disease. When lord of sixth house is in the sign of Mars, i.e., in Aries or Scorpio or is with Mars then the person suffers from eye disease.

Shortsight. When in twelfth house there are Venus and Mars with Moon then the person is short-sighted.

Eye is the most important part of our body. It is said: "Eye is the world." We cannot enjoy the world without eyes. Hence when there is any kind of defect in eye/eyes known through horoscope proper treatment should be taken.

The above said combinations taken from the book *Jyotish Shyam Sangraha* in Hindi, published in 1905 a.d. Now the great authority in astrology after Varaha Mihir well known Kalyan Verma writes in "Saravali" about eye troubles and eye diseases as following:

"Mars or Saturn in 12th house destroys the eye. Saturn is the destroyer of right eye and Mars is the destroyer of left eye. If Sun and

Moon both are in 12th house or if there are malefics in 6th and 8th houses the person born in this combination is blind. Sun in 2nd house and Moon in 12th house destroys right and left eye respectively. Rahu in *lagna* and Sun in 7th house too make the person blind. These combinations should not be aspected by benefics. In the same way Moon in 6th, Sun in 8th, Saturn in 9th and Mars in 2nd houses make the person blind.

If Moon is with Mars and Saturn in 6th and 8th houses or with malefics such as Sun, *Rahu* and *Ketu* the eye of the person is destroyed by bad influence of cough. If Moon is in 8th house then right eye, if Moon is in 6th house then left eye get destroyed but if aspected by benefics then blindness is not at birth but after some time in *Mahadasa* or *avtardasa* of lord of 8th and 6th houses respectively.

If Moon is with Saturn in 8th and 12th houses aspected by malefics then eye is destroyed by molinfluence of wind (वात/विकार).

Moon with Saturn, Sun troubles the eye with various diseases. Mantreswara in *Phal Deepika* repeats the above mentioned combination in *Rog Nirnaya Adhyay* Chapter 14 Verses 10-11.

According to *Jataka Parijata* of Vaidya Nath, verses 13-78 when Venus is in 6th and 8th houses with lord of 6th house eye disease is produced.

According to *Jatakalankar* of Ganesh Daivagya:

If lord of 2nd and 12th houses with Venus and lord of ascendant are in 6th, 8th, 12th evil houses the person born with this combination is blind. In the same way, Moon with Venus and malefics in 2nd house makes the person blind.

Ear Diseases

According to *Phal Deepika* if there are Jupiter and Mars with Saturn or aspected by Saturn in 3rd and 11th houses they cause ear disease. From 3rd house right ear and from 11th house left ear are considered. Jupiter is indicator of sky element. Saturn and Mars are indicators of sufferings. Hence when Jupiter will be with Saturn or Mars or will aspect Saturn and Mars or will be aspected by both or one of them in 3rd and 11th houses ear disease is indicated.

According to *Jyotish Shyam Sangraha* when Venus and Mars are in 2nd and 12th houses then the person suffers from ear diseases. When in horoscope malefics are in 3rd, and 5th, 9th and 11th houses unaspected by benefics then the person is born deaf.

When Mercury with lord of 7th house is in sign of Mars that is in Aries or Scorpio aspected by Saturn or be in 6th house or aspects the 6th house then the affected person is deaf.

According to *Saravali* of Kalyan Verma, if Moon aspected or combined with malefics is in 1st, 3rd and 11th houses the person suffers from ear diseases. If malefics be in 5th and 9th houses aspected by malefics the person suffers from eye disease.

If malefics be in 9th house then suffering is in right ear but when in 5th house then suffering of left ear is indicated.

According to Varaha Mihira's *Brihat Jatak,* when malefics in 3rd, 9th and 11th houses person suffers from deafness. Malefics means weak Moon, Sun and Mars.

Mouth Diseases: In mouth, tongue and teeth are the main parts. When Moon with Mars is in *lagna* or ascendant the person is like a dumb and if lord of 6th house and Mercury are in *lagna* then the tongue of the person is cut and he cannot speak properly.

When *Rahu* is in second house then the person has long teeth with disease in teeth.

When birth ascendants are Aries, Taurus and Sagittarius and malefics are posited in them then the teeth of the person are not well.

According to *Phalit Vikas* of Ramyatna Ojha if *Rahu* and *Ketu* are in 6th and 8th houses the person suffers from teeth trouble.

Malefics in 7th house too causes decomposition of teeth.

Dysentery: If Venus and Mars occupy the 7th house combined and malefics Sun, Saturn, *Rahu*, *Ketu*, weak Moon aspect them, then there is serious danger of dysentery to them in whose horoscope this combination is present.

Diseases in Secret Places

If Moon is in the *Navamsa* of Cancer or Scorpio and is in conjunction with malefics then there is possibility of diseases in secret places as sex organs, testes, anus, etc.

In the same way when lord of 6th or 8th house be in 7th house or lord of 6th house be in 8th house then the person suffers from disease in anus.

Seventh house is the house of sex organs and 8th house is the house of anus. Venus is the indicator of sex organs. So when Venus is in 7th or 8th house it denotes diseases of semen, urine, diabetes, etc.

What is Navamsa?

It has come in many places while dealing with diseases, causes of diseases, that Moon or any other planet in 1 to 9 *Navamsa* or any other planet or ascendant is in certain *Navamsa.* Hence it is necessary to know well what is *Navamsa?*

Navamsa is 9th part of 30° that 3° 20 *kalas* indicate one *Navamsa.* Ascendant and 12 signs have 30° each. To find out *Navamsa* I am giving here a short chart so that the readers may easily find out the *Navamsa* of any sign.

Navamsa Chart

Signs	*1-5-9 Aries-Leo-Sagittarius*	*2-6-10 Taurus-Virgo-Capricorn*	*3-7-11 Gemini-Libra-Aquarius*	*4-8-12 Cancer-Scorpio-Pisces*	*Degrees 0*	*Kalas 1*
1st *Navamsa*	1 Aries	10 Capricorn	7 Libra	4 Cancer	3	20
2nd *Navamsa*	2 Taurus	11 Aquarius	8 Scorpio	5 Leo	6	40
3rd *Navamsa*	3 Gemini	12 Pisces	9 Sagittarius	6 Virgo	10	00
4th *Navamsa*	4 Cancer	1 Aries	10 Capricorn	7 Libra	13	20
5th *Navamsa*	5 Leo	2 Taurus	11 Aquarius	8 Scorpio	16	40
6th *Navamsa*	6 Virgo	3 Gemini	12 Pisces	9 Sagittarius	20	00
7th *Navamsa*	7 Libra	4 Cancer	1 Aries	10 Capricorn	23	20
8th *Navamsa*	8 Scorpio	5 Leo	2 Taurus	11 Aquarius	26	40
9th *Navamsa*	9 Sagittarius	6 Virgo	3 Gemini	12 Pisces	30	00

Lagna or ascendant is seed, Moon sign is flower and *Navamsa* is the fruit. Hence in predictive astrology the last result, i.e., fruit is known through *Navamsa.* Any planet weak in ascendant such as in debilitation, combust, in inimical sign may be in *Navamsa* in exaltation, in friendly sign, in own sign hence may be powerful. So, finding out of *Navamsa* is very useful to find out the exact result.

Leprosy: (1) Moon in ascendant or *lagna* Sun in 7th house and malefics *Kuja* (Mars) and Saturn in 2nd and 12th houses denote leprosy.

(2) When Moon is in 5th *Navamsa* of Sagittarius or is in the *Navamsa* of Aries, Cancer, Capricorn and Pisces of any sign with Saturn or Mars. To make it clear suppose Moon is in Sagittarius what is 5th *Navamsa* of Sagittarius it means that in *Navamsa* of Leo, it falls between 13°-20' to 16°-40'. To make more clear it means that the Moon is between 13°-20' to 16°-40'.

In *Navamsa* of Aries, Cancer, Capricorn and Pisces mean of Moon may be in 1st *Navamsa* of Aries, Leo, Sagittarius.

Moon may be in 4th *Navamsa* of Taurus, Virgo, Capricorn.

Moon may be in 7th *Navamsa* of Gemini, Libra, Aquarius.

In the same way by degrees and *kalas* and Moon we can find out the *Navamsa* of Cancer, Capricorn, Pisces with the help of *Navamsa* chart.

(3) When Scorpio, Cancer, Taurus, Capricorn are 5th or 9th signs from any ascendant having aspect or conjunction of a malefic the person will suffer from leprosy. From Cancer ascendant Scorpio is 5th, Pisces is 9th sign. From Scorpio ascendant Pisces is 5th, Cancer is 9th sign. From Capricorn ascendant Taurus is 5th sign. From Virgo ascendant Taurus is the 9th sign, Capricorn 5th sign.

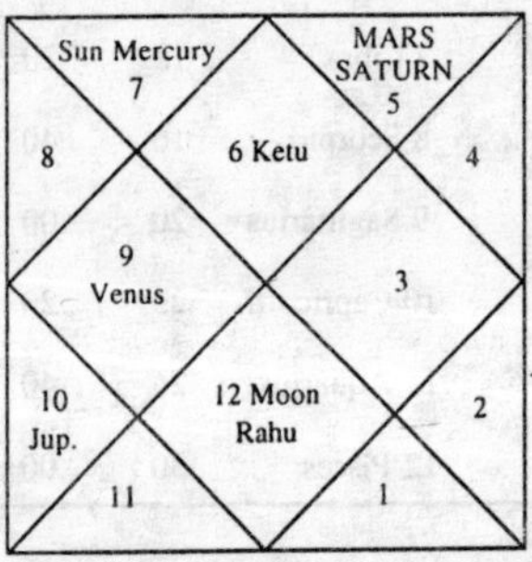

It means that persons born in Cancer, Scorpio, Pisces, Capricorn and Virgo ascendants having malefics aspect on 5th and 9th houses suffer from leprosy. Signs Cancer, Scorpio, Pisces are watery signs indicating blood. Signs Virgo and Taurus are earthy sign indicating skin.

Example of Leprosy: A male was born on 4-11-1949 at 3 a.m. at Lat. 24°-36′ north longitude 77°-13′ east in Virgo ascendant as following:

Vikrami Samvat 2006 *Saka* 1871 *Kartik Shukla* 13 Thursday 37/26 *Uttra Bhadra Pada Nakshatra* 3/56 with planetary position as following: *Rewati* 4th *Charan*.

SUN 6/18/25 MARS 4/9/52 JUP.9/3/23 SAT 4/25/10

MOON 11/28/0 MER.6/6/12 VEN. 8/3/17 *Rahu* 5/25/50

NAVAMSA

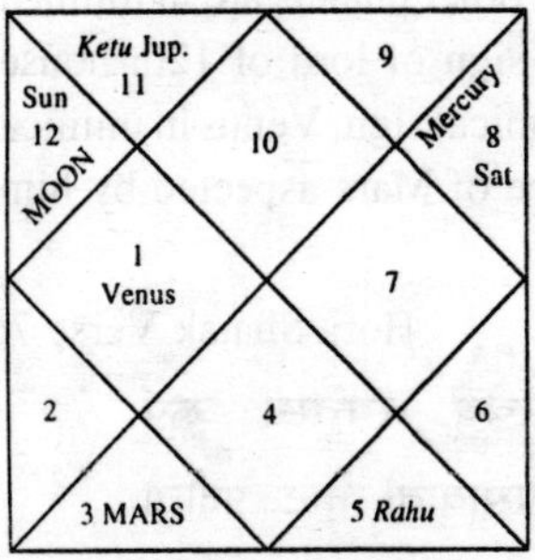

Balance of *Vimshottari Mahadasa* of Mercury. Balance 7 years, 10 months, 13 days. In the age of 39-40, i.e., in 1988-89 the person suffered from leprosy in Sun *Mahadasa*.

The combination for leprosy have been explained above. Just see the correctness of astrology in indicating the disease leprosy. I was astonished when I marked the full combination of leprosy in this horoscope.

According to *Jyotish Shyam Sangraha* Chapter 7, Verses 25-26.

पाप मध्य नव भाग गे विधौ मंद भौम युत वीक्षितेऽथवा।

मेष नक्र झष कर्कटांशगे कुष्ठवानपि भवेत्तदा नरः ।। 25 ।।

धी धर्मस्था गोकुलीरारिनक्राः क्रूरैः रवेटेः संयुता वीक्षिता वा।

ते वै नूनं सूतिकाले प्रकुर्युर्निः संदिग्धं मानवं कुष्टयुक्तम् ।। 26 ।।

It means when Moon is in *Navamsas* of Aries, Capricorn, Cancer, Pisces, between malefics aspected by Saturn, Mars then the person suffers from leprosy.

When in horoscope in 5th and 9th houses be Taurus, Cancer, Scorpio, Capricorn signs with or aspected by malefics the person suffers from leprosy undoubtedly.

Here in this case Virgo is ascendant and in 5th house is Capricorn sign in 9th house is Taurus sign. The fifth house is aspected by *Ketu* a malefic, 9th house is aspected by Saturn and Moon in Pisces is in *Navamsa* of Pisces with *Rahu* aspected by *Ketu* and Mars.

Ascendant is with *Ketu* a malefic, lord of ascendant Mercury is with another malefic Sun who is debilitated and lord of 12th house. Hence ascendant and Moon both are in *Papakartari* Yoga as ascendant in between Sun, Mars, Saturn and *Ketu*. In the same way Moon with *Rahu* aspected by Mars has been badly affected. However, Moon is in *Vargottam Navamsa* but due to evil influence of malefics it has been neutralised.

In *Navamsa* chart the *Navamsa lagna* is Capricorn, the sign of natural malefic Saturn. The lord of Navamsa lagna Saturn is with lord of birth ascendant Mercury in the sign of Mars, the bitter enemy of Saturn and Mercury. Moon with Saturn and most of the other planets are in inimical house, e.g., lord of *Navamsa lagna* in the sign of lord of 12th house, Jupiter in malefic sign with Ketu, Mars is inimical sign, Venus in inimical sign. *Navamsa lagna* is under evil influence of Mars aspected by him. Other Sanskrit texts approve leprosy thus:

Hora Shatak Verse 76

बुधो लग्नपश्चेतग्रुपमेव चन्द्रस्त्वेवं रक्तस्य रूपं
शनेर गोश्चेदृग्योगयुक्तो मलिन प्रभावात् कुष्ट प्रदौतौ
शशांक तत्पुत्र विलग्ननाथा सराहवः केतुयुतास्त्वंगे
वैश्यं तु कुष्टं मुनयो वदंति शुभेक्षितस्तत्र न भवेन्तदानीम्

Sarvartha Chintamani

Means Mercury and Moon represent skin and blood and when they are lord of ascendant aspected or with Saturn and *Rahu* then give leprosy disease,—M.S. 76. When Moon, Mercury and lord of ascending are with *Rahu, Ketu* unaspected by benefics cause leprosy. This is true in the above example of leprosy.

Causes of Diseases

Phal Deepika is the best book of predictive astrology. In its 14th chapter *"Roga Nirnaya"* details are given about causes of diseases. I am mentioning here in short the essence. According to Sun the following diseases are caused.

(1) Bile (2) Hot fever (3) Inflammation in body (4) Epilepsy (5) Heart disease (6) Eye disease (7) Diseases below navel or below *(Kakhari)* (8) Skin disease (9) Bone disease (10) Fear from enemies (11) Diseases caused by wood (12) Fire, arms or poisonous diseases (13) Psychological diseases (It wife or son is suffering from any disease or the person is psychologically disturbed by them) (14) Fear from thieves or quadrupeds (15) Serpent bite (16) Fear from king or Lord Shiva or Yama Raj.

According to Moon the following diseases are caused: 1. Sleeping disease—either insomnia or walking while sleeping, 2. Cough, 3. Dysentery, 4. Tumour, 5. Malaria, 6. Idleness, 7. Fear from animals with horns or living in water, 8. Constipation or loss of appetite, 9. No desire of food, disinterest in food, 10. Psychological problems created by ladies, 11. Jaundice, 12. Blood disturbance (leprosy, etc.), 13. Fear from water, 14. Fatigue in mind, 15. Pains from gods, ghosts, spirits, snake, Yakshini, etc.

According to Mars the following diseases are caused: (1) More thirst, (2) Wind or bile attack, (3) Bilious fever, fear from fire, arms, poison, (4) Tumour in stomach, appendicitis, (5) Leprosy, (6) Eye disease, (7) Epilepsy, (8) Bone marrow disease, (9) Itches, (10) Roughness in skin, (11) Fracture in any part of the body, (12) Fear from government, fire and thieves, (13) Conflict with friends, brothers and sons, (14) Battle with enemies, (15) Fear from planet, giants or diseases on upper part of the body.

Mercury causes the following diseases in the body: (1) Illusion in intellect, unnecessary fear, (2) Throat infection, (3) Eye disease, (4) Goitre, (5) Nose disease, (6) Cold, cough, wind fever, (7) Disease due to poison, (8) Skin disease, (9) Jaundice, (10) Itches, bad dream, (11) Fear from fire, (12) Gandharva diseases.

Diseases which are caused by Jupiter are as follows: (1) Tumour in stomach, appendicitis, (2) Typhoid, (3) Coma, cough, as Jupiter is controller of cough, (4) Ear diseases, (5) Pains from temple's property, (6) Curse of Brahmins, (7) Litigation in case of money, trust or banks, (8) Conflict or pain through *yaksha, kinnar, gandharva,* (9) Trouble due to disobeying the parents, teachers or misbehaviour with them. Such sufferings occur in *Dasa, Mahadasa* and *Antardasa* of Jupiter.

Planet Venus produces these diseases: (1) Anaemia, (2) Diseases of cough, wind and eye, (3) Urinary, diabetes, syphilis or diseases due to increase of prostrate glands, (4) Lack of semen, (5) Unable to perform sexual deeds, (6) Weakness, lack of smoothness in mouth due to excess sexual deed, (7) Constipation of the body, (8) Fear from unseen deities, (9) Loss of friendship.

Saturn is the main *karaka* or planet of diseases. The position of Saturn is like a magistrate who punishes for ill deeds due to previous life's sins. The following diseases are caused by Saturn: (1) Diseases produced by wind and cough, (2) Pain in legs, (3) Fatigue due to excess labour, (4) Illusion, (5) Bulio, (6) More heat in the body, (7) Mental shock due to servant's unwilling actions, (8) Calamities of wife and children or other family members, (9) Hurt or injury in any part of the body, (10) Hurt, wound due to trees, stones, (11) Internal heart melancholy, (12) Pain of ghosts, (13) Anticipatory troubles such as death of parents, family members by accidents or heart attack or by any other means.

Rahu is the most malefic planet. He causes the following diseases: (1) Heart disease (2) Inflammation in heart (3) Leprosy (4) Illusion (5) Hurt, injury in legs (6) Sufferings to family members or troubles due to them (7) Diseases due to self-errors (8) Diseases due to poison (9) Fear from serpents or ghosts, giants, etc.

Ketu produces such troubles which are turned into serious diseases as conflicts or struggle between two castes, unknown mysterious diseases which cannot be quickly diagnosed by doctors or due to divine anger of supernatural forces which are unknown to us.

More on Planets and Diseases

According to *Phal Deepika* the diseases are caused by planets as following:

Sun. Excess bile, secretion hot fever, inflammation in the body, epilepsy, heart disease, below navel or bubo, skin and bone diseases, fears from enemy, wood, fire, arms, poison, wife, sons, thieves, animals, serpants, government, Dharma Raj (Yama Raj), Rudra, etc.

Moon. Insomnia, excessive sleeping, walking in sleep, idleness, cough, dysentery, malignant tumour, cold fever, fear from horn bearing animals or from aquatic animals, loss of appetite, dislike food, melancholy from ladies, jaundice, impurity in blood, hydrophobia fatigue, fear of deities, as yakshini, evil spirits, etc.

Mars. Excessive thirst, due to wind or bile, bilious fever, fears from fire, arms, poison, leprosy, eye diseases, tumour in stomach, or appendicitis, epilepsy, diseases due to lack of adequate marrow in bones, itches, breaking of any part of body, conflicts, family troubles (from brothers, sons), etc.

Mercury. Illusions, diseases of eye, nose, throat, *Tridosha* (wind, bile, cough), poisonous diseases, skin diseases, jaundice, itches, bad (evil) dreams, neglecting behaviour, labour.

Jupiter. Diseases of stomach, tumours, pimples, appendicitis, typhus, coma, ear diseases, sufferings from temples, curse of Brahmins, litigation due to banks, trust, treasury, etc. unseen spirits, and negligence of parents, teachers.

Venus. Paleness due to anaemia, due to wind and cough, eye diseases, urinary diseases, sexually transmitted diseases like venereal diseases, gonorrhea, syphilis, trouble in urinating infertility incapability to copulate satisfactorily pimples on face, physical weakness due to excess sexual activity, fear from deities, loss of friendship, etc.

Saturn. Wind and cough diseases, trouble in legs and lameness, fatigue due to excess labour, illusion, bubo, excess, heat in body trouble from menials, servants, troubles to wife and sons, injury, mental trouble, injuries owing to stones, trees, evil spirits, calamities, etc.

Rahu. Heart diseases, inflammation, leprosy, defect in mental development, illusion, poisonous disease, bone diseases, injuries in legs, troublesome wife, sons, etc. fear from serpents, evil spirits, etc.

Ketu. Fear from aristocrats, mysterious diseases, unnatural and sudden deaths of family members, fear of evil spirits and many other diseases.

Diseases from Evil Houses. In the horoscope the 6th, 8th, and 12th houses are known as evil houses and their lords are called evil creator planets, e.g., if Sun is in 6th, 8th houses it causes fever, if Mars and *Ketu* are in the 6th and 8th houses they cause injury, it causes of urinary and sex diseases cases, is in the 6th and 8th houses is in the 6th and 8th houses it if Jupiter causes T.B., if Saturn is in the 6th and 8th houses it causes goitre, if Mars and *Rahu* cause wounds, tumours, if Moon is in the 6th and 8th houses it causes diseases of liver, spleen is in the 6th and 8th houses if Saturn is in the 6th and 8th houses it causes dropsy, T.B., etc.

Causes of Death. In the horoscope the 8th house is the house of longevity and death. Hence whichever planet is in the 8th house or aspects the 8th house or the lord of 8th house is in relation to other planets and houses, among them whichever is strong or aspects strongly it causes death.

If the lord of the 8th house is in the 4th house then death may occur due to stomach trouble, if it is in 5th house due to heart disease, if lord of 8th house are either Sun or Mars then death may occur due to bilious diseases, typhus, blood pressure, if Saturn is lord of 8th house then death may happen due to wind diseases. Lord of 22nd *drekkana* from birth *drekkana* causes death due to diseases or other causes prescribed from him.

Planets in 8th house. When planets sit in 8th house or aspecting 8th house, the 8th lord causes death as follows:

Sun causes death due to hot fever, bilious fever, arms or fire. Moon causes death from cholera, dropsy, other water diseases, *flurity*, typhus, tuberculosis, etc. Mars causes death due to blood diseases, fire, electricity, accident and other incidental causes. Mercury causes death due to jaundice, anaemia, illusions, nervous diseases, liver troubles, etc. Jupiter causes death due to cough, diabetes, obesity, etc. Venus causes death due to infertility, excessive sexual actions, urinary diseases. Saturn causes death due to wind diseases as goitre, paralysis, constipation. *Rahu* causes death due to leprosy, serpents, scorpions, other poisonous animals, etc. *Ketu* causes death due to accidental events, unknown, unseen, mysterious diseases, etc.

According to *Bhavartha Ratnakar*:

1. If lord of 8th house is in birth *lagna* then body is healthy.
2. If lord of 6th house is in birth *lagna* then people of our own caste, family hold enmity to the subject and thus fearful diseases are produced in the mind and body of the subject.
3. If lords of *lagna* and 6th houses are combined with Sun then the subject suffers from fever.
4. If lords of *lagna* and 6th houses are with Moon then hydrophobia and watery diseases are found.
5. If lords of *lagna* and 6th houses are with Mars then diseases due to wound, injury, arms, glands, blood, etc. are found.
6. If lords of 1st and 6th houses are with Mercury then nervous system is influenced and diseases like bilious condition, skin and nerve diseases are produced.
7. If lords of 1st and 6th houses are with Jupiter then no disease is produced and the subject is healthy.
8. If lords of 1st and 6th houses are with Venus then the diseases induced by Venus and disease to female spouse are produced.
9. If lords of 1st and 6th houses are with Saturn then Saturnal diseases, fear from thieves, menials, etc. are produced.
10. If lords of 1st and 6th houses are with *Rahu* or *Ketu* then not only fear from poison, serpents, tigers, are suddenly produced but the chances of accident are also exceed.
11. If lord of 6th house is in the 12th house with a debilitated planet and the lord of the *lagna* is strong then the person is healthy and diseases do not prevail.

3

Astrological Diagnosis: Diseases with Horoscopic Examples

While considering the relief from doctor's treatment we should see the time horoscope of the patient asked for by the relative of patient. The 1st house is known as doctor, 7th house of disease (what kind of disease afflicts the patient), 10th house of the patient and 4th house of the medicine.

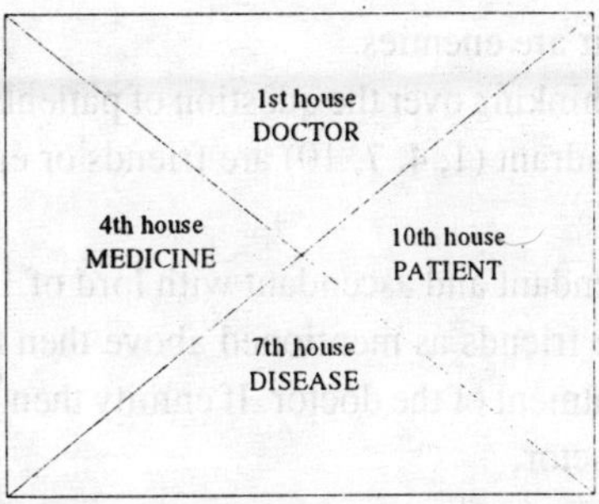

See that the 1st house is important here because if there is malefic in ascendant then the treatment of the doctor will not be beneficial. Medicines will harm the patient, and the disease will increase enormously. But if there is strong benefic in the ascendant the patient will get relief from medicine given by the doctor. In the same way malefic in the 7th house will increase the disease by medicines prescribed by the doctor or new disease will begin. Benefic in the 7th house will cure the disease prescribed by the doctor and patient will follow the instructions of the doctor.

If malefics in the 10th house patient will not follow the instructions of the doctor and the disease will increase enormously. On the other hand if there are benefics in the 10th house then the patient will get relief by the treatment and medicines prescribed by the doctor.

Malefics in the 4th house will increase the disease by the treatment of the doctor or long-termed disease will be replaced. Benefics in the 4th house will treat the patient well by the medicines prescribed by the doctor. Hence it is clear now that there should not be malefics in quadrant (1, 4, 7, 10) while asking the astrologer about the cure from illness of the diseased person.

The twelve signs are divided into four elements—Fire, Earth, Air and Water.

Aries, Leo, Sagittarius	Firey signs
Taurus, Virgo, Capricorn	Earthy signs
Gemini, Libra, Aquarius	Airy signs
Cancer, Scorpio, Pisces	Watery signs.

Earth and Water are friends.
Air and Fire are friends.
Water and Fire are enemies.
Earth and Air are enemies.

Hence while thinking over the question of patients' treatment see that all the signs of quadrant (1, 4, 7, 10) are friends or enemies mutually or not.

If lord of ascendant and ascendant with lord of 10th and the sign in the 10th house are friends as mentioned above then the patient will get relief from the treatment of the doctor. If enmity then the disease will not be cured by the doctor.

In the same way 4th house's sign, lord of 4th house has friendship with 7th house's sign Lord of the 7th house the disease will be cured. If enmity then the disease will not be cured by the doctor.

We see practically that a patient gets his disease cured by the doctor, on the other hand the patient does not get his disease cured by the same doctor. This is because there is much difference in the nature of the patients and diseases. Hence the same medicine may not cure all the patients or all the diseases. This fact must be understood well by the doctors and astrologers.

Doctor's profession is the service unto humanity. Nowadays medicines and doctor's charges are very high and beyond the reach of the general public. Hence it is necessary to propagate the cheap means of treatment like herbs, urine therapy, homoeopathy, Acupressure, *yantra*, *mantra* and astrological guidance so that the world at large may be benefited.

Advice for treatment of diseases. Through horary astrology see the position of 8th house, its lord and the planet posited there as follows:

1. If there is Sun or Mars, then the disease is caused by blood and bile. So the treatment should be conciliation of Sun or Mars by chanting their *mantras,* worshipping, donating their *yantras* and prescribed things. The doctor should prescribe medicines to stop blood pressure, faulty blood circulation and bile. The person should wear the ring with ruby or coral as the case may be. Doctor should see whether there are symptoms of heart disease or blindness.
2. If there is Mercury in 8th house then constipation, dyspepsia, coma, inflammation in the body, weakness in nervous system are observed. Then medicines of these diseases should be prescribed. The patient should be advised to wear emerald in golden ring and *japa, yantra, mantra* of Mercury should be performed.
3. If Moon is in 8th house then mental stroke is the cause of disease. Psychological treatment will help in this case. Other diseases caused by the weakness of Moon are also indicated by the attendance of Moon there. Due to weakness of Moon, brain trouble, gout or rheumatism may also attack. Hence the doctor should cautiously diagnose the disease and prescribe medicines. The donation of Moon, *japa, yantra,* ring of pearl, etc. should be utilised to eradicate diseases.
4. If there is Jupiter in 8th house then stomach trouble, elephantiasis, apoplexy, epilepsy, paralysis, etc. may be indicated. All diseases caused by Jupiter are due to divine order the creator of the cosmos. Hence *japa, yantra, mantra,* ring of topaz in gold, *maha mrityunjaya mantra*, donation, feeding of poor girls, Brahmins

should be performed. Doctors should judge the position of the disease then prescribe medicines.

5. If there is Venus in 8th house then diseases caused by Venus are cough, defect in semen, sex organs, AIDS, etc. For this, remedial measures should be applied *japa, yantra, mantra,* herbs, homoeopathy, acupressure and ayurvedic medicines, are the means to cure the diseases. *Dawa* and *Duaa* meaning medicines and grace of God both should be applied to cure the diseases.
6. If there is Saturn in 8th house then due to skin disease, disease due to wind, or death by appetite or thirst affect the person. For placation of Saturn *japa, yantra, mantra,* and herbs whichever prescribed for Saturn should be performed. Saturn is the most strong planet in producing disease as if is the *karaka* of diseases. Hence due to Saturn's position in 8th house the disease may be for long time because Saturn's period is longer than any other planet.
7. When *Rahu* or *Ketu* is in 8th house then injury, wound due to accidents or any other disease concerning blood may be treated.
8. If there are Sun and Moon in 8th house then bloody bile should be cured.
9. If there are Mercury and Jupiter in 8th house then T.B. treatment should be prescribed.
10. If there is malefic with Jupiter then *Tridosha* (wind, bile, cough) disease be cured.
11. If Saturn and Mars are in 8th house then skin diseases and leprosy should be treated.
12. If *Rahu* and Saturn are in 8th house then wind disease i.e., *Kampan ray* should be treated.
13. If Moon and Venus or Mercury with malefic *nakshatras* are in the 8th house then *Sannipat* (coma) should be treated.
14. If Venus and Mars are iln the 8th house then T.B. or defective semon should be treated.

When there is no planet in 8th house then the planets who aspect 8th house or lord of 8th house, according to their position the treatment should be taken in hand. The 8th lord and his relations with other planets and house lords should also be considered.

Planets which aspect the 8th house

1. If Sun aspects the 8th house then disease occurs due to bile.
2. If Moon aspects the 8th house then cough disturbs the subject.
3. If Mars aspects the 8th house then disease is due to blood.
4. If Mercury aspects the 8th house then disease is due to nerves and wind.
5. If Jupiter aspects the 8th house then disease is due to stomach trouble, heart disease or divine desire.
6. If Venus aspects the 8th house then defect in semen, sex organs, urine, etc. should be treated.
7. If Saturn aspects the 8th house then *Tridosha* or skin disease or cold should be treated.
8. If *Rahu-Ketu* aspect the 8th house then injury, wound, tumour or pain which is mysterious, unknown cause, etc. should be treated.

Handicapped since Birth

According to *Jyotish Shyam Sangraha* Chapter 7, Verse 44 *Henang yoga* (हीनांग योग):

वेशिस्थिते सूर्यसुते कुजेस्ते खस्थे विधौ हीनकलेवरः स्यात्

It means when in birth ascendant Saturn is in second house from Sun, Mars in 7th, Moon in 10th house then the person born thus is *Henang* or handicapped. In the same book in Chapter 7 Verse 45 शोषक्षयः दोषः combination is thus:

सूतौ मिथः क्षेत्रगतौ रवीन्दू परस्परांशोपगतौ च यद्वा
शोषक्षयं तौ कुरुने नराणामेकैकगेहोपगते तथैव

It means when in birth chart of native Sun and Moon are mutually posited thus is in either birth chart or chart of *Navamsa* Sun in sign of Moon and Moon in sign of Sun then the person is physically weak and having declined by diseased body.

These two verses tell the truth correctly as I experienced in a case given as follows. A male was born on 20-7-1979 at 11-20 p.m. at 25°–41′ north latitude and 78°-28′ longitude east.

Vikrami Samvat 2036 *Saka* 1901 *Sravana Krishna* 12 Friday 55/49 *Rohini nakshatra* 36/20 Pisces ascendant.

Planetary position : *Mrigsira* first *charan*

Sun 3-3-19	Mercury 3-16-10 (R)	Saturn 4-19-59
Moon	Jupiter 3-23-26	Rahu 4-16-0
Mars 1-24-10	Venus 2-25-4	Ketu 10-16-0

Birth Chart

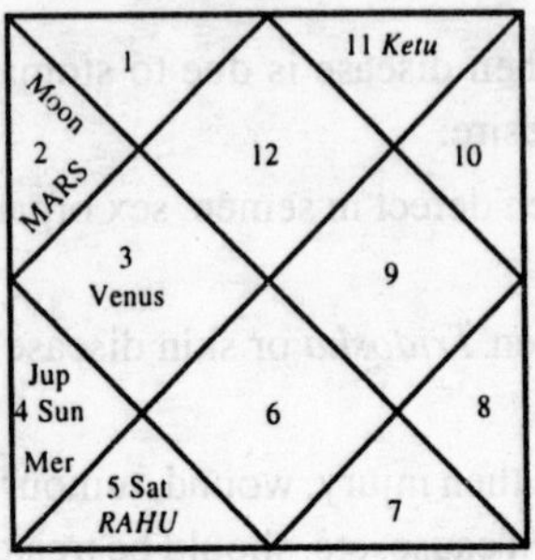

Navamsa Chart

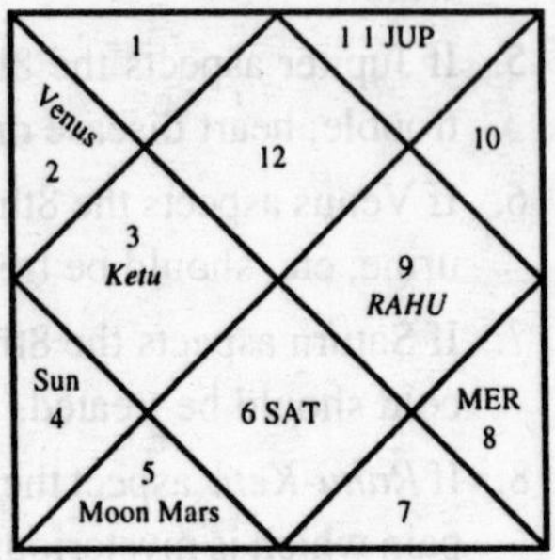

According to verse 44 in this chart Saturn is in second house to Sun in birth chart, Moon is in tenth house to Saturn Mars though not in 7th house but with Moon.

According to verse 45 in birth chart and *Navamsa* chart Sun is in sign of Moon, Cancer and in *Navamsa* chart Moon is in sign Leo of Sun that exchange of signs of Moon and Sun.

These two combinations make the person handicapped. The person since childhood neither can sit nor stand nor walk and speak properly. Though beautiful by features of the face as Jupiter aspects the *lagna,* since birth he has polio in his both legs. His both legs are thin. He takes food and does other work as urinating, or going to lavatory being taken on back or holding the hands of others.

Here too, *Vargottam Navamsa* of birth *lagna*, Sun is present but the position of *Lagna* lord Jupiter is between malefics, moon into malefic Mars both in birth and *Navamsa* chart.

Besides *Kala sarpa yoga* is present too in this horoscope as all the planets are between *Rahu* and *Ketu* which is not good.

Brain Haemorrhage

The nervous system enclosed in the skull is called brain. Brain is the inner matter of head. The head is studied through sign Aries, its lord Mars,

Sun is the controller of brain. Lord of ascendant, its lord, Moon, sign occupied by Moon and lord of ascendant, 6th house, its lord—all these should be thoroughly studied. Brain is the most important part of our body. Hence its security is most essential.

Below, I am giving two examples of persons who died of brain haemorrhage.

Example 1. Male born on 13-11-1950, Sunday at 4.40 a.m. in Libra ascendant, *Mool Nakshatra* 3rd quarter of 23°-30′ N latitude, 77-50 E longitude with planetary position as following:

Ascendant	Libra	6-2°-43′
Sun	Libra	6-26°-51′
Moon	Sagittarius	8-8°-26′, *Mool Nakshatra* 3rd Charan
Mars	Sagittarius	8-11°-56′
Mercury	Scorpio	7.03°-48′
Jupiter	Aquarius	10-05°-04′
Venus	Libra	6-26°-15′
Saturn	Virgo	5-06°-10′
Rahu	Pisces	11-02°-04′
Ketu	Virgo	5-02°-04′

Ascendant Chart

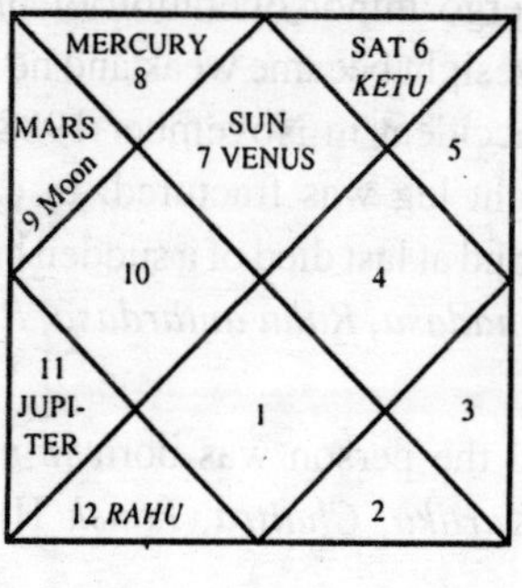

Navamsa Chart

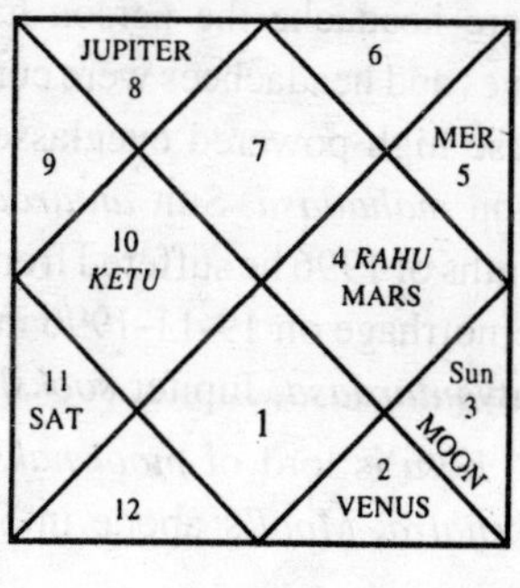

Balance of *Ketu mahadasa* at birth 2 years and 11 months. *Rahu mahadasa* commenced from 13-10-1996. Planets were in following stellars at birth time.

Planet	*Nakshatra*	*Charan*
Ascendant	Chitra	3
Sun	Punarvasa	3
Moon	Mool	3
Mars	Mool	3
Mercury	Anuradha	2
Jupiter	Dhanishtha	4
Venus	Vishakha	2
Saturn	Uttra Phalguna	2
Rahu	Poorva Bhadrapada	1
Ketu	Uttra Phalguna	1

The importance of stellers is more in predictive astrology as the prediction declaring on signs alone goes wrong because in a sign there are 3 stellers. As the lords of stellers differ then each steller is represented by a *Devta* (deity) that too plays an important role, e.g., Aries sign has 4 *charans* of *Ashwini*, 4 *charans* of *Bharni* and one *charan* of *Kritika*. These 3 *nakshatras* have lords as *Ketu*, Venus and Sun while Aries has only one lord. Then these *Devtas* differ too. So for deeper study these aspects should also be taken into consideration.

In the above case Moon and Mars are in *Mool* which is the *nakshatra* or steller of *Ketu.* Jupiter, lord of 6th house is in the *nakshatra* of Mars *Dhanishtha*. *Rahu* is in the *nakshatra* of Jupiter *Poorva Bhadrapada.*

In Venus *mahadasa* the person suffered from headache (Venus is the lord of ascendant Libra and is in the *nakshatra* of Jupiter, the lord of 6th house). Jupiter aspects Venus and ascendant from 5th house. Due to severe headache the person had to undergo minor operation of brain nerves and headachees were cured. His eyesight became weak and he had to use high powered eyeglasses. In an accident in November 1988, in Moon *mahadasa*, Sun *antardasa* his right leg was fractured. In early months of 1996 he suffered from malaria and at last died of a sudden brain haemorrhage on 19-11-1996 in *Rahu mahadasa*, *Rahu antardasa*, *Rahu pratyantardasa*, Jupiter *sookshmadasa*.

Ketu is lord of *mool nakshatra* and the person was born in *mool nakshatra*. *Mool*'s abode in *Sravana*, *Kartika*, *Chaitra*, *Paush* Hindu months and in Gemini, Virgo, Sagittarius, Pisces ascendants, i.e. 3, 6, 9, 12 signs of dual nature, is on *Bhoomi* (land) and according to astrological point of view 1 + is not considered auspicious. Besides there is *Kalasarpa yoga* too being all the planets between dragon's head *Rahu* and tail *Ketu*. His birth ascendant Libra is in the Libra, the self *navamsa*, i.e., *vargottam navamsa* and in *Chitra nakshatra*, the stellar of Mars, the strong malefic and killer (*Markesh*) for Libra ascendant's born person. The lord of ascendant Venus is in Libra in *Vishakha nakshatra* in Taurus *navamsa* and is combust due to being in the same degree 26' with Sun. Hence Venus, lord of *lagna* is much too weak, Venus is also the lord of 8th house, the house of longevity and death.

Due to combust Venus, Sun could not get cancellation of debilitation (*Neecha Bhanga*). Thus Venus, the lord of ascendant, the most important planet in horoscope has become malefic with *neech* Sun. This benefic planet has turned malefic due to bad and evil influence of the Sun, the *atmakaraka* planet.

These two malefics aspect adversely Aries the sign of Mars. Aries represents the head and the brain. The lord of Aries Mars is with the lord of 10th Moon in 3rd house in Sagittarius. Moon and Mars both are in *mool nakshatra* whose lord is Ketu the mysterious planet. Hence, the lord of Aries too has become too weak being in the house of Jupiter, the lord of 6th house, the house of diseases Jupiter being the lord of 6th house and being a malefic (अकारक) to Libra ascendant's the person aspects the ascendant with inimical point. Both signs of Jupiter, the Sagittarius and the Pisces are occupied by the super malefics Mars and *Rahu* sign. Sagittarius is also aspected by other malefics Saturn and *Ketu*. This, due to occupation of *Rahu* in 6th house the subject died of a sudden brain haemorrhage in *Rahu mahadasa, Rahu avtar*, *Rahu pratyavtar*, Jupiter *sookshma*. On 19-11-96, Tuesday day of Mars, the lord of Aries and in *shatbhisha nakshatra* whose lord is too *Rahu,* for Libra ascendant Mars, Tuesday, Aries proved fatal.

In *navamsa* chart Venus, lord of ascendant, is aspected by lord of 6th house Jupiter and *Ketu.* Thus square aspect of Jupiter and Saturn on Venus affected longevity. All the malefics *Rahu*, Mars, *Ketu*, Saturn, Sun are in quadrant and trinal houses which also is not good.

The disease of brain haemorrhage is a serious and mysterious disease about which no one can say beforehand. *Jyotish Shyam Sangraha* says:

कुलीर कीटांश गते हिमांशौ पापान्विते गुह्यरूजार्दितः स्यात्

J.S.S. 7/43

which means when Moon is in *Navamsa* of Cancer and Cancer with malefics then the person suffers from secret disease. Here Moon is in *Navamsa* of Scorpio with *Rahu*. So, the mysterious disease sets in.

Example 2. Male child was born on 21-10-1955 at 7.30 a.m. *Vikrami Samvat* 2012 *Saka* 1877 *Ashwin Shukla Paksha* 5 Friday 3/21 *Mool Nakshatra* 53/16. Second phase of birth time with the planetary position as follows:

Sun	6-3-20	Mercury	5-18-55	Saturn	6-24-35
Moon	8-3-55	Jupiter	4-14-16	Rahu	7-25-47
Mars	5-11-02	Venus	6-14-53	Ketu	1-25-47

Birth Ascendant 6-19-06

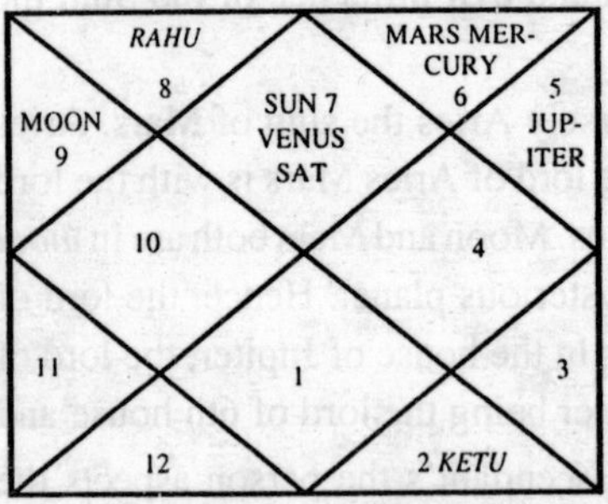

Navamsa Chart

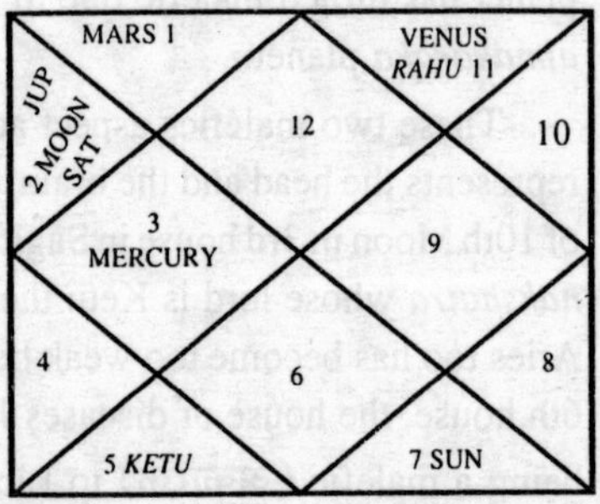

In this case the same ascendant Libra is occupied with Sun (*neecha*) Venus (between two malefics—Sun and Saturn) and Saturn. Saturn and Sun have adverse aspect on Aries.

The lord of Aries, Mars is with an evil lord's house in 12th with Mercury. Mars as killer (*Markesh*) for Libra ascendant being lord of 2nd and 7th houses and Jupiter *akarak* for Libra ascendant being lord of 3rd and 6th evil houses both aspect Moon. Moon's position is in trine to Aries.

Hence, Aries, its lord Mars ascendant, its lord Venus, Moon are afflicted by malefics. Ascendant too has *Papakartari yoga* being surrounded by four malefics and cruel planets Mars, Sun, Saturn and *Rahu*.

The subject expired on 29-12-1996 due to brain haemorrhage in Moon *mahadasa*, Venus *antardasa*, *Ketu pratyantardasa*, *Rahu sookshma*. Moon is under malefic influence of three planets aspect of Jupiter, Mars and Saturn. The sign Aries (representing head and brain) its lord Mars, ascendant, lord of ascendant, lord of 4th and 5th houses are badly afflicted. The *atmakarak* Sun is in debilitation and *atmakaraka* according to Jaimini Saturn is also afflicted by Mars and *Rahu* in the 2nd and 12th houses.

The brain haemorrhage disease is a disease which attacks at random mysteriously. Hence, death due to sudden brain haemorrhage is clear. In *Navamsa* chart, the sign of 6th house of birth *lagna* is *Navamsa lagna*. Lord of *lagna* Venus in 12th house with Rahu is indicating the sudden attack of disease. *Ketu* is aspecting Aries where Mars is posited aspected by *neecha* Sun. At the time of death the *Navamsa lagna* Pisces was occupied with Saturn, *Ketu* aspected by Mars and Rahu in Virgo. Jupiter too proved *maraka* being in 3rd house of *Navamsa* chart with Moon and Saturn.

In these two examples birth ascendant and birth *nakshatra* are the same Libra and mool.

Dumbness since Birth

I am giving here an example of a person who is dumb since birth and mentally weak but still is able to understand a little bit by physical actions.

A male was born on 29-9-1969 at 4.00 a.m. in the second quarter of *Bharani Nakshatra* with a balance of Venus *mahadasa* of 10 years, 4 months and 5 days.

Birth Chart

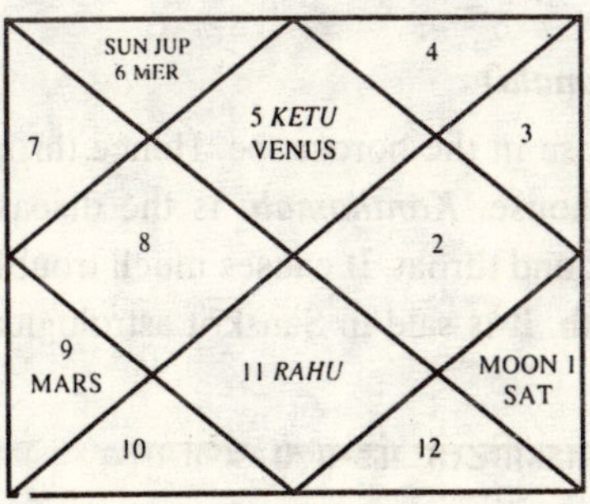

Navamsa Chart

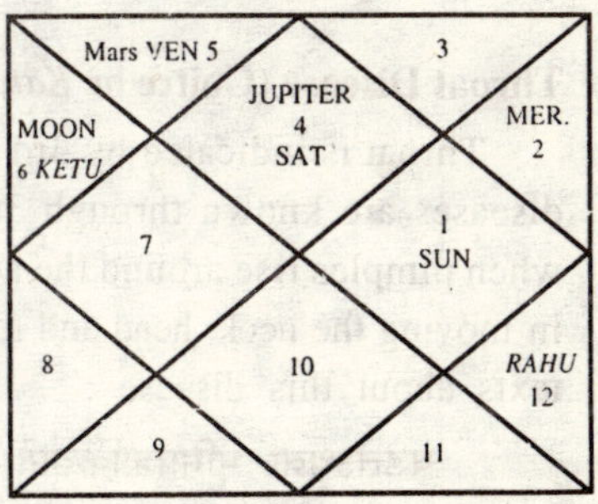

Mercury and Saturn are in retrogression. Dumbness in a person is indicated through the position of Mercury, 2nd house, its lord, 5th house, its lord both from birth chart, Moon. From *navamsa* and Sun's position too it should be considered. First of all we see that *lagna* Leo is heavily afflicted by occupation of Venus and *Ketu* and aspect of *Rahu*. These planets are enemy of the lord of *lagna,* the Sun. In Moon sign Aries, the bitter enemy of lord of Moon sign, Saturn is posited. Saturn is in debilitation and retrogression. In *navamsa,* Cancer is sign of *navamsa lagna* and Moon is heavily afflicted by *Rahu* and *Ketu* by aspect and combination. From Sun sign we see that Mercury, the lord of Sun sign is retrograded and is weakening the Sun sign and 2nd house of speech from birth ascendant.

Mars is posited in 5th house in Sagittarius and in *navamsa* Mars is the lord of 8th house where Scorpio is the sign. In 2nd house in *navamsa* Mars and Venus are destroying the 2nd house (house of speech). From Moon in 5th house there are Venus and *Ketu* both enemies of 5th lord Sun.

Hence, considering the 2nd and 5th houses from birth *lagna*, Moon and Sun signs, *navamsa* we see that the 2nd and 5th houses, their lords along with *lagna* and *lagna* lord are under heavy malefic influence.

In birth sign the aspect of debilitated Saturn on 6th house (house of diseases) in retrograded position is not good. All the benefics Venus, Jupiter, Moon and, Mercury are hemmed in between malefics. So it is proved here that houses of speech, mind (2nd, 5th) and their lords are not in favourable position causing the patient dumbness and mental sickness.

Throat Disease (Goitre or *Kanthamala*)

Throat is indicated by 3rd house in the horoscope. Hence throat diseases are known through 3rd house. *Kanthamala* is the disease when pimples rise around the neck and throat. It causes much trouble in moving the neck, head and mouth. It is said in Sanskrit astrological texts about this disease :

षडेतेऽथवा भूमिपुत्रार्कियोगे शुभाऽहाष्टितो गंडमाला व्रणायम्

J.S.S. 7 – 55

The means when there is combination of Saturn and Mars in 6th or 12th house then the subject suffers from or Goitre.

I am giving below an example of the person who suffered from this disease.

Birth Lagna

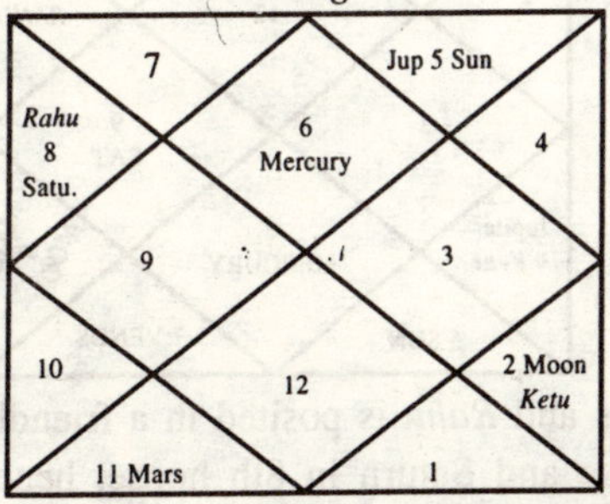

A male was born on 30-8-1956 in Virgo ascendant, *Rohini nakshatra* with balance of Moon *mahadasa* 0 year and 6 months. This person suffered from goitre in Moon *mahadasa* in *antardasa* of *Rahu*, Jupiter and Saturn for about 3 years from the age of 1 year 6 months to 4 years 6 months. Here in the 3rd house there are Rahu and Saturn aspecting Moon. Mars is in 6th house in the sign of Saturn, Aquarius aspecting Moon in 9th and Jupiter and Sun in 12th house. The lords of 3rd and 6th houses Mars and Saturn are exchanging their signs. Hence the 3rd and 6th houses are under malefic influence denoting goitre disease.

Saturn and Mars are connected to 6th house as in Saturn's sign Aquarius, Mars, in 6th house.

Pulmonary Diseases

There are so many cases of diseases which are not particularly described in old textbooks but which draw our attention for research work in such cases. I am giving a case of fluid getting accumulated in the lungs of a child at the age of 13 years.

A male was born on 23-11-82 at 5.00 p.m. in the 4th quarter of *Dhanishtha Nakshtra* in *Vikrami Samvat* 2039, *Kartika Shukla 7*, Tuesday. Planetary position as following:

Sun 7-6-24	Mercury 7-8-33	Saturn 6-7-12
Moon 10-5-6	Jupiter 7-1-35	Rahu 2-12-15
Mars 8-25-11	Venus 7-11-45	Ketu 8-12-15

Balance of Mars *mahadasa* of the subject 6 and years, 11 months 6 days. The Pisces sign is watery by nature. The last *navamsa* of Cancer and Pisces is not considered auspicious as regards health. Here is the last *navamsa* of Pisces, i.e., Pisces, though it seems that it is *Vargottam navamsa*. The ascendant is weak as those in Dosha of *lagna goudant* that is Pisces ending and Aries rising hence this is also not auspicious as regards health.

Pisces Ascendant

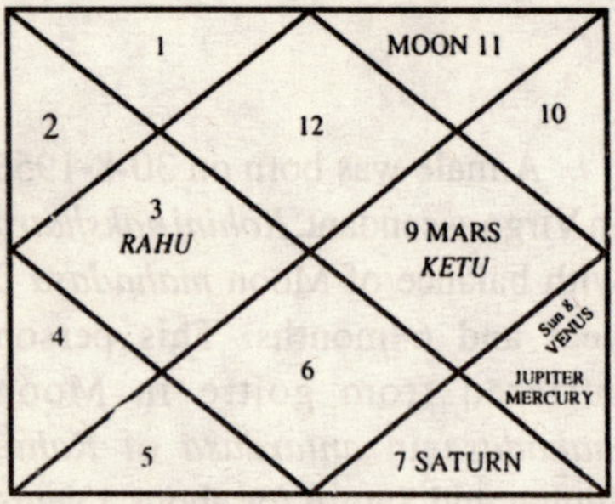

Navamsa

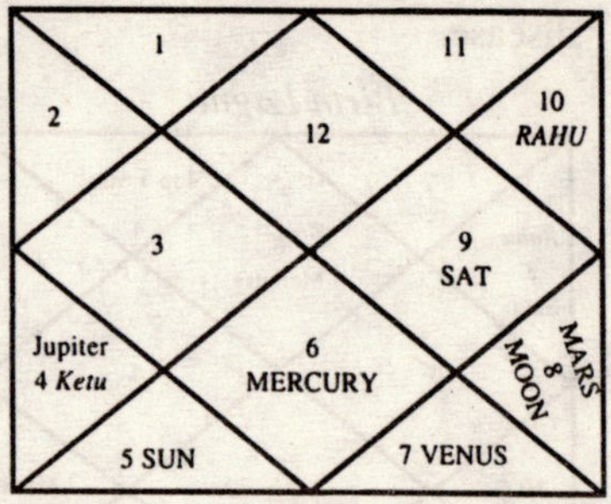

The 4th house represents lungs and *Rahu* is posited in a friendly sign aspecting Moon in 12th house and Saturn in 8th house, hence the Moon is under malefic affliction. The lord of 4th house Mercury is in inimical sign in 9th house with lord of 8th Venus and lord of 6th house Sun, lord of ascendant Jupiter. Mars aspects the 4th house from 10th house. Thus the 4th house, lord of 4th house, ascendant, lord of ascendant and the 4th sign Cancer of *Kalapurusa* being aspected by Mars and Saturn two malefics. Cancer is also a watery sign Mars aspects *lagna* too. *Rahu* is famous for sudden events, and calamities. Hence the child felt trouble in lungs and was taken to in Hospital on 15-3-1993. There was fluid accumulation in lungs and so the case was a serious one. The child was admitted for 8 days and the doctors drained the fluid from lungs. This happened in *Rahu mahadasa, antardasa* of Mercury which was running w.e.f. 11-10-1991 to 29-4-1994. The boy's body slowly became pale and unconscious. But thanks to Jupiter, lord of ascendant who is posited in 9th house with Mercury and in 5th house in *navamsa* exalted unaspected evil planets and malefics like Saturn, Mars, etc.

Consequently, the child is survived but his health problem is due for proper treatment and nursing. Jupiter in *navamsa* is highly strong having full aspect on birth *lagna*, *navamsa lagna* and Moon in *navamsa*, who is debilitated and whose debilitation is cancelled by being with strong Mars in his own sign and benefic aspect of Jupiter, a divine planet who indicates the grace of God. In *navamsa Rahu* is aspected by Jupiter who is ordering him to minimise his malefic influence in the horoscope. Besides there is *Gaja Kesari Yoga* too who gives divine courage to the subject to tolerate troubles and pains.

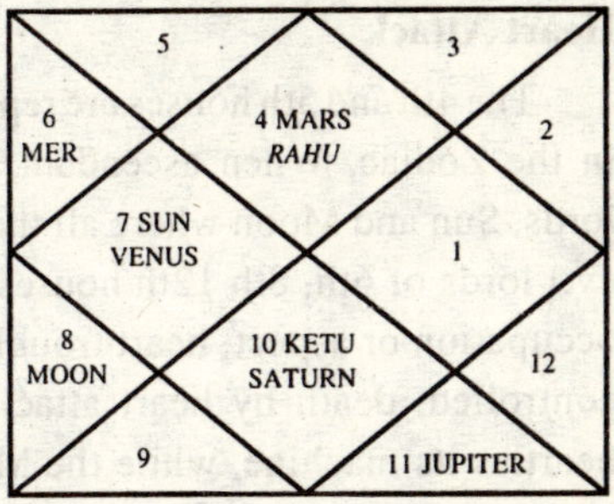

Example 2. The person was born on 1-11-1962 at 11.30 p.m. *Jyeshtha Nakshatra* in the second quarter of Cancer ascendant with three planets in debilitation (*neecha*).

In this horoscope lord of ascendant Moon is in Scorpio in debilitation but its lord Mars (lord of Moon sign) is in a quadrant *lagna* hence there is *Neecha Bhanga Yoga* or cancellation of debilitation too. Lagna is occupied by Mars in debilitation (*neecha*) with *Rahu* aspected by Saturn (lord of 7th and 8th houses and *Ketu*). The lord of 2nd house (*markesh*) Sun is also in debilitation but with Venus in own sign in a quadrant (4th house) debilitation is somehow cancelled, though Venus too is combust and retrograded. Hence, the dosha of *markesh* of Sun has been lesser.

The 4th house denotes lungs and heart, upper part of stomach. This house is occupied with a malefic and *markesh* Sun aspected by two other malefics Mars (*neecha*) and Saturn hence the subject is always having some or the other types of diseases, sometimes suffering from pain in stomach, heart and chest. Thanks to lord of 9th Jupiter (house of luck and grace of God) who aspects the 4th house, thus minimising the bad influence of these malefics.

Besides Mars is a *Karaka* for Cancer *lagna* and *Rahu* too is beneficial to Aries, Cancer and Leo *lagnas* as and when occupying these *lagnas* he helps in times of trouble to these *lagna's* subject as king allows grace to criminals and arrested persons getting the punishment of jail.

Even then Mars and Saturn aspect each other and the subject is always restless and in hypertension. Shri Ganesh Daivagya says in *Jatkalankar*, "क्रूरे केन्द्रालयस्थे यदि शुभ विहगैर्नक्षिते रोगवान स्यात्" meaning if there are cruel malefics in *kendra*, i.e. in 1st, 4th, 7th and 10th houses unaspected by benefics the subject suffers from diseases. Here Mars, *Rahu, Ketu* and Saturn—four malefics are in 1st and 7th houses unaspected by malefics hence diseases are occurring.

Heart Attack

The 4th and 5th houses are representatives of heart of *Kalapurusha* in the Zodiac. When ascendant, its lord, 4th and 5th houses, their lords, Sun and Moon where all these are afflicted by malefics only by evil lords of 6th, 8th 12th houses in any way either by combination, occupation or aspect, heart trouble is indicated and if not checked or controlled, death by heart attack results. Sun represents soul with heart as its machine, while the Moon represents mind. Jupiter too is related to heart as it is also called *Jiva* or life in human beings.

The heart is the centre of vitality and longevity. The work of heart is to supply strength through purifying blood circulation to all the parts of the body and strengthen the brain through nervous system. Nerves in the root of thumbs of both the hands are the barometer of life. As long as there is breath in heart the man is alive. Doctors use stethoscope in ausclation of heart and lungs. Sanskrit texts tell us about heart and stomach trouble as follows:

क्षितिजसकलदृष्टयाभ्यार्दिते देवपूज्ये
यदि दिव जननेऽस्मिन् भूमिपुत्रे विनष्टे
अशुभ शुभसमेते शत्रुनाथेऽलिगेऽर्के
प्रभवति किल शूलं चोदरेत्हृत्प्रदेशे J.S.S. 7-59,

It means when Mars aspects Jupiter, birth day time, Mars less strengthen or *nashtabali* means strengthless, lord of 6th house with benefics and malefics, the Sun in inimical sign or in the sign of malefics then the subject suffers from stomach and heart troubles. Similarly,

हृच्छूलरोगमुपयाति सुखे फणीशे पापेक्षिते गतवले यदि लग्ननाथे
शूलमर्यमनुपतो रिपुनचि राशौ भौमे सुखे रविसुते यदिपाप दृष्टे

which means if lord of ascendant is weak aspected by malefics and 4th house is occupied by *Rahu* then the subject suffers from heart trouble. Lord of ascendant in evil signs, debilitation, influenced by malefics, Mars with malefics or aspected by Saturn in 4th house give heart trouble.

Heart is the most sensitive part of the body. Mental pressure, fear, sufferings, anger, failure, etc. increase the palpitation of heart and blood pressure, breakage in blood, etc., ensue which may lead to heart attack.

Symptoms of Heart Disease

According to Charaka the symptoms of heart disease are as follows:

वैवर्ण्य मूर्च्छा ज्वर कास हिक्कांश्वासास्य वैरस्य वृषा प्रमोहः

छर्दि कफोर्रक्लेशर, जोड़रूचिश्चय हृदोगजा स्युर्विविधास्तया उन्ये

which means that being colourless (due to internal discourage) this is due to lack of courage, fainting fits, fever, cough, bronchitis, involuntary audible spasm of lungs, high breathing, vomiting, trouble by cough, disinterest and trouble in breathing, etc. are seen when heart disease, or when heart attack begins. There is also pain in heart and check in palpitation of heart.

Kinds of Heart Disease

Heart diseases are caused by drinking hot tea or coffee, hot and fatty food, liquors, excessive work, insomnia, and stressful thinking. In Ayurveda, five kinds of heart diseases are recorded:

1. Gastric heart disease, e.g., pain, palpitation, fits, etc.

2. Bilious heart disease, e.g., hotness, inflammation, vomiting.

3. Coughy heart disease, e.g., trouble in breathing, no taste in mouth.

4. Threefold defective heart disease: Severe pain troubles and heart failure, tension.

5. Warmal heart disease : itches, sudden darkness in vision, swelling, etc.

Signs denoting heart diseases—Aries, Taurus, Leo, Virgo, Libra, Scorpio and Pisces.

Stellars denoting heart trouble—Bharni, *Kritika*, *Aridra*, *Jyestha*, *Magha*, *Poorva Phalguna*, *Uttra Phalguna*, *Swati* and *Vishakha*.

In heart disease simple food, adequate rest, free from cares, and desisting from stressful thinking is necessary. Heart is the centre of all the human activities—mental, physical, psychological as Sun is the lord master of solar system. In *Bhagwat Geeta* Lord Krishna said to Arjuna:

क्षुद्रं हृदयदौर्बल्यं त्यक्त्वोत्तिष्ठ परंतप

which means oh Arjun! Leave the thinking of weakness of heart and get up. Again he said:

"ईश्वरः सर्वभूतानां हृद्देशेऽर्जुन तिष्ठति

which means oh Arjun! God lives in the heart of all beings. Which goes to show that the heart is the abode of God and that is soul or life which we feel by inspiration of air. Hence heart is the most important part in human body without which we cannot think of a human being.

Examples of Heart Attacks and Heart Troubles

Example 1. The great revolutionary poet of Hindi Prof. Shri Krishna 'Saral', who wrote 112 books in which 12 are epics, was born in *Vikrami Samvat* 1978, *Jyeshth* month Tuesday *Shukla Paksha Panchmi* 9/14 Birth *Nakshtra Aridra* 3rd quarter Aries ascendant. Aries ascendant and *Aridra nakshatra* indicate the probability of heart disease. Planetary position is as following:

	S	D	M
Lagna	0	20	05
Sun	1	23	44
Moon	2	16	20
Mars	2	00	21
Mercury	2	16	10
Jupiter	4	20	28
Venus	0	09	26
Saturn	4	28	38
Rahu	6	02	38
Ketu	0	02	38

Birth Ascendant

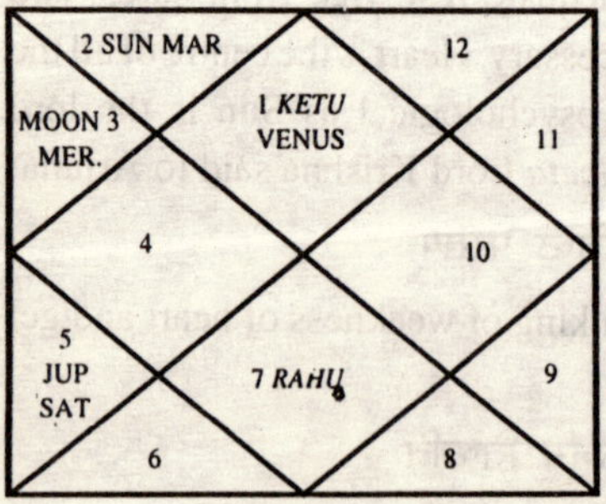

Navamsa Chakra

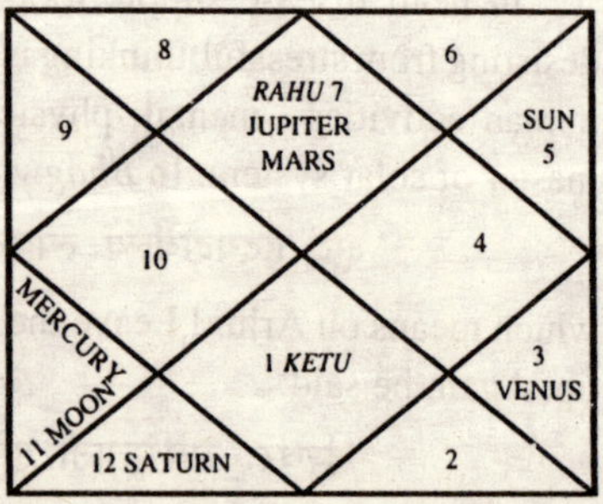

For knowing the strength of *lagna* and planets we see *Sapta Varga* chart as follows:

	Rasi	*Hora*	*Navamsa*	*Trim-sansa*	*Drekan*	*Sapta-mamsa*	*Dwada samsa*	*Benefic Vargas*
Asc.	1	4	7	3	9	5	9	5
Sun	2	5	5	10	10	12	11	3
Moon	3	4	11	9	11	11	9	3
Mars	3	5	7	1	3	3	3	2
Mer.	3	4	11	9	11	6	9	5
Jup.	5	4	7	3	1	9	1	5
Venus	1	5	3	11	1	3	4	4
Saturn	5	4	12	7	1	11	4	4
Rahu	7	5	7	1	7	7	8	4
Ketu	1	5	1	1	1	1	8	6

Here we see that in Aries, Venus and *Ketu* are posited, *Rahu* in 7th house in Libra in friend's sign, Jupiter in 5th in friend's sign, Saturn in 5th inimical sign *lagna* and 5th house are under malefic influence. Sun is Venus's sign in Taurus. Lagna has fivefold strength, so Jupiter too has fivefold strength. Jupiter is lord of 9th (*trikona* house) is in trine (5th house) aspecting the other trine (9th house) and ascendant. *Ketu* in friend's sign aspected by Jupiter and with Venus has been highly strengthened and has made the horoscope strong and the subject's life is long.

Prof. Shri Krishna Saral has suffered from heart attack on a few occasions but due to the grace of Jupiter (lord of 9th house, the house of God and His blessings) he survived on all occasions. The last heart attack took place in January, 1998. *Vimshottari Mahadasa*: Balance of *Rahu Mahadasa* at birth 6 years and 8 months w.e.f. 7-6-21 to 6-2-1928.

Jupiter *Mahadasa* w.e.f.	7-2-28 to 6-2-1944
Saturn *Mahadasa* w.e.f.	7-2-44 to 6-2-1963
Mercury *Mahadasa* w.e.f.	7-2-63 to 6-2-1980
Ketu Mahadasa w.e.f.	7-2-80 to 6-2-1987
Venus *Mahadasa* w.e.f.	7-2-87 onwards

The last heart attack took place in January 1998, in *mahadasa* of Venus, *antardasa* of Jupiter, *pratyavtardasa* of Saturn (w.e.f. 15-8-97 to 17-1-98). But due to the grace of Jupiter he survived. As can be seen in *Gochara Rahu* is in Leo aspected by Jupiter since 1-1-1998. Lord of 5th Sun is in inimical sign since 14-1-1998 till 14-3-98. The other thing is that in January 1998 the lord of *lagna* Aries, Mars was in Aquarius aspected by *Rahu* hence the heart attack in January, 1998 is clear.

Example 2. Second example of heart attack is of Leo *lagna* and birth *nakshatra kritika* 4th quarter. Male born on 6-9-1928 Thursday Kritika nakshatra 4th Quarter. Balance of Sun *mahadasa* at birth 2 years 6 months and 15 days.

Birth Ascendant

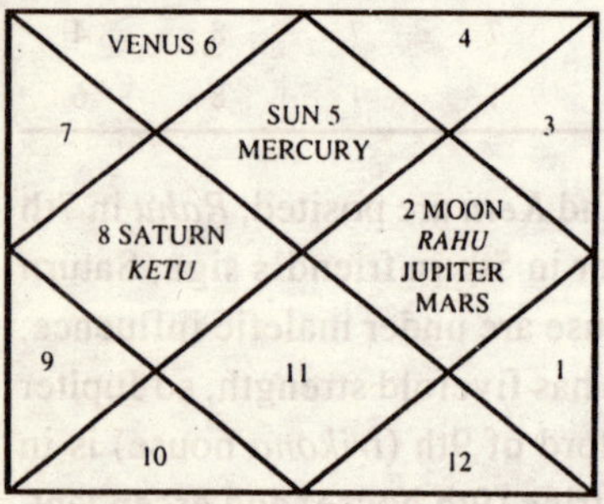

Moon Sign

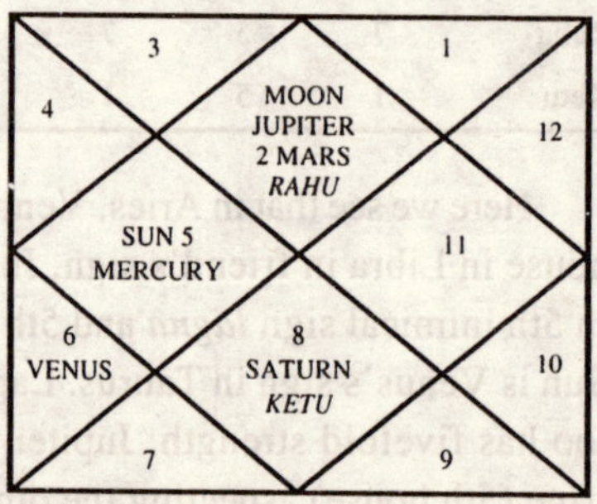

In this horoscope birth *lagna* Leo, lord of *lagna* Sun, Moon sign, lord of Moon sign Venus, lords of 4th and 5th houses both from birth *lagna* and Moon sign are badly afflicted by malefics.

The aspect of inimical signs Saturn and Mars on birth *lagna* make the heart sign Leo and its lord Sun weak. Moon is under malefic influence of *Rahu*, Mars, Saturn, *Ketu,* the four malefic planets.

The 4th and 5th houses from birth *lagna* Scorpio and Sagittarius signs and their lords are in inimical houses, occupied and aspected by Saturn and Mars. The 5th house from Moon is occupied by the debilitated Venus besides there is *Kalasarpa yoga* present in this horoscope due to the occupation of all planets between *Rahu* and *Ketu*. Lord of 8th house Jupiter and 12th house lord Moon are in 10th house among malefics. Thus lord's 6th and 7th houses Saturn fully aspects *lagna* and its lord, Moon and Jupiter, 4th house is occupied with two malefics *Ketu* and Saturn aspected by Mars, *Rahu*, Jupiter and Moon. Moon and Jupiter are the two benefics which are under affliction of four malefics Saturn, Ketu, Mars and Rahu. 5th house is also aspected by Mars and lord of 5th house Jupiter too is with two malefics Mars and *Rahu* aspected by two other malefics Saturn and *Ketu*. These 4th and 5th houses, their lords, *lagna, lagna* lord, Moon, its sign lord Venus all are under malefic affliction. Hence, heart trouble is clearly seen.

Due to these combinations the subject expired by heart attack in Saturn *mahadasa*, Mercury *antardasa* on 16-11-1985. Saturn *mahadasa* commenced from 21-10-1982. Saturn is the lord of 6th and 7th houses *maraka* and *markesh*. Besides Mercury too is *markesh* for Leo *lagna* being lord of second house.

Example 3. The third example of heart disease is that of Aries *lagna* and *Jyeshtha Nakshatra*, who died of heart attack.

A female born on 29-1-1946 Tuesday, *Jyeshtha Nakshatra* 4th quarter, Balance of Mercury *mahadasa* at birth time 0 year, 4 months and 4 days.

Birth Ascendant

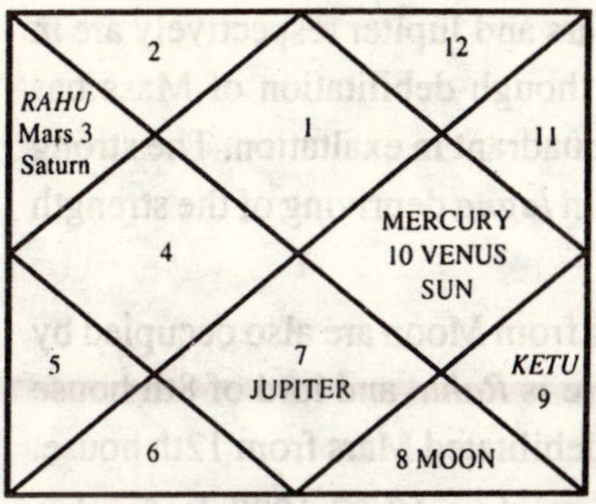

This female expired on 5-8-1997 by heart attack in *Rahu mahadasa. Rahu antardasa. Rahu mahadasa* from 3-6-1996 in *antardasa* of *Rahu* and *prtyantar-dasa* of Saturn resulted in the death of this female. Sun lord of 5th house is in inimical sign Capricorn in 6th house from the 5th house of his own sign Leo. Moon lord of 4th house is in 8th house debilitated (*neecha*). Cancer sign 4th house is aspected by malefic Sun, Mercury (lord of 6th) and Venus (being lord of 2nd and 7th *Markesh*). Sign Leo (5th house) is aspected by the *Rogakarak* Saturn from 3rd house. Sun and Saturn both are in 6th and 8th position to each other. Lord of ascendant Mars is under malefic affliction of *Rahu* and Saturn being itself in inimical house in Gemini.

Hence Sun and Moon and their signs, 4th and 5th houses along with lord of ascendant Mars are under heavy malefic affliction. Not only this but Jupiter a benefic planet is lord of 12th house being in inimical sign aspects the *lagna* and *lagna* lord which is not favourable. This lady was married to a widower.

Example 4. A female was born on 10-10-1949 with Leo *lagna* and *Kritika Nakshatra* 3rd quarter. *Vimshottari mahadasa* balance of Sun *mahadasa* one year, 6 months and 15 days. Here too there is Leo ascendant as in Example 2.

Birth Ascendant

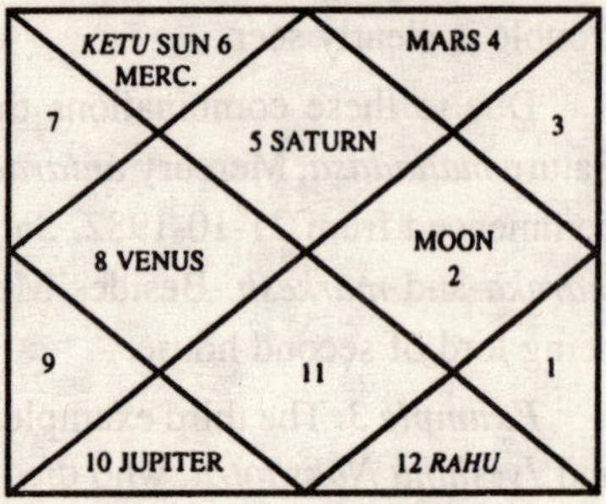

In this horoscope the signs Cancer and Leo both are occupied by two great malefics—Mars in debilitation and Saturn in great enemy's house, i.e. Leo. Lord of ascendant Sun is with *Ketu*, the great enemy of Sun. The lagna is under *papa, kartari yoga*. Moon is aspected by 8th lord Jupiter which is in debilitation (*neecha*) in 6th house. *Rahu* aspectation *lagna* lord Sun and 4th house, its lord Mars. Venus, the lord of 10th and 3rd houses is in inimical sign of happiness (4th house) in Scorpio. Moon is also the lord of 4th house though in 10th house in exaltation sign.

The lords of 4th and 5th houses, Mars and Jupiter respectively are in debilitated sign aspecting each other, though debilitation of Mass has been cancelled due to her position in a quadrant in exaltation. The strong enemy of *lagna* lord Sun, i.e., Saturn is in *lagna* depriving of the strength of Sun and *lagna*.

In the same way 4th and 5th houses from Moon are also occupied by Saturn, Sun and *Ketu*. In 8th house there is *Rahu* and lord of 8th house Jupiter is in debilitation is aspected by debilitated Mars from 12th house.

This lady died from a sudden heart attack on 19-07-1997. Before her expiry there was a sign of wound on external part of heart, i.e. in the chest. Thus this case may be an example of heart cancer too. Death occurred in Saturn *mahadasa* and Saturn is lord of evil houses of 6th and 7th. Saturn *mahadasa* was in force w.e.f. 25-4-1997. At the time of her death there was running *antardasa* of Mercury who is lord of 2nd house (*markesh*) and 11th house (house of obstacles).

Thus for Leo ascendant Saturn and Mercury both are *marakas* and death too occurred in *mahadasa* of Saturn, *antardasa* of Mercury.

Example 5. A male born on 22-11-1933 at 3 p.m. in the first quarter of *Swati nakshatra*. *Vimshottari mahadasa*—balance of *Rahu mahadasa*

14 years, 8 months and 23 days. Here in birth ascendant Capricorn lord of *lagna* Saturn is posited in retrogression aspecting the sign Cancer in opposition. In Leo sign *Ketu* is posited and *Rahu* aspects Leo too. From Moon too 4th and 5th houses are occupied by the two famous malefics Saturn and *Rahu* respectively.

Birth Ascendant

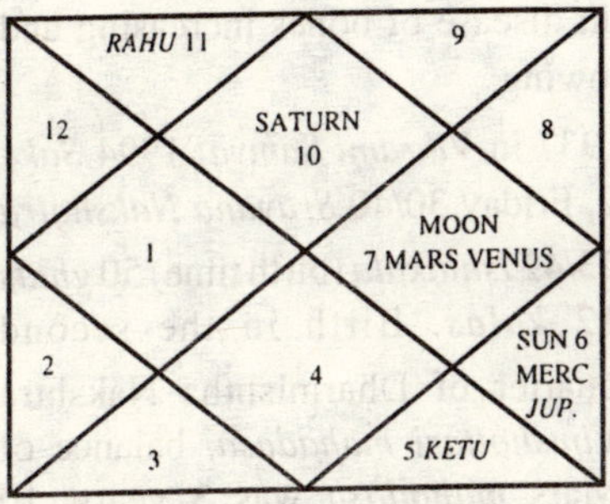

Hence, Cancer sign, Moon, Leo sign, Sun (between two malefics *Ketu* and Mars) are badly afflicted by malefics. Lord of 5th house from *lagna* Venus is in inimical sign and with strong malefics Mars. Lord of 6th house Mercury and lord of 6th house from Moon, i.e., Jupiter are with Sun who is the lord of another evil house, i.e. , 8th house.

Besides there is strong *Kalasarpa yoga* being all the planets between *Rahu* and *Ketu*. This person died from heart attack on 13-7-1988 at 4.00 p.m. in Mercury *mahadasa*, *antardasa* of Venus, *pratyantardasa* of Jupiter. Mercury lord of 6th Jupiter lord of 12th, Venus lord of 5th afflicted being with Sun lord of 8th, with Mars lord of 4th and 11th respectively. Ascendant has become weak by lagna lord Saturn being in retrogression respectively and aspected by Mars and Jupiter the lord of 12th.

Death Horoscope 13-7-1988

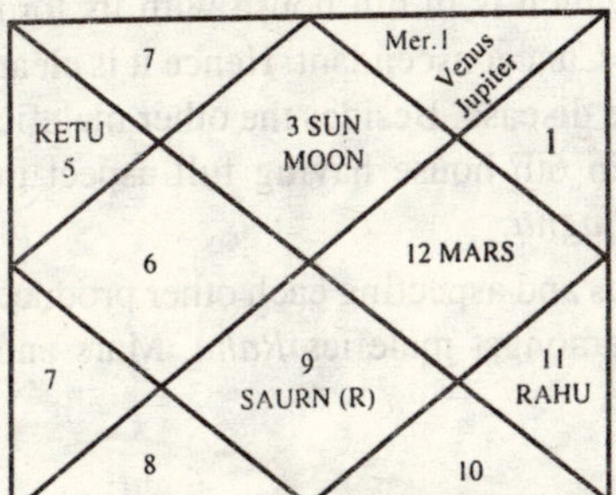

Ketu is in inimical sign in 8th house Leo which indicates sudden and mysterious death. At the time of death of this subject Gemini was rising which is 6th house sign in this horoscope. Saturn was in Sagittarius in retrogression aspecting the *lagna* Gemini in transit, Moon and Sun therein. *Rahu* aspects *lagna* Sun, Moon from 9th house. The lord of *mahadasa*, lord of *antardasa* Venus, lord of *pratyantardasa* Jupiter are in Taurus in 12th house. *Rahu* and *Ketu* are in same signs as in birth horoscope. 4th and 5th houses are aspected by Mars the lord of 6th and 11th houses along with Sun and Moon. Cancer is between malefics Sun and *Ketu*.

Bone Diseases

In the human body bones play an important role. Any kind of trouble in bones, marrow or blood deficiency is known through the Sun's position in horoscope and Sagittarius sign. Both of them are representatives of bones along with lord of Sagittarius Jupiter and Sun's sign Leo should also be considered. I am giving here the example of a female subject who is suffering from disease of bones increasing and breaking. The particulars are as following:

The subject was born on 17-9-1937 in *Vikrami Samvat* 1994 *Saka* 1859 *Bhadrapada Shukla Paksha* 12, Friday 30/40 *Sravana Nakshatra* 23/42 *Ishtakala* (birth time) 50 *ghats* 12 *kalas*. Birth in the second quarter of Dharmishtha Nakshtra *Vimshottari mahadasa,* balance of Mars *mahadasa* was 3 years, 10 months and 27 days. Birth ascendant Cancer and Moon sign Capricorn.

Birth Ascendant

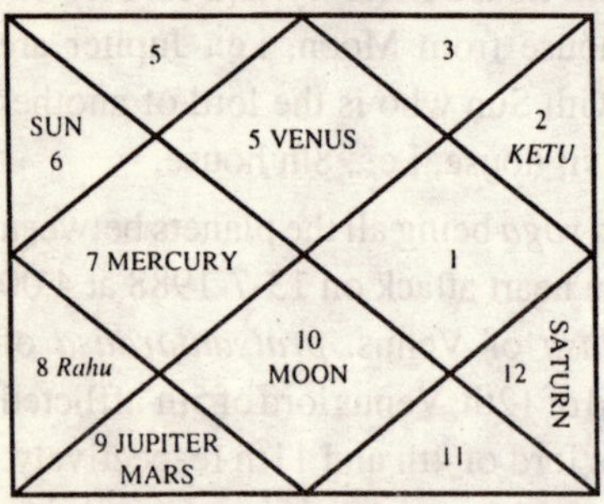

Mercury, Jupiter, Saturn are retrograded "प्रत्यक्षं किं प्रमाणं" which means when the case is clear then no question of proving it arises. The truth of astrology is present in this horoscope. We have mentioned earlier that Sun and Sagittarius sign represent bone. Saturn lord of 7th (*Markesh*) and 8th houses has full aspect on Sun and Sagittarius sign which is in 6th house with its lord Jupiter in natural house of disease for Cancer ascendant. Hence it is clear that the subject is suffering from bone disease. Besides the other malefic Mars is with Jupiter in Sagittarius in 6th house having full aspect in *Rogakaraka* Saturn, 12th house and *lagna*.

Saturn and Mars both are malefics and aspecting each other produce hypertension. Moon is hemmed in amongst malefics *Rahu*, Mars and Saturn. *Rahu* also aspects the *lagna*.

Bone Cancer

Bone declining case. I am giving below a case of bone declining case of a patient, that was not cured and death was at last due to this disease.

Male was born on Sunday date 25th February 1935 in Vishakha 2nd quarter ascendant Scorpio balance of Jupiter *mahadasa* for 9 years, 2 months and 24 days.

Birth ascendant

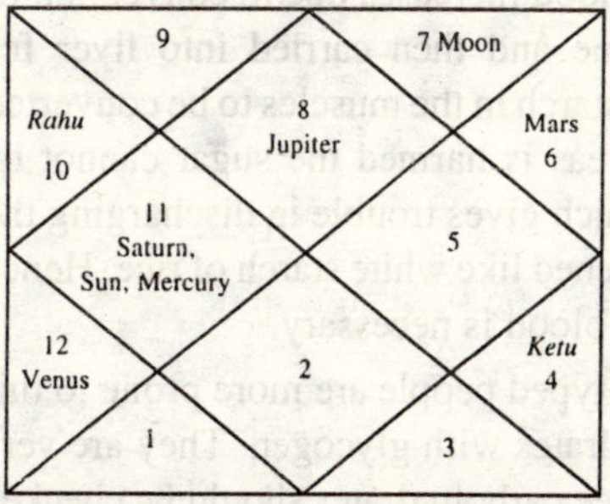

In an accident the person's shoulders were injured in September 1993. There was fracture in right shoulder in bone and special treatment was taken still the condition of the bone of the shoulder began to decline. It became incurable and the patient died in November 1993.

Here in Scorpio ascendant Jupiter is posited and the lord of the ascendant Mars is in enemy's sign in 11th house in Virgo. In 4th house there is lord of 8th house Mercury with lord of 10th house Sun and lord of 4th house Saturn. Mars is the lord of 6th house too. 6th house is the house of disease. Hence accident occurred due to Mars and became the cause of fracture of bone and could not be treated because Mars is in the house of enemy.

Sun is the *karaka* for bones and is posited in 4th house in inimical sign Aquarius with great malefic Saturn and natural *karaka* for diseases too. Sun and Saturn both are enemies. There is 6th 8th relation amongst Sun, Saturn and Mars. *Rahu* is in the 3rd house. 3rd house denotes shoulder, 11th house too denotes shoulder (left). Hence the injury of shoulders through sudden accident is proven here by two malefics in 3rd and 11th houses.

Mahadasa of *Rahu* began since 31st March 1992 and from the same say *Rahu antardasa* commenced. *Rahu* is famous for sudden accidents. *Rahu* is posited in right shoulder, 3rd house aspecting the left shoulder, 11th house where lord of ascendant is posited. So death occurred in *mahadasa,* and *antardasa* of *Rahu* because it is posited in the house which is 8th to 8th house and in 12th house from the location of lord of 8th house Mercury.

Why the fractured bone could not be cured is because combination of Sun (bone) and Saturn is not good. The 4th house from ascendant and Moon are occupied by malefics. From ascendant there are Sun and Saturn in 4th house and from Moon there is *Rahu* in 4th house. Mars is also aspecting the 6th house (house of disease). This is also a case of bone cancer.

Diabetes

When the quantity of sugar in blood increases due to conversion of carbohydrates into sugar in intestine and then carried into liver for conversion into glycogen, a form of starch in the muscles to be converted to sugar when needed. When pancreas is harmed the sugar cannot be stored and increases in the blood which gives trouble in discharging the urine. In this condition urine is thickened like white starch of rice. Hence test for contents of uric elements in blood is necessary.

According to astrology, Jupiter typed people are more prone to this disease as they are fond of carbohydrates with glycogen. They are very fond of sweet foods and starch. Hence carbohydrates should be checked and not to be allowed to increase sugar in the blood. People born on Thursday in Sagittarius/Pisces signs of Jupiter afflicted are prone to this disease. The main planet Jupiter afflicted by malefics either with them or aspected by them may cause diabetes.

Birth Ascendant

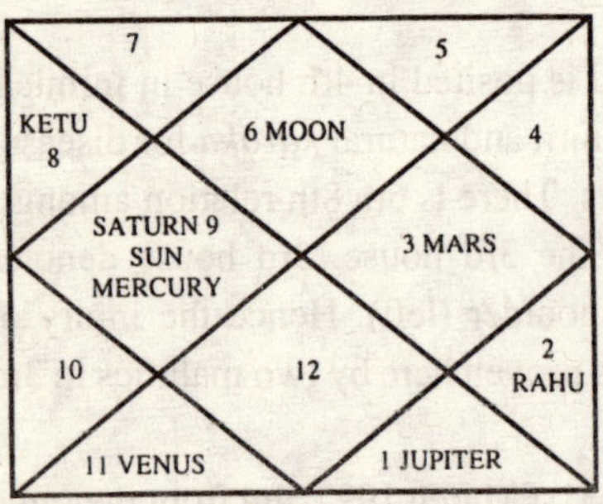

Example. A female was born on 3-1-1929, Thursday at 11.50 p.m. *Chitra Nakshatra*. Birth ascendant Virgo. In this example birth day is Thursday/Sun in Sagittarius with Saturn, Mercury and *Ketu* aspects Pisces. Mars aspects Sagittarius. Jupiter in 8th house in Aries sign of Mars (lord of 8th house). This female generally suffered from diabetes after the passage of 40 years of age. In her last days she got much trouble and remained in unconscious condition for 15 days prior to breathed her last on 21-3-1997.

Kidney Trouble

In our body kidney and liver are the two glands which are very important parts in abdomen. Liver is a gland from which bile is secreted while kidney is a pair of glands in abdomen which purifies the blood and separate urine. Kidney is disturbed when the salt indicated by Libra, i.e., sodium phosphate is not absorbed.

Lord of Libra is Venus and Venus is concerned with urine so when Libra is afflicted by malefics and Venus is adversely aspected by malefics or is with malefics then the kidney gets disturbed and stops working properly. This turns into a serious case because kidney disease is one of the serious diseases if it is not cured and checked at an early date and the patient has to live on dialysis . In dialysis the patient cannot be kept to live for a long period of time and transplantation becomes necessary. If proper kidney of the patient's blood group is not available the patient dies soon. Kidney donors charge between two to five lakh rupees generally. Hence, it is not a surety to find a suitable kidney in time and often transplantation too it is not a surety that the patient will survive.

When 6th house is aspected by Saturn and lord of 6th house has any relation with Jupiter then kidney trouble increases. Irregularities in taking proper diet and food at proper times and in proper proportion, exhaustive work, insomnia, melancholy, lack of appetite, are some of the main causes. So when this disease spreads blood turns into water and dialysis becomes necessary to extract the excretory matter mixed in the blood which causes trouble.

Kidney is divided into two parts—the right and the left. When kidney transplantation becomes necessary the donor donates one kidney and thereafter he has to live on one kidney. I am giving here some examples of kidney disease and transplantation of kidney.

Example 1. A male was born on 30-8-1955, Tuesday at 6.30 p.m. in Aquarius ascendant in the first quarter of *Sravana nakshatra* at 25°-41′ north and 78°-28′ east. Balance of Moon *mahadasa* was 2 years 10 months and 11 days at birth time.

Birth Lagna

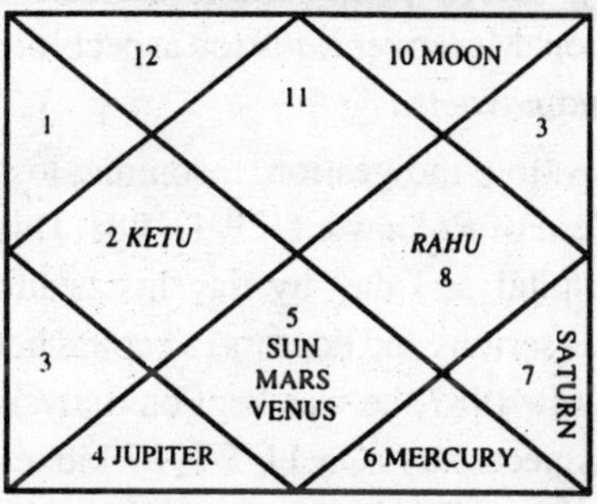

Navamsa

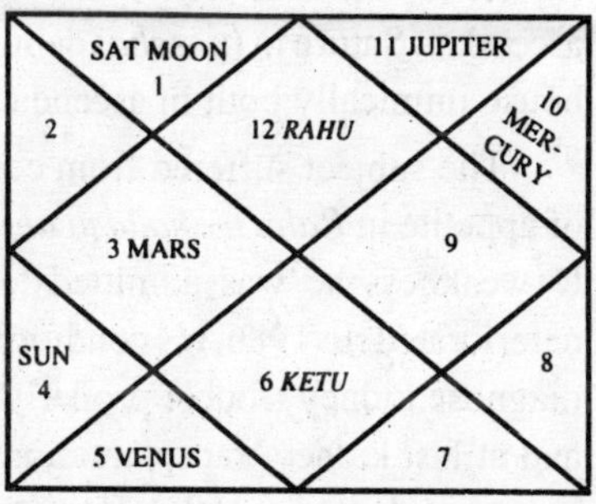

This man was born in *nakshatra antardasa* when *uttrashada nakshatra* was in last degree and *Sravana nakshatra* was rising. His birth time was *sandhikal* means end of day and beginning of night. The *lagna* Aquarius is not regarded auspicious in birth but Chanakya regards auspicious due to benefic *navamsa* not afflicted with malefics.

Here lord of ascendant is in Libra in exaltation but in *navamsa* in Aries in debilitation (*neecha*). 6th house is occupied by Jupiter in exaltation and is aspected by *karaka* of diseases Saturn, the lord of ascendant Libra is occupied by malefic Saturn and lord of Libra Venus is in inimical house with two malefics Sun and Mars in Leo and is combust too. 7th house is a *maraka* house for Aquarius ascendant born people and lord of 7th Sun is *markesh*. In the same way Jupiter being the lord of second is too *markesh*. Libra is occupied with malefics. Besides Jupiter is highly related with 6th house aspecting the lord of 6th house Moon in 12th house. The evil houses 6th, 8th and 12th are occupied by natural benefics that is not good.

In *navamsa* too Libra is aspected by Saturn and lord of 6th Moon. Venus is hemmed in between two natural malefics Sun and *Ketu*. Jupiter in exaltation 6th house (an evil house) has lost his good quality and in *navamsa* being lord of *navamsa* is in 12th house in Aquarius being in malefic sign of disease giver Saturn. In this horoscope Mercury, Jupiter, Saturn are the three planets in exaltation. There is *Ashubha yoga* strong due to occupation of malefics in trines and quadrants both in birth ascendant and *navamsa*.

The notable thing to be seen is that Venus is in *vargottam navamsa*. But in inimical sign this *vargottam* has been turned into bad position giving the worst possible disease, kidney trouble. Mercury, Jupiter, Saturn are exalted but in *navamsa*, Mercury, Jupiter is in Saturn's sign, Jupiter in Aquarius turned into highly malefic planet and lord of Libra ascendant Saturn in (*neecha*) debilitation. Moreover *Rahu* too aspects 6th house inimically both in ascendant and *navamsa*.

The subject suffered from constipation, indigestion, insomnia, loss of appetite in *Rahu mahadasa antardasa* of *Rahu* w.e.f. 29-1-1984. Due to weakness he was admitted to hospital and day by day his health deteriorated. In 1986, his condition was serious and doctors too could not diagnose kidney trouble properly. But in 1987, he was kept on dialysis and at last kidney transplantation was necessary. On 11-5-1987 kidney was transplanted at Jaslok Hospital Bombay. The kidney was donated by his wife she was and the transplantation was successful. But after 17 months in October, 1988 the kidney stopped working and the patient breathed his last on 3-11-1988.

The horoscope of patient's wife is as follows:

She was born on 30-3-1957 at 3.00 a.m., *Vikrami Samvat* 2013, *Saka* 1878 *Chaitra Krishna Paksha,* and Friday 13-49, *Shatbhisha nakshatra* 8-20. Then after *Poorva Bhadra pada* 3rd quarter with balance of Jupiter *mahadasa* 4 years 4 months 28 days at birth time.

Birth Lagna Chart

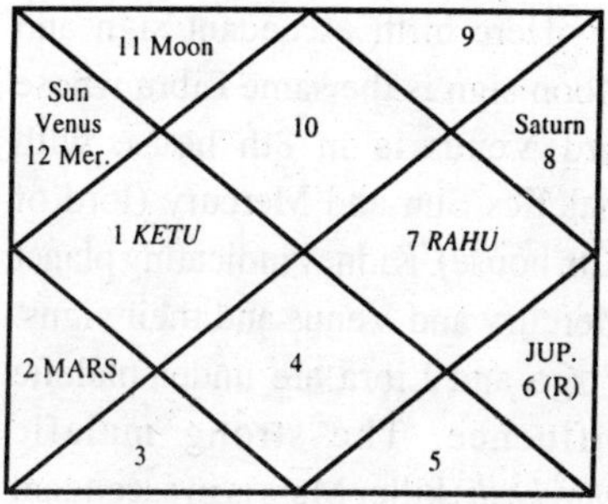

Navamsa Chart

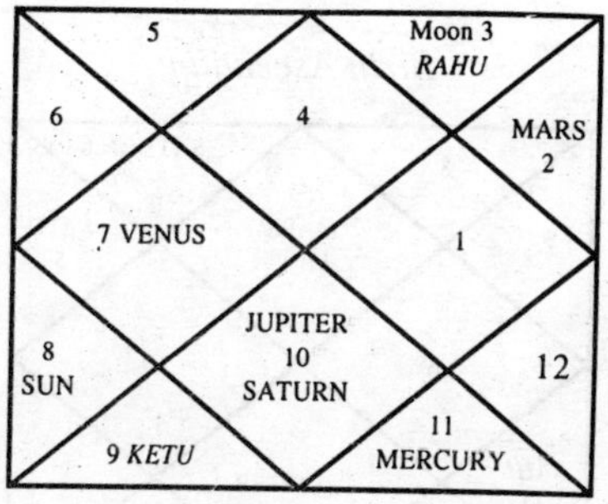

In this horoscope the 6th house lord Mercury is in debilitation in 3rd house in Pisces with lord of 8th Sun and Venus lord of 5th and 10th aspected by retrograded Jupiter from 9th house. Jupiter is the lord of 12th house too with lordship of 3rd house. 6th house is being aspected by malefic *Rahu.* Virgo and Libra both signs indicating kidney and their lords Mercury and Venus have weak position under malefic influence. Mercury is in debilitation and Venus is combust, though in exaltation sign. Virgo aspected by lord of 6th and 8th houses, 12th house has fallen weak, Libra is under malinfluence of Rahu. Besides Saturn being in inimical sign and Mars too in inimical sign aspect the 8th house, the house of *saubhagya* for ladies. Hence this combination indicates harm to matrimonial happiness and affects the longevity of life of husband. Mars in 5th aspecting Leo indicating operation of kidney for the sake of husband's life security.

In *navamsa* 7th house, the house of husband is occupied by Jupiter (lord of 6th house) and Saturn lord of 7th and 8th houses. Seventh house is hemmed in between two malefics *Ketu* and Mercury (lord of 12th house). Saturn's aspect on 4th and 9th houses when Venus is posited is proving fatal to the subject's happiness and luck. Mars have too aspects Leo in 2nd, 5th and 6th houses. Moon's position is bad in 12th house with Rahu. Hence the subject had to donate her kidney. She donated her kidney on 11-5-1987 to save the life of her husband in *Budh* (Mercury) *mahadasa, antardasa* of Sun. Mercury is lord of 6th house indicating kidney (disease) and Sun is lord of 8th house (longevity and happiness of husband). Hence it is clear proving the sacrifice of kidney for saving the life of husband.

Example 2. A male was born on 4-6-1952 at 4.00 p.m., Wednesday in Libra ascendant, 4th quarter of *Chitra nakshatr*. Balance of Mars *mahadasa* was 1 year 8 months and 18 days.

Birth Ascendant

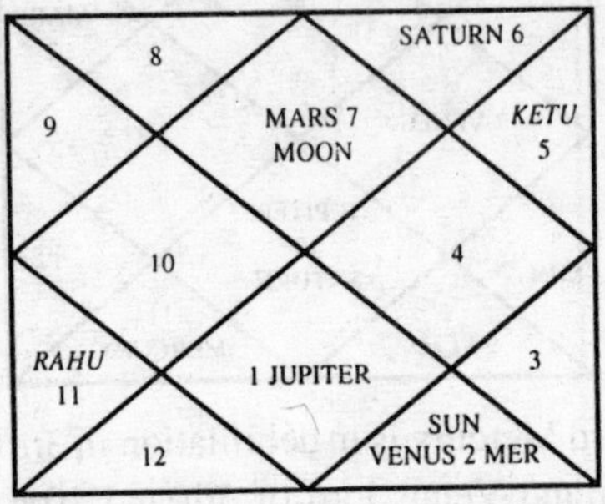

Here birth ascendant sign and Moon sign is the same Libra whose lord Venus is in 8th house with malefics Sun and Mercury (lord of 12th house). Kidney indicating planet Mercury and Venus and their signs. Virgo and Libra are under malefic influence. The strong malefic (*markesh*) killer Mars is in ascendant with Moon therein. Virgo is in 12th house occupied by malefic Saturn and Mercury and Venus are ill posited in 8th house, the house of longevity and death indicating clearly that death will be due to kidney trouble. Besides Jupiter lord of 6th house Jupiter in Aries aspects the Moon and birth ascendant. Saturn aspects the 6th house. The combination in this horoscope is similar to the combination in example 1.

Saturn *mahadasa* from 22-2-1988 in order and *antardasa* of Saturn was running. He felt uneasiness in July 1989 owing to constipation, loss of appetite, nausea, indigestion. Doctors declared kidney trouble. He was kept on dialysis in November 1989. But delay occurred in finding out a suitable kidney for transplantation and he could not be survived and expired ultimately on 2-2-1990.

Paralysis

When lagna, Sun, Moon and Mercury are under malefic and affliction and attack the person then paralysis disease in the body. Rahu and Saturn represent paralysis of nerves hence aspect of Saturn and Rahu on ascendant increases this disease. Mercury rules over skin and nervous system. Below is given an example of paralysis disease.

A male was born on 25-3-1932, Friday, *Vishakha Nakshatra* in the third quarter of birth time at 0.45 a.m. Balance of Jupiter *mahadasa* was 10 years, 6 months and 10 days.

Birth Ascendant

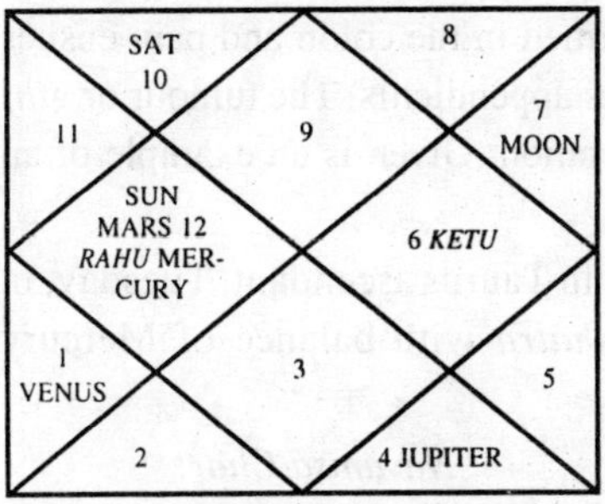

Navamsa

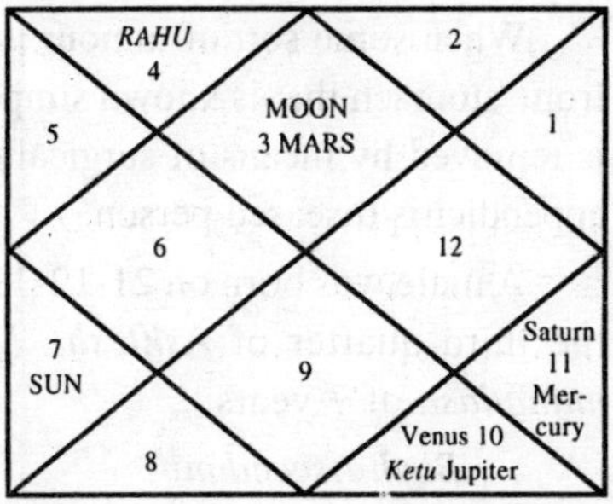

Here the lord of *lagna* Jupiter is in 8th house in Sagittarius in exaltation, but retrograded and aspected by a malefic and *maraka* (being lord of second house) Saturn.

Sun is in the 4th house with three malefics—*Rahu*, Mars (lord of 12 house) and Mercury the lord of 7th house, a *marak* and aspected by the another malefic and *maraka* Saturn. The greatest malefic and disease supplying planet Saturn has full aspect on Sun, Jupiter and Moon. From Moon in 6th house are Sun, Mercury, Mars and *Rahu*. Moon is aspected by Venus (lord of 6th house) and Mars.

In *navamsa* Mercury is with Mars and Jupiter, lord of ascendant is in debilitation with *Ketu* aspected by Mars and *Rahu*. Hence, *lagna, lagna* lord, Mercury are under malefic influence of Saturn, Mars and *Rahu*.

The subject was attacked by paralysis in 1989 in Venus *mahadasa, antardasa* of Saturn. After 3-4 months' relaxation the disease again attacked in 1990. Between 1989 and 1991 two attacks were suffered in right part of the body as the 2nd to 6th houses represent the right side of the body.

At last the subject died from paralysis in March 1991 in Venus *mahadasa, antardasa* of Mars. Venus is the lord of 6th house and Mars is the lord of 12th house. The subject was firstly attacked by paralysis at the age of 57 and died in his 59th year of age in March 1991. The planetary position mentioned above is generally seen in the cases of other paralytic diseases suffered patients. Note the influence of Saturn and *Rahu* on Jupiter, the lord of *lagna* having free aspect. Besides Mercury is in debilitation with Sun and *Rahu* in 4th house. Saturn too aspects Mercury. Thus Jupiter, the *lagna* lord, Moon, Mercury are under malefic influence hence paralysis is proving here itself.

Appendicitis

When some sort of tumour is formed in the colon and pain ensues from stomach that is known simply as appendicitis. The tumour or *gilti* is removed by means of surgical operation. Given is an example of an appendicitis diseased person.

A male was born on 21-12-1937 in Taurus ascendant, Tuesday, in the third quarter of *Ashlesha Nakshatra* with balance of Mercury *mahadasa* of 7 years.

Birth Ascendant

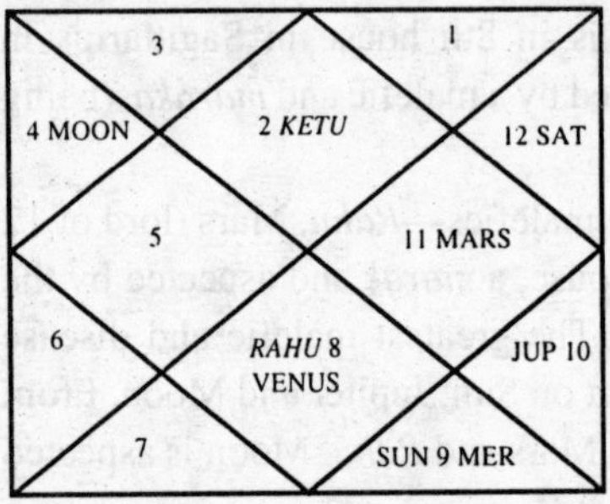

Navamsa Chart

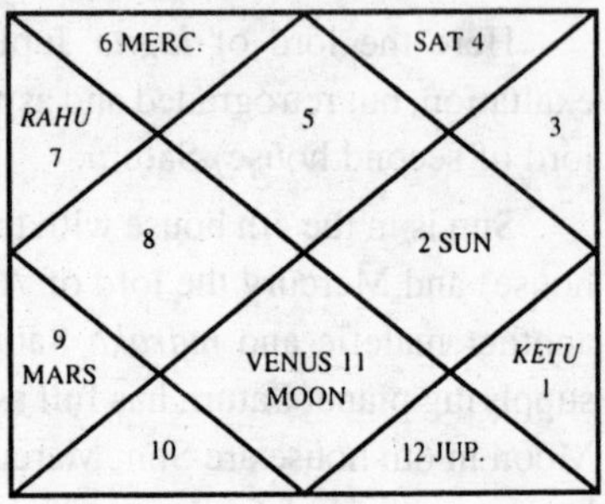

The 5th house is aspected by Mars in birth ascendant and its lord is Mercury in 8th house with Sun (lord of 4th house) in *navamsa* Mars is in 5th house, 5th lord is in 8th house in *navamsa* Jupiter. Hence it proves itself by the position of 5th lord and Mars, Jupiter that there is some kind of trouble and pain in stomach due to Mars' relation with 5th house and 5th lord's position in 8th house in both the charts.

Mantreswara in *Phal Deepika* says that all the tumours in stomach are formed due to influence of Mars and Jupiter. Being in 5th house in Sagittarius in Jupiter's sign and Jupiter is in inimical sign of Virgo in 2nd house. In *navamsa* Mars is in inimical sign. Virgo being. The lord of 5th house and Jupiter in *navamsa* though exalted but with Saturn lord of 7th and 8th houses has become afflicted.

The operation of the patient for appendicitis took place on Tuesday dated 28-1-1975 in Sun *mahadasa* and Saturn *antardasa*. Sun is the lord of 5th sign of *Kalapurusha* in Zodiac, i.e., hence the operation was successful.

Example 2. A female was born on Sunday dated 29.10.1950 in the first quarter of *Mrigsira nakshatra,* in Leo ascendant with balance of Mars *mahadasa* of 6 years and 3 months.

Birth Ascendant

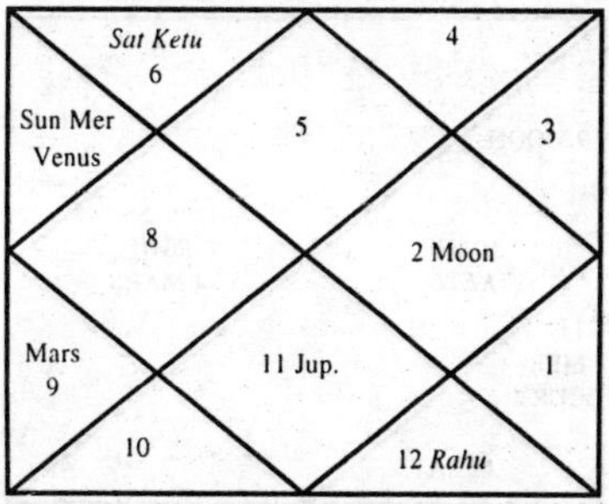

Navamsa

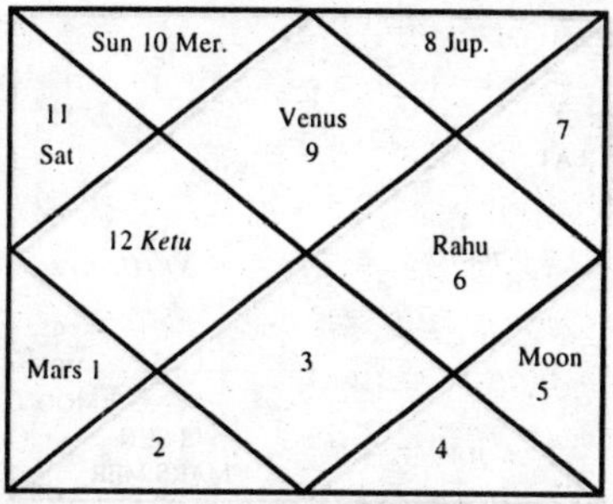

As in example one here also Mars is in 5th house (house of stomach) in both the charts. Jupiter aspecting the birth *lagna* and Mars aspecting the Jupiter in *navamsa* again Jupiter aspects the 4th house in *navamsa* where *Ketu* is posited. Saturn aspects the 4th house in birth *lagna* and 5th house in *navamsa*. The lord of 5th Leo of *Kalpurusha*'s sign of stomach is in debilitation in Libra *lagna* and in inimical sign Capricorn in *navamsa*. Hence operation for appendicitis is justified. The operation took place on Saturday dated 29-1-1994 in Saturn *mahadasa* and Mercury *antardasa*. Mercury's both signs are under malefic influence as Mars aspects Gemini and Virgo is occupied with Saturn, *Ketu* the two malefics in birth chart and in *navamsa* Mercury is in sign of Capricorn (lord of Saturn). In Virgo is *Rahu* and on Gemini aspect of lord of 6th Venus is to be noted.

Accidents

Sudden accidents by train, bus or by any other vehicle also cause accidents. They are generally due to vehicle (Venus) and 4th house and its lord's position in the horoscope. Mars represents blood. Hence Mars, position should be studied to find out the actual cause of accidents. Given below is an example of train accident.

A male was born on 20-11-1944 in Aries ascendant in the first quarter of *Uttrashada nakshatra* with the balance of Sun *mahadasa* of 4 years, 9 months and 18 days.

The train accident happened on Thursday dated 26.5.1988 in *Uttra Phalguna nakshatra* after which *Hasta nakshatra* was in order and *mahadasa* of Jupiter was running *antardasa* of Saturn was in force till 8-5-1989. Lord of *lagna* Mars with lord of 5th Sun and 6th Mercury in 8th house denotes accident because from 4th house *Rahu* is aspecting these

Birth Horoscope

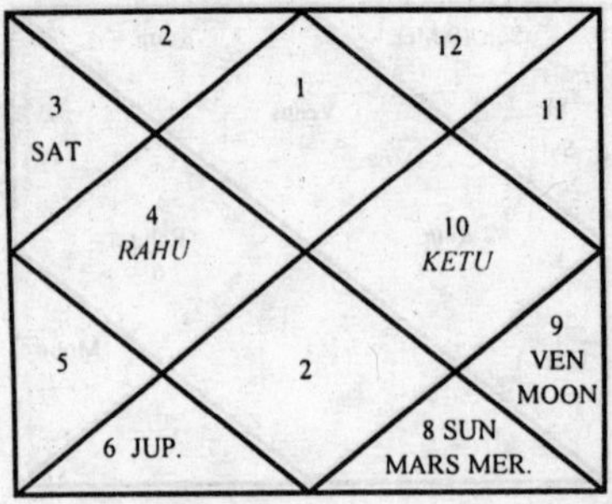

Navamsa

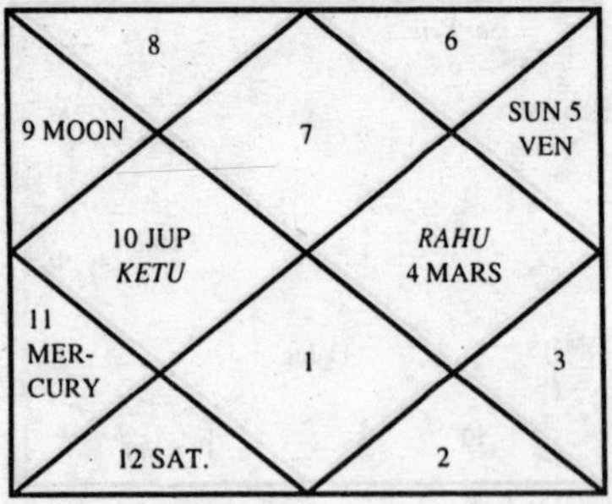

three planets in 8th house. *Rahu* is expert in creating accidental events. 4th house is the house of vehicle and 7th house is the house of travel. The lords of 4th and 7th houses Venus and Moon respectively are in 9th house aspected by great malefic Saturn retrograded. In *navamsa* chart Jupiter is in 4th house with *Ketu* aspected by two malefics *Rahu* and Mars debilitated. Saturn is aspecting the 4th hous by retrograded aspect. Hence the 4th and 7th houses are under affliction. The *Karaka* for vehicle is Venus who is with Sun in 11th house in *navamsa* combust, so weak. The day on which accident happened was Thursday and the transit horoscope was as following:

Transit Horoscope 26-5-1988

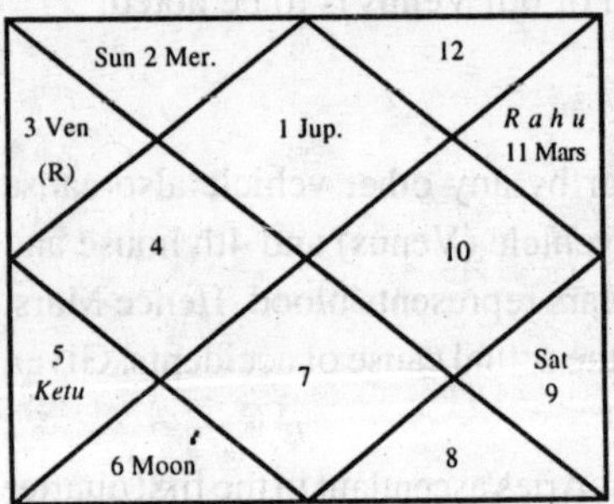

Jupiter is in 6th house in birth horoscope being lord of an evil house (12th) and occupying an evil house (6th). Hence Jupiter has been turned into a malefic planet because on his other sign Sagittarius is his bitter enemy and Venus is posited with Moon. Besides 9th house is surrounded by malefics *Ketu* and the Sun, Moon and Mercury in birth chart.

In transit horoscope Jupiter is in birth *lagna*. As *navamsa* is the fruit of the birth horoscope when Jupiter was in transit in first house aspecting 7th house, Venus in 3rd, Moon in 6th, Mars and *Rahu* in 11th, Mars aspecting true Moon, *Rahu* aspecting the 7th house of travel.

The *navamsa* chart of this horoscope is telling that when Jupiter will be in *Kendra* and *Rahu* and Mars comming together in a sign, Moon aspected by Saturn, the accident may happen.

At birth time Jupiter is in *Uttra Phalguna nakshatra* and on the date of accident, i.e., on 26.5.1988 the day was Thursday, *nakshatra* was *Uttra Phalguna* than *Hasta*. The victim was hurt heavily in head, shoulder, hands and leg was fractured but by the grace of God he survived. Jupiter is a divine planet and in transit was in (*Tanmanav*) *lagna* aspecting the 9th house (God's grace). Hence Jupiter became *Maraka* and *Karaka* both. Though Jupiter is a natural benefic and *Karaka* for Aries born victim due to his position in birth horoscope was turned into malefic, but ultimately saved the life being in *lagna* in transit.

Renal Diseases

Many combinations are found in old Sanskrit texts of astrology experienced by our great *rishis* and *munis*. For urinary diseases see the following line of verse:

कुजेस्ते संस्थे खलु युक्त दृष्टे स्यान्मूत्रकृच्छीपुरूषोपिहीनः

J.S.S. 7–50

which means Mars in 7th house with or aspected by malefics the patient will suffer from urinary diseases. One aspect of urinary disease owing to formation of stone which stops the urine from coming out.

Birth Ascendant

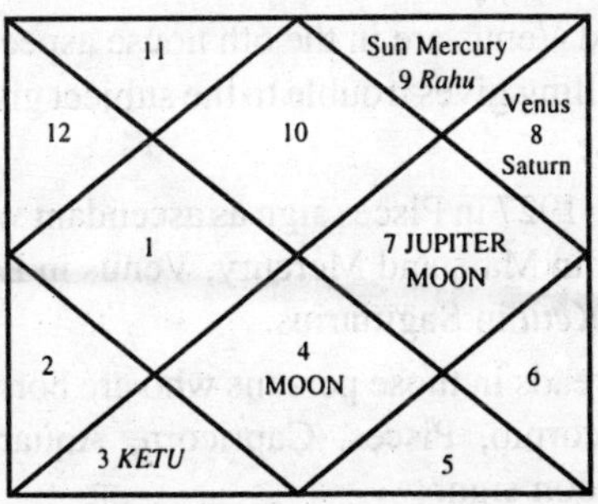

Example. A male was born on 9-1-1898 A.D. *Vishakha Nakshatra* in the first quarter of 7.45 a.m. in Capricorn ascendant. Balance of Jupiter *mahadasa* was 13 years, 10 months and 12 days.

In this horoscope Mars is in Cancer in debilitation (*neecha*) sign. Mars' position without aspected by malefics or combined is very weak and critical. The 8th house (house of urine) is occupied by Saturn, a supermalefic in inimical sign. Eighth sign in Zodiac of *Kalapurusha* is Scorpio, whose lord Mars is in debilitation hence urinary disease is confirmed according to the verse mentioned above. Venus too is weak in inimical sign. Not only this but the 8th lord from Moon is too (Taurus lord) Venus who is with Saturn in sign of Mars a bitter enemy of Venus and Saturn. Mars aspects Moon and *lagna* too.

The subject went for pilgrimage to Uttarakhand, i.e., Haridwar, Rishikesh, Badrinath in the summer season in 1962 in Venus *mahadasa antardasa* of *Rahu*. There he took strong mineral water. After coming back from pilgrimage he felt trouble in passing urine. Then he consulted doctor who diagnosed the malady as formation of stones in the kidneys. After undergoing operation for removal of stones he passed urine at the age of 65 years for some time but could not live for more time and breathed his last in February, 1963.

Besides all the above-mentioned combinations there is *Gaja Kesari Yoga*, being Jupiter, Moon in 10th house. The subject was always having happy mood. There is *Kala Sarpa Yoga* too in the horoscope being all the planets between *Ketu* and *Rahu*. Though *Kala Sarpa Yoga* has been turned into *"kalamrit yoga"* according to the work of Kalidasa "Uttar Kalamrit" wherein he opined that when there is *Ketu* from 1st to 6th houses with all the planets between *Rahu* and *Ketu Kala Sarpa Yoga* is cancelled.

This man was married in 1926. He had five children. His wife expressed at the age of 44 years in 1942.

Swelling

सिते गष्पितौ षष्ठगे पापदृष्टे स शोथो J.S.S. 7–55

This line explains when Jupiter and Venus are in the 6th house aspected by malefics then the disease of swelling gives trouble to the subject given below is an example of this disease.

A male child was born on 14-7-1927 in Pisces sign as ascendant with Jupiter there Sun *Rahu* in Gemini, in Mars and Mercury, Venus in Leo, Saturn in *Scropi'o* and *Moon and Ketu* in Sagittarius.

Swelling disease generally spreads in those persons who are born in watery signs such as Cancer, Scorpio, Pisces, Capricorn, Aquarius whether it may be ascendant or Moon sign.

Birth Ascendant

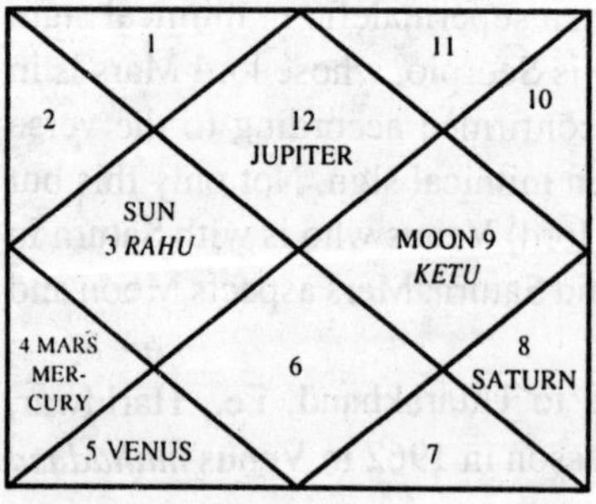

This person struggled with disease of swelling for one and a half years in *mahadasa* of Mercury *antardasa* of *Ketu* and Venus in 1995-96. Here Venus in 6th house in Leo is fully aspected by Saturn. When water increases abnormally in the body and is not absorbed due to the deficiency of concerned salts to the relative sign then swelling increases in the body and blood decreases and there is also fear of kidney trouble, liver trouble, etc. Hence swelling must be treated as soon as possible.

Asthma

According to *Jataka Tatwa* of Mahadev Pathak "भौमार्क्य दृष्टे लग्नेश्वास क्षयादिः" means when Mars and Saturn aspect the *lagna* then the diseases of asthma, T.B., etc. attack the subject. Generally when Venus and Moon are in 3rd, 6th and 11th houses, or in watery signs birth in January or February, then the person's nature is windy and coughy and they are commonly prone to cold, cough, lungs disease, T.B., etc. an example of is patient of Asthma is given below.

A male was born on 22nd January, 1927. Saturday, in the third quarter of *Uttra Phalguna.*

Here the month is January which is the cool season. Birth sign is watery, Saturn is in *lagna*, Scorpio and Mars aspect it from the 6th house. Asthma is also considered from the second sign of *Kalapurusha* in

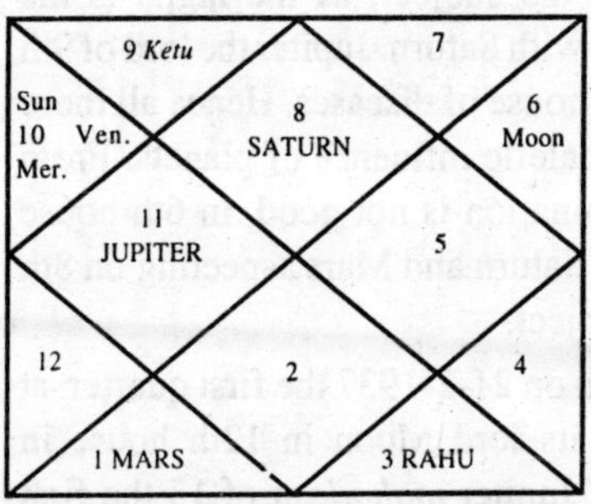

Taurus. Here Taurus is aspected by the disease supplier Saturn. Besides Taurus is surrounded by two malefics, Mars and *Rahu* are producing *Papa Kartari Yoga* for Taurus. The third sign of *Kalapurusha* in Gemini. From second to second hence Gemini is also considered the *Karaka* or representative of asthma. Gemini is occupied by *Rahu.* From Moon 2nd house is aspected by *Mars* and in 3rd house there is Saturn. In 2nd house from *lagna* there is *Ketu.* Jupiter, though aspected by *Rahu* from 8th house is in *kendra* being the lord of a trine, the 5th house hence strong. The lord of trine if posited in *kendra* gets double strength. Hence the disease is under control due to Jupiter.

Example 2. A male child was born on 2-7-1934, in *Vikrami, Samvat* 1991, *Ashada* month, *Krishna Paksha* 4, Saturday 49/35, *Sravana nakshatra,* 8/22 *Ishtakala* 52, *ghapi* 30, *palas* in Aries *lagna* with balance of Mars.

Mars *mahadasa* was 1 year, 6 months 10 days.

Birth Chart

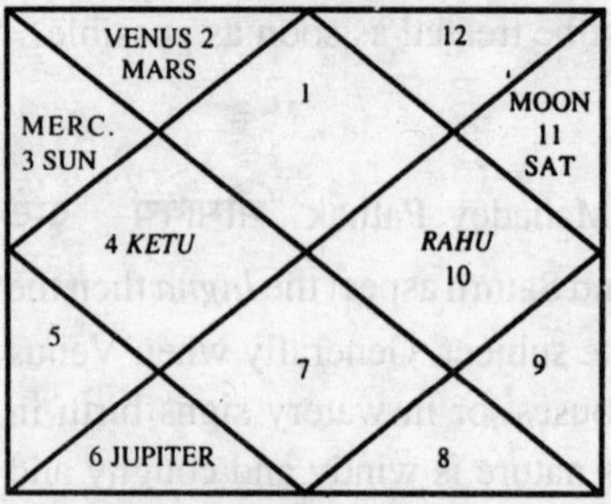

In this horoscope the lord of *lagna* Mars is with *marakesh* Venus in 2nd house aspected by *Rahu* from 10th house and by Jupiter from 6th house, Saturn aspects the *lagna*. The *Ragakaraka* Saturn (supplier of diseases) is with Moon. The 2nd house is the house of *Swas*. Venus and Mars are bitter enemies hence this combination produces asthma disease.

The combination of 1st and 2nd house lords made the subject's life full with suffering. This man suffered for long with asthma and died of this disease on 25-2-1989 at the age of 55 years. The disease increased in Saturn *Mahadasa* and death occurred in Mercury *mahadasa*, Mercury *antardasa*. Mercury is the lord of 3rd and 6th houses, the 3rd house is 8th house from 8th house in birth chart.

Saturn's aspect inimically made the subject, as the lagna is the debilitated sign for Saturn. Moon too is with Saturn. Jupiter the lord of 9th and 12th houses is inimical sign in the house of diseases. Hence all these things made the horoscope weak by malefic influence of planets. From moon in 4th house Venus-Mars combination is not good, in 6th house there is *Ketu*, a bitter enemy of Moon. Saturn and Mars aspecting on 8th house and show shorten life of the subject.

Example 3. A male child was born on 21-2-1937 the first quarter at 3.00 p.m. in Cancer ascendant with its lord Moon in 12th house in *Punarvasu nakshatra* with balance of Jupiter *mahadasa* of 13 the first quarter years, 9 months and 8 days.

Birth Ascendant

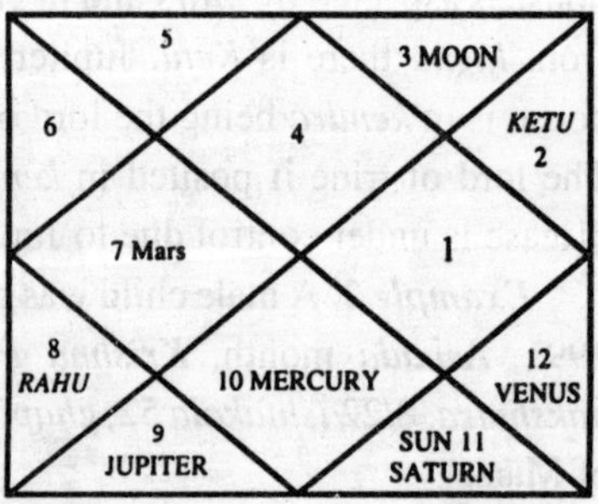

In this horoscope Moon is aspected by lord of 6th house Jupiter in his own house Sagittarius. Lord of 2nd house Sun is with his great enemy Saturn in 8th house of death. From Moon 2nd house in her own house Cancer aspected by lord of 12th and 3rd Mercury. Saturn aspects the sign of Taurus, the 2nd house of *Kalapurusha* in Zodiac. Besides

Rahu also aspects Taurus and *lagna* with Venus in 9th house. Thus Venus and Moon whose nature is cold and cough are under malefic influence causing bronchitis. This produced asthma to the subject.

The subject also suffered too much in *mahadasa* of *Ketu* by asthma and breathed his last in Saturn *mahadasa* in *antardasa* of Sun in 1980 at the age of 43. In this horoscope Moon, Mars, Jupiter—these are the three lords of trinal houses, i.e. 1-5-9 and are badly afflicted by their position, e.g. Moon in an evil house of 12th, Jupiter in another house of evil—the 6th, and Mars though in *Kendra* but in inimical house in the sign of Libra. Mars in the house of Venus in 4th house has lost his utility. Thus the 2nd house from *lagna*, Moon, Aries (1st sign of *Kalapurusha* in Zodiac) are under malefic influence causing the patient with asthma disease and poor longevity.

Epilepsy

Epilepsy is a disease of the nervous system. Near wells, rivers, dams, *kund*, etc., water attracts the victim and then there is foaming in mouth, giddiness and the victim falls down. In such victims horoscope water sign, water planet such as Moon and Venus play an important role in causing this disease. I am giving examples of two persons here suffering from this disease.

A female was born on 30-10-1959 at 8.30 p.m. in Taurus ascendant, in the first quarter of *Chitra Nakshatra,* balance of Mars *mahadasa* of 6 years, 1 month and 15 days.

Birth Chart

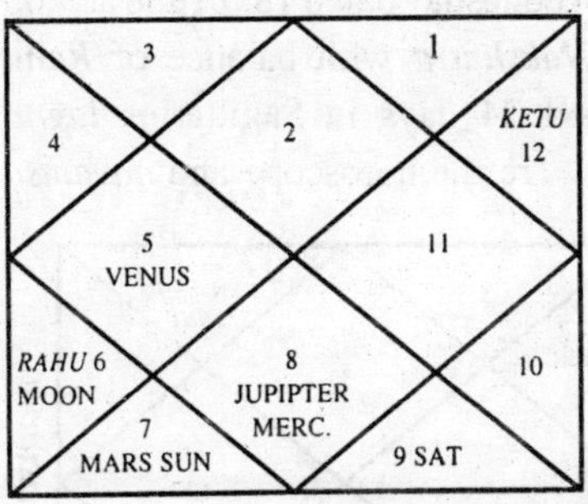

Navamsa Chart

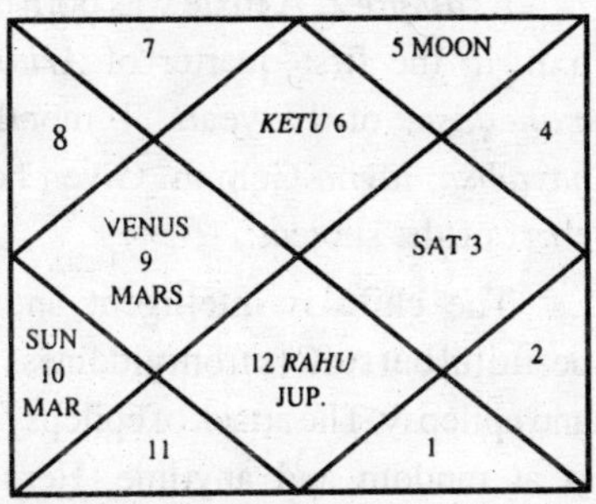

In this horoscope lord of *lagna* Venus in enemy sign, Moon too is in enemy sign with *Rahu* aspected by Saturn are heavily afflicted. Both of these, are watery planets, 5th house is occupied by Moon and *Rahu,* its lord Mercury is in watery sign with lord of 8th house. 5th lord is under

Papakartari yoga being between Mars and Sun, and Saturn aspected by *Ketu*. Hence heavy load on nervous system is seen here. So when nervous disturbance is made by Moon, Mercury by malefic aspect or occupation epilepsy occurs.

In *navamsa* too *lagna,* and 5th house both are under malefic influence afflicted by *Ketu*, Sun, Mars and Moon in 12th house (in an evil house) aspected by Saturn and Mars is hemmed resulting in epilepsy.

After marriage this lady was rejected by her husband when he came to know about her disease, so she lived in her parents' house for some years and died in Jupiter *mahadasa*, Venus *antardasa* in 1992. In *navamsa* in 4th house Venus-Mars combination is not auspicious for happy life. In 7th house *Rahu*-Jupiter combination is unauspicious for happy married life. Hence Jupiter being lord of the 8th house in birth chart and lord of the 7th being a *marakesh*, Venus in 4th house malefic Mars in enemy sign gave short and unhappily diseased life.

Birth Chart

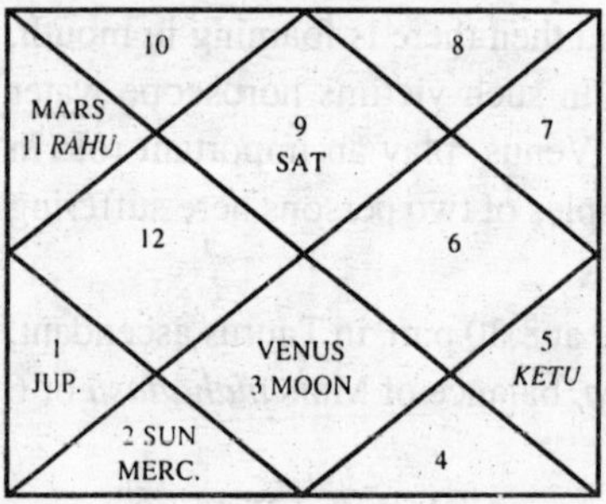

Moon Chart

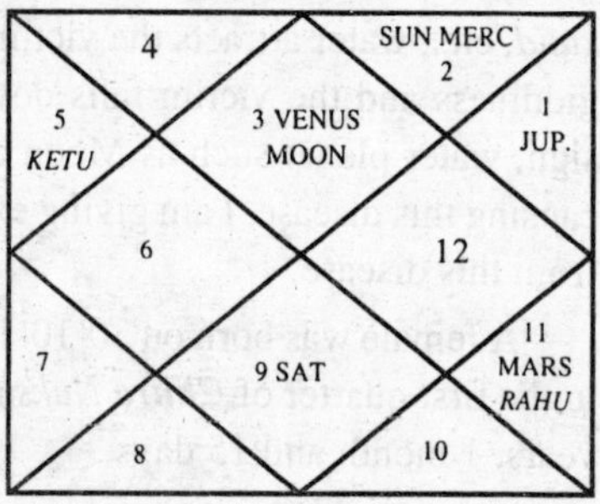

Example 2. A male was born on Wednesday dated 18.5.1988 at 9.00 p.m. in the first quarter of *Aridra Nakshatra* with balance of *Rahu mahadasa,* of 17 years, 1 month and 24 days in Sagittarius *lagna navamsa, lagna* Gemini. Given below are the horoscope and *navamsa* chart of the subject:

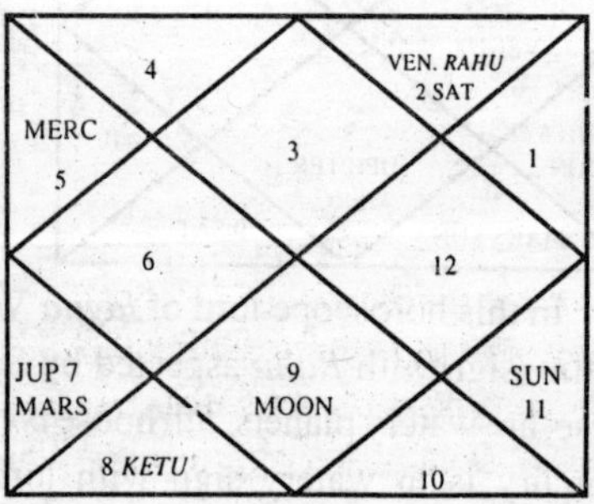

Navamsa Chart

The child is intelligent and beautiful but suffers from giddiness and epilepsy. The attack of epilepsy is at random and anytime. Here watery planets Moon and Venus are in quadrant in 7th house, sign of Gemini aspected by Saturn (*markesh*) and *Rahu*. In 5th house there is Jupiter aspected by Mars from 3rd house. Mars also aspects 6th house (house of diseases) where Sun and Mercury are posited.

In Moon chart lord of 8th Mars aspects the Moon sign, lord Mercury in 12th house. Moon and Venus are aspected by Saturn. In navamsa 6th lord Mars is in 5th house with Jupiter *marakesh* and lord of birth ascendant. Thus 5th house and its lord are under malefic influence. Moon is between two malefics Sun and *Ketu*. Mars in 5th house gives hypertension and mental disturbance too much.

It seems that perhaps in Jupiter *mahadasa* the subject may be out of the grip of this disease because Jupiter aspects the *lagna* being *lagna* lord. Saturn (*markesh*) is not giving good result though in texts it is said that Saturn in Sagittarius and Pisces in *Kendras* give Rajyogas or good result.

Piles

Piles is a disease which gives painfully persists for many years and even then the patient lives. It is of two kinds : (1) bloody piles (2) constipated piles. In bloody piles blood passes through anus. When wind and bile cough are disturbed they make moles inside the rectum. These moles are the root of constipated piles.

This disease is due to excessive intake of spices, oil and salt in food, wine, lack of proper sleep at night, disturbance of liver, etc. I am giving an example of blood piles in which a male was born on 3-7-1937 in Capricorn ascendant with balance of Venus *mahadasa* and 14 years, 8 months and 5 days and in the second quarter of *Bhrami Nakshatra*.

Birth lagna

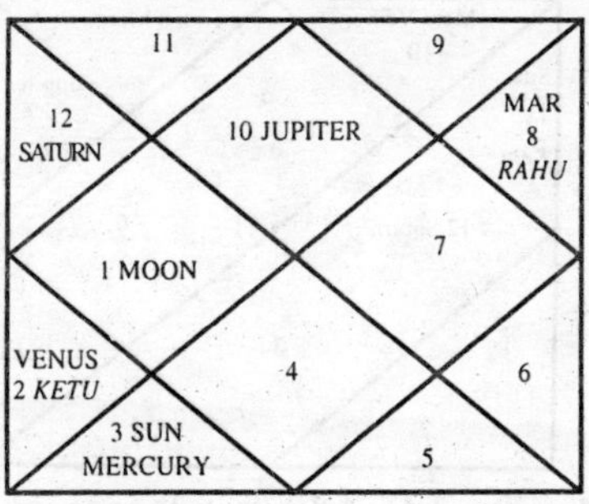

Navamsa

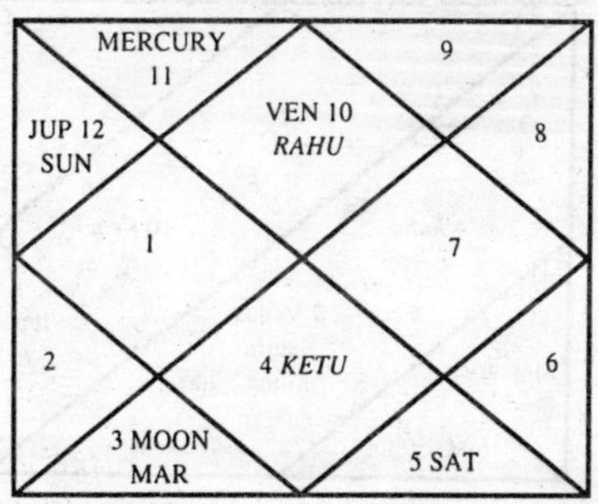

Here anus is in the 8th house where Leo sign and his lord Sun is in 6th house (disease's house) with house lord Mercury. There is exchange of Saturn (*lagna* lord) and Jupiter (lord of 6th and 9th houses). The lord of 8th house Sun is aspected by lord of 4th and 11th Mars. Mars represents blood as Mar's sign Aries is occupied with Moon representing water and Venus has too been aspected by Mars. Thus watery planets are related to Mars hence they both are under Mars indicating flow of blood through anus. This person lived near my house for many years and was known by me to take a lot of spices and oil in his food. Hence when Mars *dosha* began in 1967-68 he was troubled with this disease, i.e., bloody piles. I advised him not to take excess oil, spices and restrain taking *tambakoo* after meals. He used to take Ayurvedic medicines but it was again in order to make him suffer.

Some more Examples

A male child was born on Sunday 20-9-1925, *Ishtakala* 37 *ghatis* 10 *palas* Balance of *Mahadasa* Mars 1 year 7 months, 27 days. *Chitra* IVth quarter.

रंध्रस्वामी संस्थितो यस्य चांशेमृत्यु which means lord of 8th house is in which *navamsa*, death occurs in *dasa, antardasa* of that lord of *navamsa*.

Here 8th lord is Mars who is in *navamsa* in Capricorn, whose lord is Saturn hence the person died of stomach disease in Saturn *mahadasa* and Moon *antardasa*, because Mars is in Saturn's house and aspects the 8th house in *navamsa* where Cancer is the sign whose lord is Moon. Besides there is *Kalasarpa yoga* or that all the planets are between *Rahu* and *Ketu*.

Birth Lagna 0/26/03

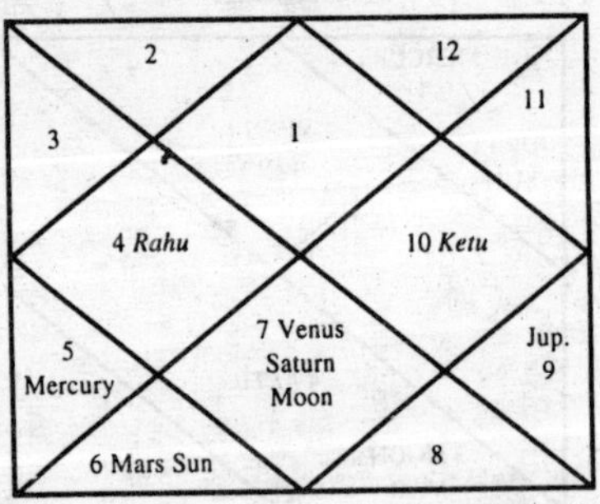

Navamsa

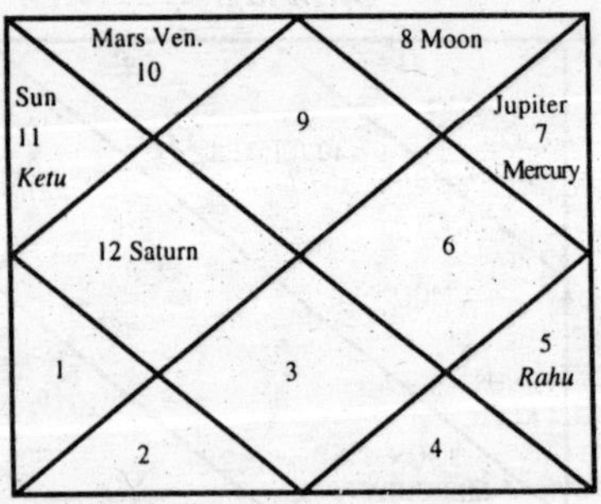

A male child was born on Sunday dated 15-4-1928 in ther second quarter of *Dharmishtha Nakshatra* balance of Mars *Mahadasa* of 3 years, 8 months and 29 days.

Birth Lagna

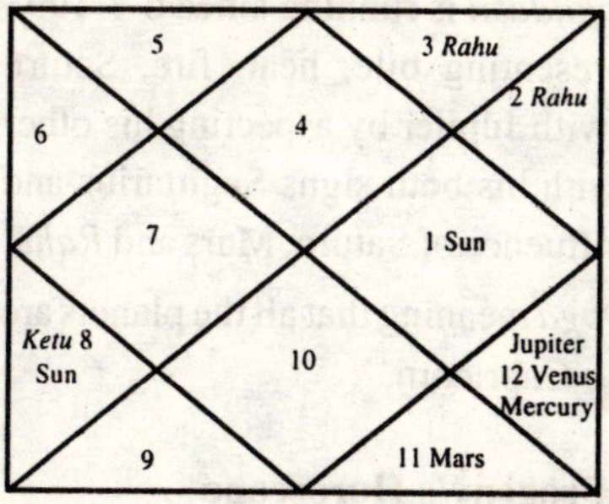

In this horoscope there is *Kalasarpa yoga* too. This subject died on 7-2-1980 by beating with sticks and stones by his enemies. If there is Mars in 8th house then unnatural death occurs by stones and sticks and other arms. Death occurred in Saturn *mahadasa, Rahu antardasa* and *prtyandardasa* of *Rahu*. Saturn aspects *Rahu* and *Ketu* aspects Moon. Mars is in 8th house in inimical sign.

A male child was born on 13th October 1925 at 4.30 a.m. in Virgo ascendant, in the first quarter of *Magha,* with balance of *Ketu mahadasa* of 6 years, 7 months and 24 days.

Birth Lagna

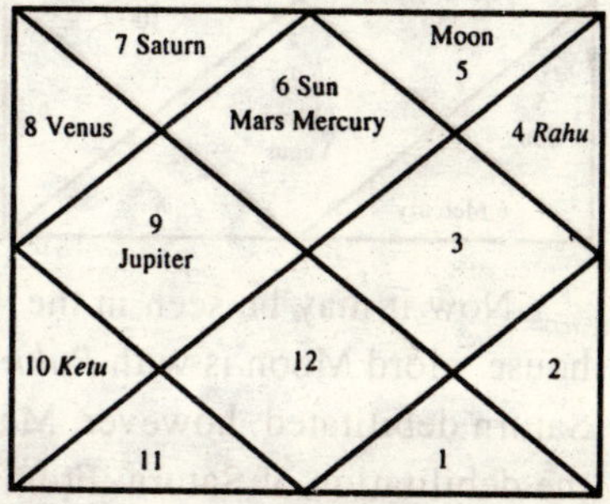

In this horoscope too there is *Kalasarpa yoga* means all the planets are between *Rahu* and *Ketu*. Saturn aspects *Rahu* and *Rahu* aspects Saturn's sign Capricorn hence Saturn and *Rahu* have been closely related with each other and these are the main planets influencing paralysis. Mars and Saturn both aspect 8th house. Sun and Mars in *lagna* made the person bilious in nature. Mercury with these two malefics affects the nervous system. Jupiter in *Kendra* has *Kendradhipati Dosha* and has been aspected by Mars and Saturn. Though there is *Hansa Yoga* in this horoscope due to Jupiter in quadrant in own sign Sagittarius but due to *Kendradhipati Dosha* and aspect of Saturn and Mars, Jupiter is losing its benefic influence. Such Jupiter aspects the 8th house and moon in 12th house too.

Moon is hemmed in amongst three malefics *Rahu,* Sun and Mars.

This person in 1991 came under the paralytic attack by all these above-mentioned things. Since 1991 he is unable to sit, stand and walk. Now he passes his time lying on the *cot* and sits by holding a hanging rope's end on the *cot*. Everything that he does is with the help of others.

The paralysis effect began in *Rahu mahadasa, Chandra antardasa*, then Mars *antardasa*. Now Jupiter *mahadasa* is running since 6-7-1993 as Jupiter is aspected by Mars representing bile, heat, fire, Saturn representing wind. *Rahu* has relation with Jupiter by aspecting his other sign of Pisces. Mars aspects Jupiter with his both signs Sagittarius and Pisces. Thus Jupiter is under malefic influence of Saturn, Mars and *Rahu*.

There is *Malika yoga* or *Ekawali yoga* meaning that all the planets are in seven houses sitting from Cancer to Capricorn.

Parent's Diseases known Through Progeny's Horoscope

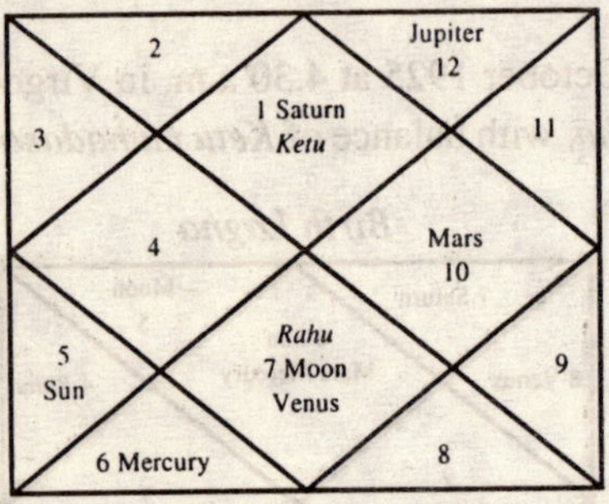

This is the horoscope of a person who is B.A., L.L.B. and is an agriculturist. For some years he also practised as advocate. After giving birth to this only son his mother became senile and began to wander here and there clothless. She lived up to the age of 15 years of the subject.

Now it may be seen in the 4th house (the house of mother). 4th house's lord Moon is with *Rahu* and Venus in 7th house aspected by Saturn debilitated, however, Mars in 10th in exaltation is cancelling the debilitation of Saturn. From Moon in 4th house is Mars exalted, aspected by Saturn. Saturn is the lord of 5th house (the mind of mother) from Moon is in debilitation and from 4th house 5th house is the 8th house in horoscope which is exalted but aspected by debilitated Saturn has lost the good qualities of exaltation. Hence due to 4th house, its lord from birth *lagna* and Moon, malefic influence is seen clearly showing the causes of senility of the mother. Jupiter, the lord of 9th is in 12th house in own sign but he has been weakened by aspecting the 6th and 8th houses (evil houses) is itself too in an evil house, i.e., 12th house. Moon *karaka* for mother is heavily malaffected.

This is the horoscope of a lady whose father's hands and face have white spots. *Pitrakaraka* Sun is with debilitated Mercury is in 4th house. 10th house is the house of father whose lord is Mercury.

Birth Lagna

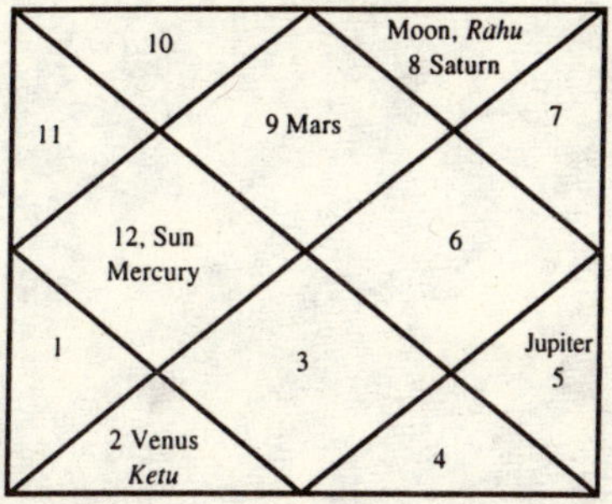

These two planets concerning father have aspect of Mars. From 10th house (the house of father) the lord of 6th house is Saturn (disease supplier to father) is with Moon, *Rahu* in 12th house. Hence 10th house (face of the father) aspected by debilitated Mercury and Sun reveals spotted white colour. Mercury controls the skin and nervous system. *Poorva Phalguna nakshatra* represents right hand which is in the reign of Leo sign and *Uttraphalguna Nakshatra* represents left hand which is in the reign of Virgo sign. The sign Leo with Jupiter is aspected by *markesh* Saturn from 12th house (an evil house) and Virgo sign is aspected by Sun and the lords of Leo and Virgo both are aspected by Mars and *Rahu*. Hence the face and hands of the father are white spotted as is proved here.

Birth Lagna

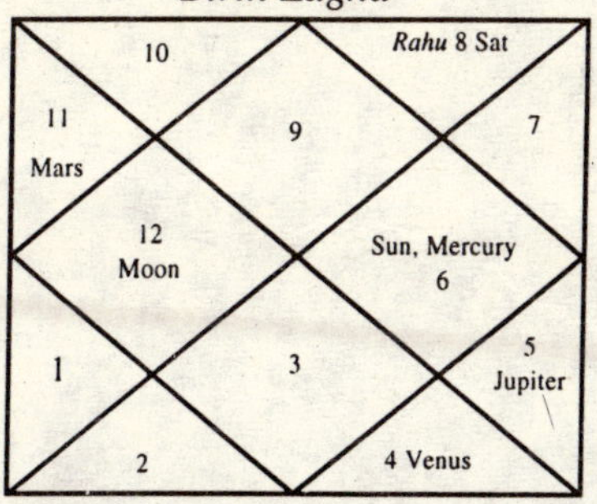

This horoscope belongs to another lady whose father also has white spots on face. Mars the lord of 12th house aspects the 9th and 10th houses being in the sign of Saturn. Saturn too aspects the 9th house. Moon is aspected by *Rahu*. From the house of father (10th house) in 6th house (the house of disease indicating father's disease) is occupied by malefic and evil house lord Mars and the lord of 6th house and Saturn is in 12th house with *Rahu*.

4

Horary Astrology, Numerology, Palmistry

Knowledge of Diseases Through Horary Astrology

Horary astrology is the branch of astrology which is useful to all, especially for those persons who have no horoscopes or birth particulars. Hence by putting questions before the astrologer, the knowledge of diseases, death of the person can be gauged.

When anybody asks the astrologer about the cure of disease of patient or will the patient survive or not then in such cases, Time Horoscope is cast in which the time when the question was put before the astrologer is taken into account. According to horary astrology the following comes as the result:

Death. When there are malefics in 2nd, 7th and 12th houses and Moon is in ascendant, 6th or 8th house then in this position the patient dies soon. Malefics on both sides of Moon also indicate death of the patient. Here see that ascendant has malefics on both sides being malefics in 2nd and 12th houses.

Secondly, when Sun is in ascendant and moon in 7th house then that also causes death.

Thirdly, if ascendant is in evil sign (sign of malefics) such as Aries, Scorpio (Mars), Leo (Sun), Capricorn, Aquarius (Saturn) and malefics aspect ascendant or in ascendant and moon is in 8th house with malefics then patient dies soon.

Fourthly, if malefics in 8th and 12th houses and Moon in 1st, 6th to 8th houses then patient dies soon.

Fifthly, malefics in 7th house and lord of ascendant combined or aspected by malefics then too patient dies early.

Sixthly, if lord of ascendant is weak, lord of 8th is strong, Moon in 6th and 8th houses patient dies soon.

Seventhly, lord of 8th in ascendant and lord of ascendant and Moon in 8th house then patient dies soon.

Eighthly, lord of 8th in quadrant and lord of ascendant in *dwadasamsa* of Sun then the patient dies or get death-like trouble.

Ninthly malefics in 1st, 7th, 8th houses, benefics are weak Moon in 4th and 8th houses and Moon is between malefics or malefics are in 2nd and 12th houses from Moon then patient dies.

Cause of Death

According to Indian scholars of astrology 22nd *Drekkana* from ascendant denotes cause of death. This means how death will come. A *drekkana* is equal to 10° and each sign has 3 *drekkanas*. In this way 36 *drekkanas* show the causes of death.

CAUSE OF DEATH: CHART OF 22ND DREKKANA: COUNT FROM BIRTH ASCENDANT

Sign	*Ist Drekkana*	*2nd Drekkana*	*3rd Drekkana*
Aries	By water, serpent, poison, bile	Water, bath in water, wild animals	By drowning into the water, river, tank, dam, etc.
Taurus	By ox, dog, ass, camel, etc.	By bile, fire, wind or by thief	In battlefield, conflicts, or falling from vehicles
Gemini	Bronchitis, perspiration	By buffaloes, poison or *sannipat* (coma)	Wild animals, quadrupeds
Cancer	By thorns, dreams, urine, goh (poison in living being)	By hurt or poison	By bronchitis, guluc, diabetes, blood, hard labour, coma
Leo	By water, poison or disease of feet	By disease of water as dropsy, in forest	By poison, arms, false charge, falling from high place
Virgo	By brain, head trouble or wind trouble	By serpent in forest, on mountains, prince or government	Camel, ass, arms, water, pit, lady, by eating excessively

Sign	*Ist Drekkana*	*2nd Drekkana*	*3rd Drekkana*
Libra	Lady, quadrupeds or falling	Stomach trouble	By serpent or aquatic animal
Scorpio	Poison, lady, arms, excessive eating, drinking water	By clothbound or under heavy luggage	Brick, stone hurt or by breaking thigh
Sagittarius	Disease of arms or by wind disease	Poison, ripe food, wind disease or by old tumour, etc.	Drowning in water by aquatic animal or stomach disease
Capricorn	By king, tiger, lion or violent animal, breaking of thigh, aquatic creature, poison, horse, snake bite	Fire, arms, thief, fever or by any other being than man	On account of lady
Aquarius	Lady, water, stomach pain, disease, in forest by wild animals	By lady or by secret diseases	By animal, disease of mouth, sexual intercourse
Pisces	Diarrhoea, diabetes, by lady, diseases of stomach or thigh, tumour, elephant or planets	Drowning of boat in river, sea, etc.	By dangerous or unknown (mysterious) diseases

Other Causes of Death—Planets in 8th house

Planets in the 8th house denote death as following:

If Sun is in horoscope in 8th house then death will occur from fire. If Moon in 8th house death occurs from water, if Mars in 8th house death occurs from arms, if Mercury in 8th house death occurs from fever, if Jupiter in 8th house death occurs from diarrhoea, if Venus in 8th house death occurs from thrust, if Saturn in 8th house death occurs from appetite or hunger. If more than one planets are in 8th house then among them whichever planet is strong from *Dhatu* (cough, bile, wind) of that strong planet death will occur. If there is no planet in 8th house then the planet/ planets aspecting the 8th house will cause death.

If there is movable *(chara)* sign as Aries, Cancer, Libra, Capricorn then in land other than motherland or foreign country and if even *(sthira)* sign as Taurus, Leo, Scorpio, Aquarius, then in own country or motherland and if in dual sign *(Dwiswabhava)* then death will occur while travelling or going somewhere.

There are so many other reasons of death described in astrological texts exhaustively.

Examples of horary astrology. Below I give some examples experienced by me on horary astrology regarding patient's illness.

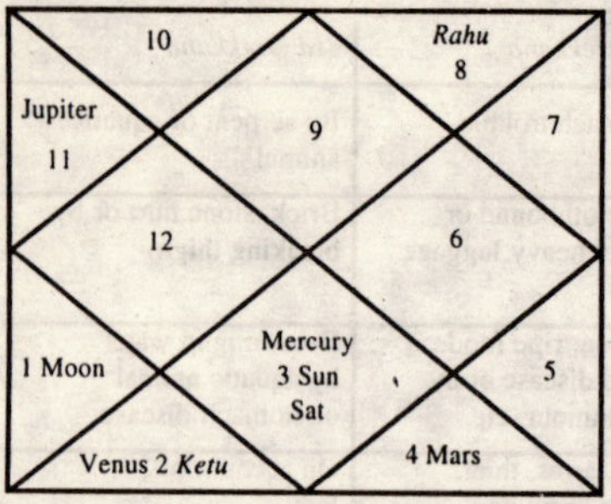

Example 1. On 14-7-1974 a person came to me who was father of a girl patient at 6.00 p.m. in Sagittarius *Lagna.*

The question was when the patient would be free from disease. See in this horoscope Moon is in 5th house, and Jupiter, lord of lagna aspects 9th house. 5th house is house of progeny and according to *Bhavat Bhavam* principle the 9th house is 5th house from 5th house hence 5th and 9th houses both deal with progeny. This denotes that the question is about progeny. The 1st house is of doctor, 4th house is that of medicine, 7th house is of disease, 8th house is of disease cure and 10th house is of patient. We have written earlier that malefics in 4th, 8th, 12th houses denote death soon. Here in 8th house lord of 5th (progeny) Mars is in debilitation unaspected by any benefics. In the same way *Rahu* is in 12th house, this is another malefic, thirdly 4th house is also aspected by another malefic Saturn. In 8th house lord of 5th Mars *(neecha)* is aspected by *Rahu*, which is bad position. The moon is weak in *Pakshabala. Lagna* has been aspected by two malefics Sun and Saturn which is very bad position. Lord of ascendant too is in malefic planet's sign Aquarius aspected by the malefics Mars. On the other hand from Moon too in 8th house is *Rahu.* The girl expired on 5-8-1974.

Example 2. On 22-10-1974 the question was asked about the good health of the subject at 7.15 p.m. Now see the cause of bad health and treatment.

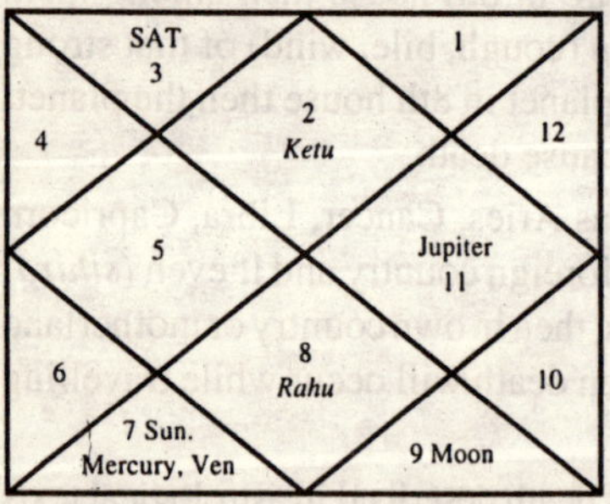

The subject was suffering from the severe stomach pain. In this chart *Ketu* is posited in *lagna* aspected by malefic *Rahu.* It means that the pain was felt suddenly. Jupiter is the lord of 8th and Moon is in 8th house in Sagittarius. Leo represents belly and Leo is in 4th house aspected by lord of 8th Jupiter along with Saturn from 2nd house. The lord of 4th Sun is in 6th house with lord of 5th Mercury, lord of *lagna* Venus, lord of 12th Mars denoting stomach trouble. Moon is aspected by Saturn. Here Jupiter also aspects Saturn, Sun, Mars, Mercury and Venus.

See that Saturn is benefic for Taurus *lagna* being lord of 9th.and 10th. Mars and Venus is 6th house denoting surgical operations and Saturn though a malefic but *karak* and benefic for Taurus has related to Moon and lord of 8th Jupiter is aspected by Jupiter.

See that the subject was born on 21-12-1937 in Taurus *lagna* with *Ketu* and aspected by Venus from 7th by Jupiter from 9th. *Lagna* is aspected by 2 malefic Saturn from 11th and Mars from 10th house. Mars and Saturn aspect the 5th house. Hence the indications for operation are clear.

Birth Lagna

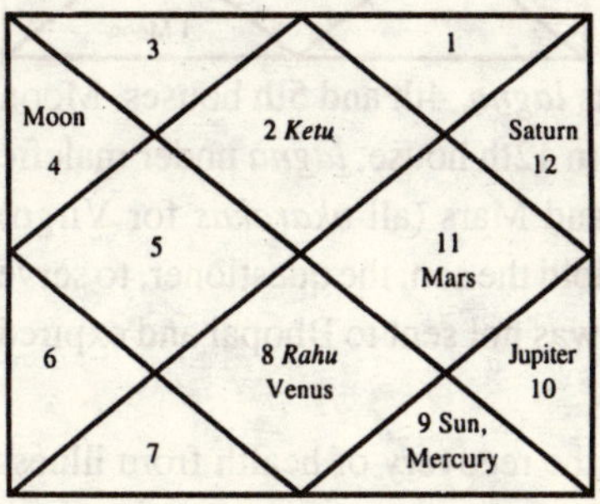

The lords of *lagna* and 10th are friends and lords of 4th and 7th are also friends. Hence indication is favourable for treatment. The person underwent surgery of appendicitis on Tuesday dated 28-1-1975. Tuesday was also on 22-10-1974, the day on which the question was put. The operation was successful.

Example 3. On 21-3-1985 at 10.30 a.m. the question was asked about the health of her father by a lady at Vidisha (M.P.) in Taurus *lagna* in 4th *Navamsa* of Aries whose lord is Mars.

Question Horoscope

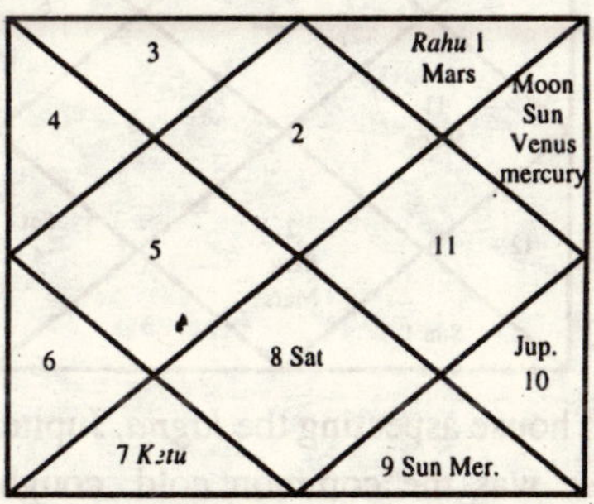

Here *lagna* is aspected by Saturn, who, though *karaka* for Taurus but being in enemy sign turned a malefic. The 8th lord Jupiter aspects the *lagna*. Moon and lord of *lagna* Venus both are with malefic Sun and *markesa* Mercury (being lord of 2nd house). Malefics in 6th and 8th houses *Ketu*, *Rahu* and Mars are not favourable. There is *Kala Sarpa yoga* because all planets are in between *Rahu* and *Ketu*. Moon is extremely weak in *pakshabala* lord of *lagna*. Venus is combust and retrograded. Jupiter aspects *lagna* and sign of Moon being lord of 5th house.

Hence there are no chances of recovering health. The subject was suffering from gout for a long time. The father of the lady expired on

1-4-1985 and could not recover health because the medicines did not show good result (house of medicines is 4th, its lord Sun is in 8th house from 4th house, Saturn aspects the 4th house).

Example 4. On 22-8-1981 a gentleman came to me at 8.30 a.m. regarding the illness of his mother. We went to visit her at Bhopal .A per chart, the *lagna* is Virgo and Venus *(neecha),* Saturn and Jupiter are in *lagna*.

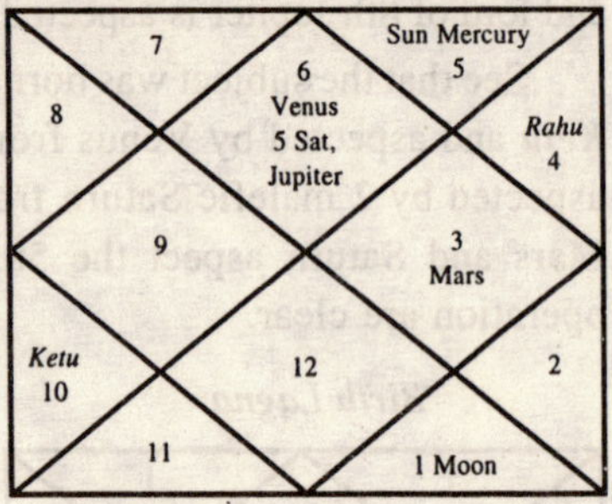

Venus and Jupiter are *markesh.* The lord of *lagna* Mercury in 12th house. Lord of 8th house Mars aspects *lagna,* 4th and 5th houses. Moon is in 8th house and Sun, Mercury are in 12th house, *lagna* under malefic influence of Saturn, Venus, Jupiter and Mars (all *akarakas* for Virgo) indicates very short life, near death. I told the son, the questioner, to serve his mother till her death. The mother was not sent to Bhopal and expired on 31-8-1981.

Example 5. A lady asked about the recovery of health from illness of her mother on 18-12-1972 at 2.45 p.m.

Question Horoscope

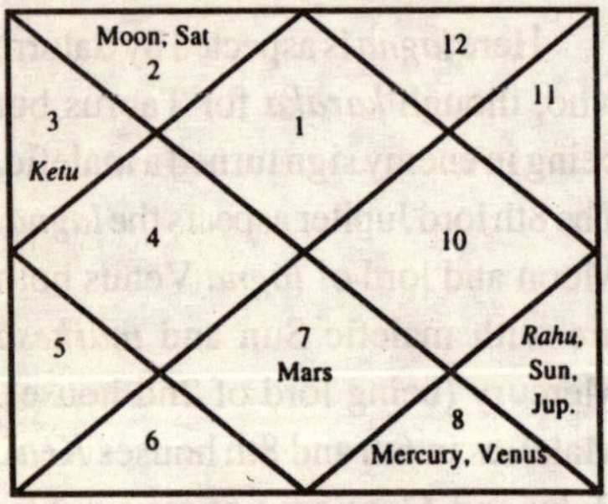

Navamsa

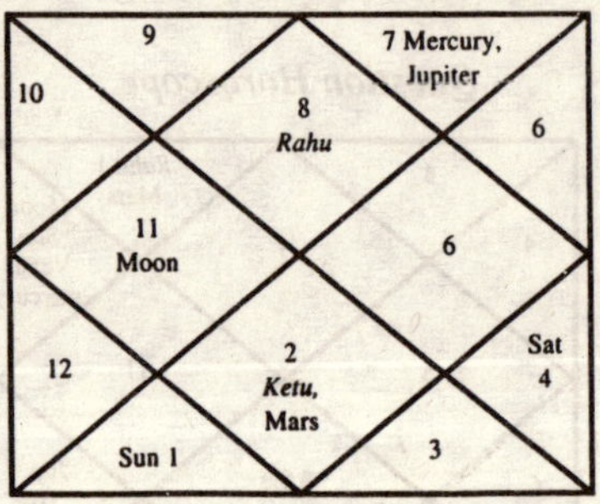

Here lord of *lagna* is Mars in 7th house aspecting the *lagna*. Jupiter is also aspecting the *lagna*. Disease was the common cold, cough, constipation fever as Mars is in the sign of Venus (cough). Moon is in the sign of Venus (cough). First house denotes doctor which means the patient's condition is worsening instead of curing. 4th house is of medicine (Moon's house, Moon is in exaltation). 7th house is that of disease whose lord Venus is aspected by Moon, Saturn, which means disease is increasing. 10th house is that of patient (Saturn, lord of 10th aspected by Venus, Mercury) the Venus patient could not maintain *pathya* hence the disease increased.

Disease gripped the patient on 20-11-1972. From 24-11-1972 it spreaded more. On 18-12-1972 it seemed out of control. But thanks to God (Jupiter in 9th indicates grace of God, and Jupiter in *navamsa* aspects the Moon) when Moon transited in Gemini aspected by Jupiter, disease began to decrease and after a week could be in control, though in recovering complete health it took about a month.

Diseases Known Through Numerology

Number One. Those who are born on 1-10-19-28 of any month are called number one persons. The lord of number one is Sun. Sun is the lord of Leo sign which represents heart. Hence number one persons generally suffer from heart disease, palpitation of heart, high blood pressure, eye disease. They should take raisins, camomile, saffron, clover, garlic, nutmeg, gentian root in daily use. Caution should be observed garlic in the months of January, February, October, November.

Number Two. Persons born on 2-11-20-29 of any month are called number two persons. Moon is their lord, the lord of imagination. They suffer generally from constipation, stomach pain, weak digestive system, wind, inflammation and tumour, swelling, etc. Number two persons should take in food lettuce, cabbages, turnips, cucumber, linseed, water plantain, melon, rapeseed, etc.They generally come in the grip of cold. Be cautious about your health in the months of January, February, July.

Number Three. Persons born on 3-12-21-30 are known as number three persons. Lord of number 3 is Jupiter. They generally suffer from nervous weakness, neuritis, sciatica. They should take in food or use as medicine dandelion, endive, apples, peaches, sage, olives, grapes, mint, saffron, nutmeg, cloves, almond, etc. They should take special care of health generally in December, February, June and September every year.

Number Four. Those born on 4-13-22-31 of any month are called Number four persons. Their lord is Hanshal, the hot newly discovered planet. They feel pain of various kinds in body. Wind, headache and generally eye disease is seen in them. They should take amla, kamalgatta (seeds of lotus), milk, etc. They should exercise a little daily or undertake morning walk. They should not think on any topic excessively. Generally January, February July, September, are seen as bad for them and should be cautious in these months.

Number Five. Those born on 5-14-23 of any month are known as number five persons. The lord of five is Mercury. They have strong mental power because Mercury is lord of intellect. Though Mercurians are always smiling, yet in adverse circumstances they show anger which is bad for their health. They are victims of nervousness and high blood pressure. Excessive speech, mental burden, diplomacy lead them to brain haemorrhage. For them deep slumber is necessary and should take more vitamin B and D in food.

Number Six. Those born on 6-15-24 of any month are known as number six persons. Their lord is Venus who gives them all comforts of life, i.e., vehicle, prosperity, good bank balance, etc. They are generally lovers of beauty. Hence diseases like sex, intense feelings, dropsy, cough, hydrocele, etc. are found common in them.

Palmistry and Diseases

Thumbs—Thumb is an important part of the hand. It is the symbol of man's intellectual power. Nails on thumb and fingers indicate of various diseases. Lines on nail of thumb denote fear of paralysis.

Nails—Below I am giving the shape of nails causing diseases:

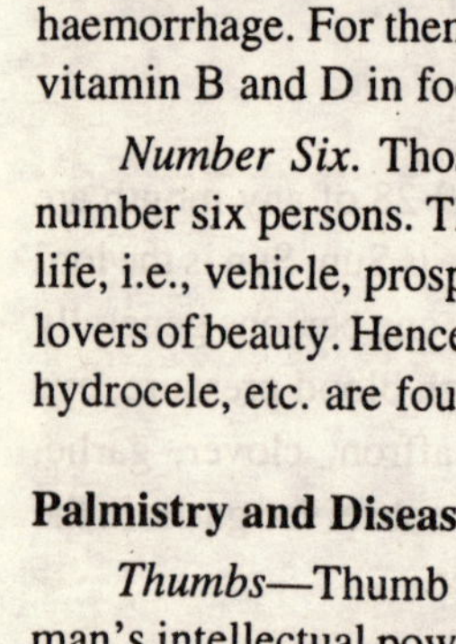

This type of nails denote the weakness of heart.

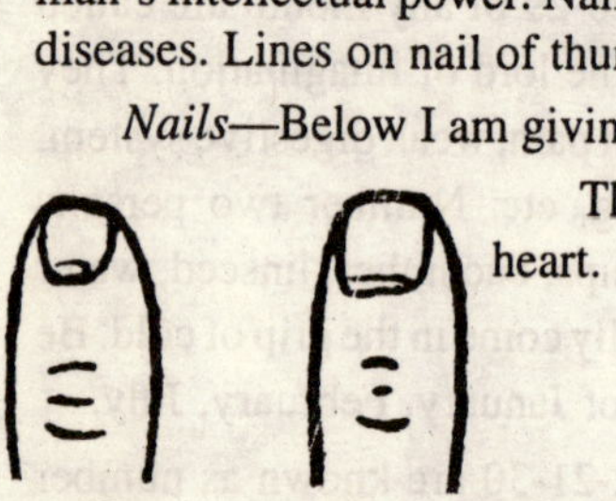

This type of nails denote that the person will suffer from paralysis.

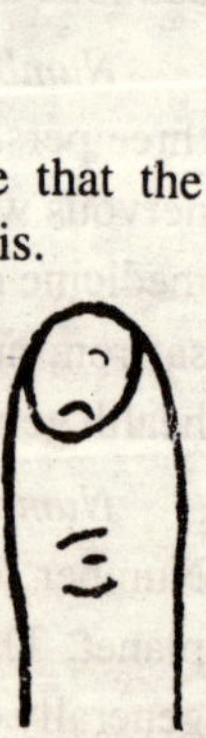

This type of nails denote the disturbance in throat or bronchitis

This type of nails denote the defect in chest.

Long nails denote the defect in lungs.

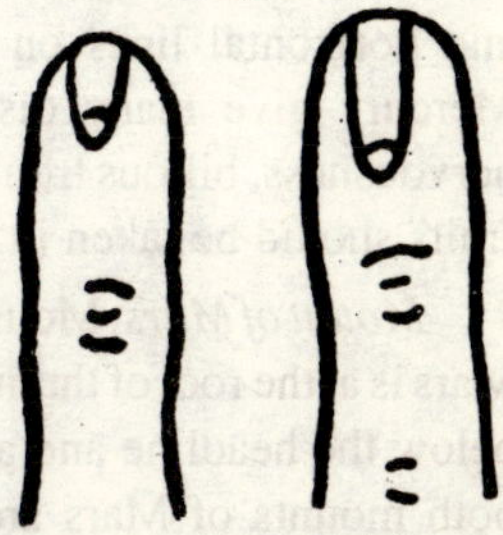

Such type of nails denote the defect

I have observed in my experiences such type of nails with above-mentioned diseases practically are found correct.

Third Phalange of First Finger. The first finger is known as the finger of Jupiter. Hence when third phalange is long and fat then apoplexy, paralysis may end the life. Such person eats excessively. But if the third phalange is long and thin like waist then hopelessness, disease in throat and lungs may happen. Besides if third phalange of first finger is fat and red in colour then paralysis is sure and the person eats excessively.

Mount of Saturn. Mount of Saturn should not be much developed. If it is more developed it produces bad qualities of Saturn in man as disappointment, melancholy, sadness, etc. Saturnian is bilious and windy, not smooth in nature. In his blood excess bile is found owing to which hand and nails are yellow. He may be victim of paralysis. Gout is another disease for him. If there is dot on the mount of Saturn then diseases of teeth and ear are generally seen. Mount of Saturn should not be crossed or many lines cutting each other show bad health. If any line from mount of Saturn goes towards life line and there is island on it in between, paralysis is sure to set in.

Mount of Sun. See the lines on mount of Sun and in finger number four. If nails are yellow on 3rd finger on both hands with lines, crossing and many lines cutting each other on mount of Sun it denotes heart and eye troubles. White colour of nail too is not sign of good health. If nail of third finger is blue coloured then there should be some disturbance or difficulty in heart.

Mount of Mercury. Mercurians though clever and cunning are sensitive and hence become nervous soon in adverse circumstances. He is more successful in the field of medicine. Their Jupiter standing lines on the mount of Mercury give good qualities to the subject. If mount is in centre and below the little finger then it is good. If there is network of lines and horizontal lines on the mount of Mercury then bad qualities of Mercury give many diseases to the subject. The main diseases are nervousness, bilious trouble, paralysis, etc. For Mercurian milk and light fruits should be taken in meals.

Mount of Mars. Mount of Mars has two places in the palm. First lower Mars is at the root of thumb near life line below Jupiter's mount. Secondly below the headline and above the upper part of Moon mountain. When both mounts of Mars are with cross, nets, cuts, stars, etc. then fever, disturbance in blood circulation, bronchitis, inflammation with perspiration and swelling are due to net of lines on upper Mar's mount.

The disease of intestines also attacks the subject which turns into T.B. Hence in such position subject should make a habit not to cheat others, not to speak a lie, not to get angered. For this he should wear coral ring in 3rd finger in gold and should fast on Tuesday and feed bread to red dogs.

Mount of Moon. Mount of Moon has been divided into three parts—upper, middle and lower. If on the upper part of Moon mountain net of vertical and horizontal lines is seen then bronchitis, inflammation in intestines, disturbance in blood circulation are indicated. If there is cross then the diseases of kidney, bladder and below navel are indicated. If Moon mount area is white in colour then weak palpitation of heart, less appetite, dropsy, etc. are indicated.

If there is cross on middle part of mount of Moon then disturbance in intestines, appendicitis, cholera, gout are indicated. More developed mount of Moon is not good as it indicates excess imagination which may turn the person to insanity.

In this way upper Moon mount indicates bowel trouble, middle Moon mount gout, rheumatism and lower Moon mount kidney, bladder, female trouble if there are cross, net of lines, island, etc. on these three parts of the mount of Moon.

Mount of Venus. Mount of Venus is at the root of thumb widely spread. Venus is the planet of joy and happiness. It is said, "A thing of beauty is joy forever," so is the case with persons who are Venus minded. Persons whether male or female attract the opposite sex for passion.

Net of straight and acute lines found on the mount of Venus in a lady's hand indicates attraction towards males. Venusians have will-power of Jupiter, wisdom of Saturn, kindness of Saturn, activeness and cleverness of Mercury.

If more lines with square disturbed, black dots are found on the mount of Venus they make them passionate and sexual diseases are commonly found in them.

5

Death and Drekkana

Examples of Death

Example 1. Date of birth of a male born in *Vikrami Samvat* 1934, IInd *Jyeshtha Krishna Ekadasi* and the third quarter of *Ashwini Nakshatra*.

Birth Lagna

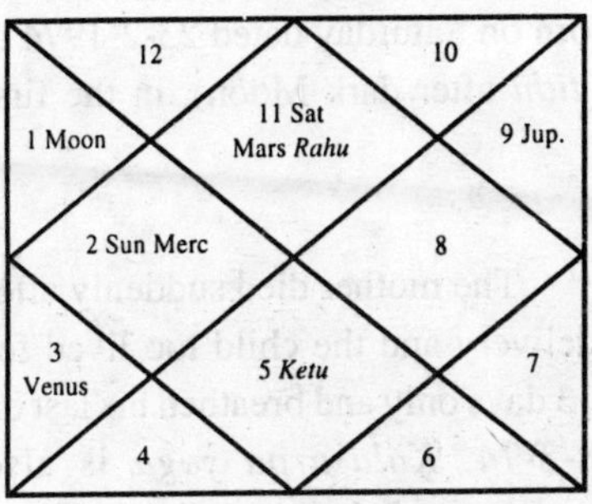

Moon Lagna

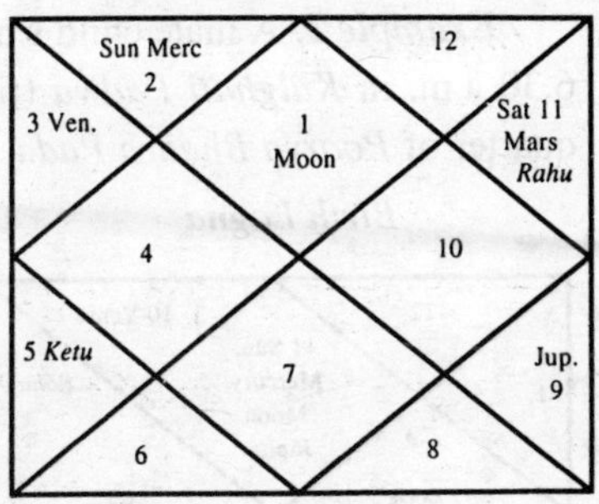

The subject (my father) died from goitre on 23-9-1939 due to bloody piles plus wind represented by 8th Lord Mercury with Sun (piles), blood (Mars in *lagna*), wind (Saturn in *lagna* with *Rahu*) at the age of 62 years, 3 months and 15 days. Death in *Rahu* major Moon minor *dasa*. Female born on Wednesday dated 8-4-1964 in the second quarter of *Dharmishtha nakshatra*. *Navamsa lagna* is Pisces (last *navamsa*).

Birth Lagna

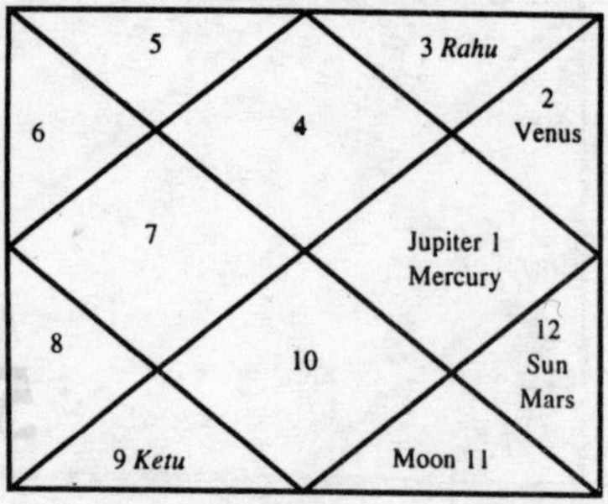

Moon Lagna

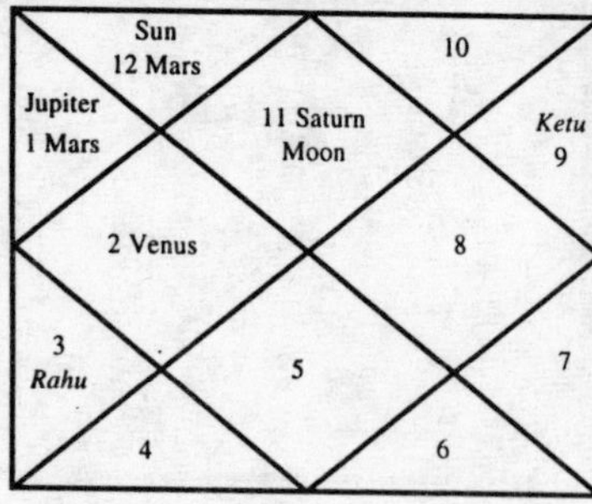

Example 2. This lady died suddenly within two hours of giving birth to a girl child on 27-7-1996 at about 10.00 a.m.

According to astrology the *navamsa lagna* Pisces is not auspicious for a person born in Cancer *lagna* . This is the case of a sudden heart attack as Mars, lord of 5th is with Sun (*karaka* of heart). *Rahu* in Moon sign in 5th house aspects Moon and Saturn in 8th house in birth *lagna. Ketu* aspects the 5th lord Mercury from Moon sign. Besides all planets are between *Rahu* and *Ketu* causing *Kalasarpa yoga* within civil houses (6th to 12th). In Moon sign in 5th *Rahu* is not auspicious. The case of death occurred in first delivery.

Example 3. A male child was born on Saturday dated 23-2-1974 at 6.30 a.m. in *Kalghati Padwa* (first *tithi* after dark Moon), in the first quarter of *Poorva Bhadra Pada.*

Birth Lagna

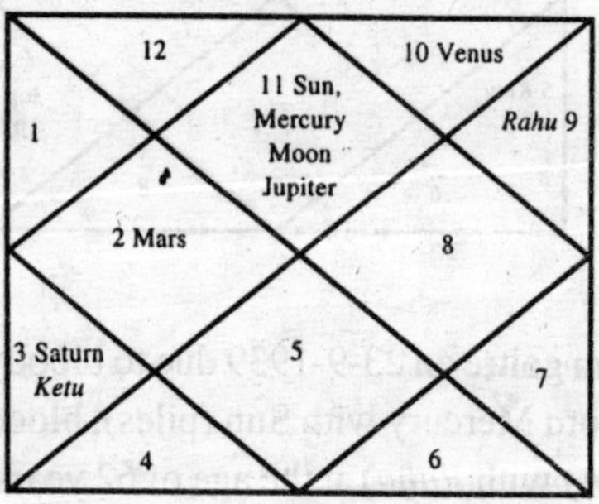

The mother died suddenly after delivery and the child too lived for 13 days only and breathed his last on 8-3-74. *Kalasarpa yoga* is also present here showing all the planets between *Rahu* and *Ketu*. Death occurred due to sudden stoppage of function of heart. It is seen that the 5th house (Heart) is occupied by two malefics Saturn and *Ketu* aspected by *Rahu* and combust Jupiter. Saturn is the lord of birth ascendant with malefic and *lagna* is occupied by Sun, Jupiter (*karakas* of Heart) combust with lord of 8th Mercury combust,

Moon. Saturn is *lagna* lord and Moon sign lord is in the sign of 8th lord Mercury, Moon (lord of 6th) and Mercury (lord of 8th) both are in *lagna* which is not auspicious. The birth on *pratiyada* (प्रतियदा) with Saturday in *Kalghati* is not auspicious.

Besides birth is in *lagna gandanta* and *nakshatra gandanta* as both are beginning, leaving the last sign and *nakshatra*, hence *Balarishta* (बालारिष्ट) is present. The mother died suddenly after delivery because 4th house denoting mother is occupied by malefic Mars aspecting the 4th house from 4th house, i.e., 7th house. Lord of 4th house Venus is in no evil house in 12th house among malefics *Rahu*, Sun, Mercury and Moon.

Example 4. A male child was born on Wednesday dated 27-7-1922 in the fourth quarter of *Magha Nakshatra* in balance of *Ketu mahadasa* of 3 months and 24 days in *Gemini lagna*. This person died on 22-2-1996 of heart failure suddenly without any disease prior to it.

Birth Lagna

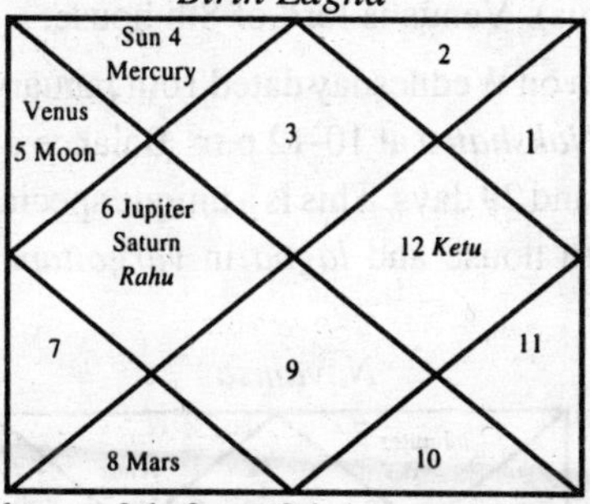

This is the special case where the subject had no disease but early in the morning as usual he bathed at a well and was coming to home when all of a sudden he fell to the ground and died.

Here the lord of 5th Venus is with Moon in inimical and *maraka* house 8th from 8th house. Mercury *lagna* lord is aspected by *Ketu* and *lagna* is aspected by 8th lord Saturn. From Moon 5th house lord Jupiter is with two malefics Saturn and *Rahu. Lagna* is also aspected by lord of 6th Mars besides the aspect of Saturn from 4th house.

This mishappening all of a sudden occurred in *Rahu mahadasa* and *antardasa* of Venus. Venus is in 12th house to *Rahu* in birth *lagna* and 8th house from 8th house, i.e. in 3rd house. The 8th lord Saturn is with *Rahu* and *Rahu* aspects the 8th lord's house Capricorn too. 8th house is also being aspected by Sun too who is an enemy of 8th lord.

Example 5. A female child was born on Saturday dated 23-4-1966 at 6.05 p.m. in the first quarter of *Rohini Nakshatra*. Death occurred from jaundice on 2-3-1990 at the age of 23 years, 10 months and 9 days in a very short life.

Birth Lagna

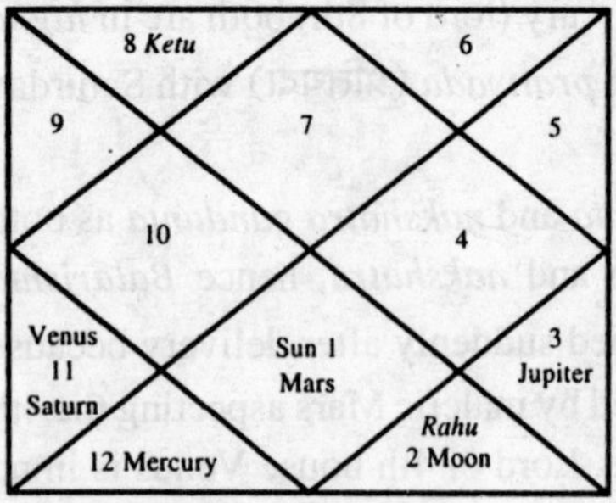

Three malefics Sun, Moon and Jupiter (lord of 6th house) and enemy of the *lagna* lord Venus are aspecting the *lagna*. Sun and Moon both are bilious and both are strong malefics due to exaltation (Sun) own sign (Mars). In 5th house lord of *lagna* Venus and lord of 5th Saturn both are aspected by Jupiter lord of 6th. In 6th house there is Mercury (debilitated) indicating nervousness.

In 8th house *Rahu*-Moon combination is inauspicious. Moon is hemmed in between Rahu among Sun, Mars and lord of 6th house Jupiter. Death occurred in *Rahu mahadasa* and *antardasa* of Venus as Rahu is occupying the house of Venus (Taurus). Venus is lord of 8th house.

Example 6. A male child was born on Wednesday dated 16th January 1934 in the third quarter of *Sravana Nakshatra* at 10-12 p.m. Balance of Moon *mahadasa* is 5 years, 9 months and 29 days. This is a unique special horoscope where 7 planets are in 5th house and *lagna* in *vargottama navamsa*.

Birth Lagna

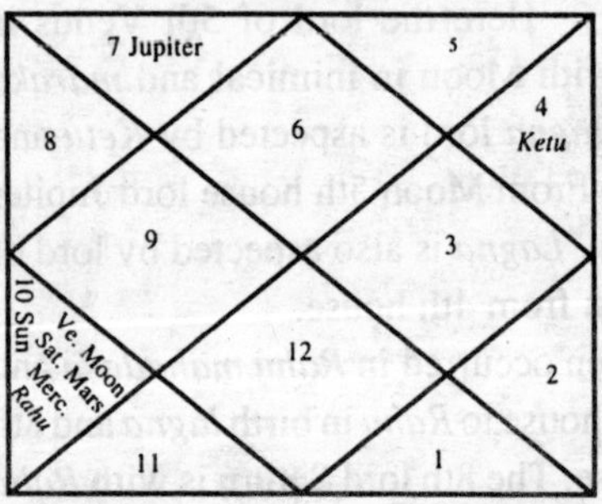

Navamsa

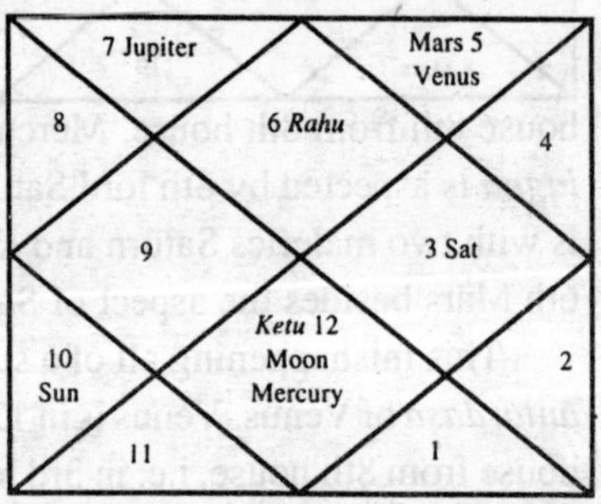

In this horoscope *lagna,* Sun, Jupiter are in *vargottama navamsa.* The subject was a gazetted officer in the Education Department and held a Ph.D. degree and was an intellectual giant but remained mentally disturbed for most part except 2 or 3 months in a year.

It can be noted that seven planets are in 5th house, among them Sun, lord of 12th is in inimical sign and Mars exalted. Eight planets aspect the

8th house whose lord is exalted. In *navamsa lagna* is occupied by malefic *Rahu* aspected by *Ketu*, Moon and Mercury (debilitated) stars aspecting the 6th house. Saturn is the 6th house lord. Hence this combination gives mental trouble by disturbances.

The subject died in June 1996, in Saturn *mahadasa* and Jupiter *antardasa*. Jupiter aspects the 8th house and 6th house. Lord of 8th house is in 12th in *navamsa* in Leo sign. The subject died of sudden heart attack due to the fact of 5th house's combination of seven planets. 5th house is the house of heart governed by Sun, Jupiter and lord of 5th house Saturn.

Drekkana Chart

Aries	*Taurus*	*Gemini*	*Cancer*	*Leo*	*Virgo*
1	2	3	4	5	6
5	6	7	8	9	10
9	10	11	12	1	2

Libra	*Scorpio*	*Sagittarius*	*Capricorn*	*Aquarius*	*Pisces*	*Degrees*
7	8	9	10	11	12	10
11	12	1	2	3	4	20
3	4	5	6	7	8	30

According to *Saravali* of Kalyan Verma:

Drekkana of 8th house indicating cause of death: Drekkana is the 1/3 part of a sign of 10°. Each sign has in this way 3 drekkana. Hence 12 signs have 36 drekkana. The drekkana falling in the 8th house indicates the cause of death as follows:

Ist Drekkana of Aries - Death occurs by disease of spleen, poison or by disturbance in bile.

IInd Drekkana of Aries - Death occurs by means of water.

IIIrd Drekkana of Aries - Death by falling into well or reservoirs of water.

Ist Drekkana of Taurus - Death by animals as horses, donkeys, who walk on four legs.

IInd Drekkana of Taurus - Death by disturbance of bile, fever or by thieves.

IIIrd Drekkana of Taurus	- Death by falling from high place or from horse.
Ist Drekkana of Gemini	- Death by disturbance of wind or breathening.
IInd Drekkana of Gemini	- Death by Tridasha wind, bile, cough.
IIIrd Drekkana of Gemini	- Death by falling from high place as hill, roof, or anywhere high or in forest.
Ist Drekkana of Cancer	- Death by drinking non-drinkable things or by thorns.
IInd Drekkana of Cancer	- Death by poison or by dysentery.
IIIrd Drekkana of Cancer	- Death by illusion, coma, spleen, liver or tumour.
Ist Drekkana of Leo	- Death by poisoning through water.
IInd Drekkana of Leo	- Death by filling of water in respiratory tract or in lungs.
IIIrd Drekkana of Leo	- Death by accident from vehicle, poison, arm's sufferings.
Ist Drekkana of Virgo	- Death by diseases of head, brain, bleeding in head or by disturbing wind element.
IInd Drekkana of Virgo	- Death by falling from fort, hill, mountain or by anger of king.
IIIrd Drekkana of Virgo	- Death by asses, camels (animal) by arms or by falling in water or water falling on man or wetting in rains, by pneumonia or by any other diseases caused by rain.
Ist Drekkana of Libra	- Death by falling, bad women, animals.
IInd Drekkana of Libra	- Death occurs by stomach diseases such as ulcer, tumour, hernia, worms, etc.

IIIrd Drekkana of Libra	- Death by snake bite or by water.
Ist Drekkana of Scorpio	- Death by poison or arms.
IInd Drekkana of Scorpio	- Death by carrying luggage or by fatigue or pain in waist.
IIIrd Drekkana of Scorpio	- Death by falling mud, wood, stone, etc.
Ist Drekkana of Sagittarius	- Death by wind trouble, or by piles diseases of arms.
IInd Drekkana of Sagittarius	- Death by attack of arrows, arms, or by poison.
IIIrd Drekkana of Sagittarius	- Death by water or by aquatic animals or by stomach troubles.
Ist Drekkana of Capricorn	- Death by lion, scorpion, pig, etc.
IInd Drekkana of Capricorn	- Death by snake bite.
IIIrd Drekkana of Capricorn	- Death by thieves, fire, arms, by fever, etc.
Ist Drekkana of Aquarius	- Death by diseases of contact through bad women, by sexual diseases as AIDS, or by stomach diseases.
IInd Drekkana of Aquarius	- Death by secret diseases.
IIIrd Drekkana of Aquarius	- Death by poisons, gonorrhoea, urinary diseases.
Ist Drekkana of Pisces	- Death by diseases of semen, or by stomach diseases.
IInd Drekkana of Pisces	- Death by water filling in body or by elephant, crocodile, fish, or by navy.
IIIrd Drekkana of Pisces	- Death by hateful diseases such as leprosy, gonorrhoea, etc.

***22nd Drekkana from Drekkana of ascendant also indicates cause of death*:**

If 22nd Drekkana is:	- Death by water, snake, poison, pile, etc.

Aries Ist Drekkana -	-	Combined or aspected by malefics
Aries IInd Drekkana	-	Death by water, wild animal, worm, snow, etc.
Aries IIIrd Drekkana	-	Death by drowning in well, lake, pond, etc.
Taurus Ist Drekkana	-	Death by ox, dog, donkey, camel.
Taurus IInd Drekkana	-	Death by bile, fire, thief.
Taurus IIIrd Drekkana	-	Death by falling from horse or by arms in fighting.
Gemini Ist Drekkana	-	Death by bronchitis, breathing.
Gemini IInd Drekkana	-	Death by buffalo, poison or *Tridosha*.
Gemini IIIrd Drekkana	-	Death by wild animal, quadruped (four-feeted animal).
Cancer Ist Drekkana	-	Death by goh wine, thorn.
Cancer IInd Drekkana	-	Death hurt or by poison.
Cancer IIIrd Drekkana	-	Death by respiration, gonorrhoea, wound, blood disturbance, coma, etc.
Leo Ist Drekkana	-	Death by water, poison, disease of feet.
Leo IInd Drekkana	-	Death by disease of water or in forest.
Leo IIIrd Drekkana	-	Death by poison, arms, false charge or by falling from high place.
Virgo Ist Drekkana	-	Death by disease in head, by wind.
Virgo IInd Drekkana	-	Death by snake, mountain, forest or royal person.
Virgo IIIrd Drekkana	-	Death by camel, donkey, arms, water, pit, woman, corn, betel leaf, etc.
Libra Ist Drekkana	-	Death by woman, animal, fall.
Libra IInd Drekkana	-	Death by stomach disease.
Libra IIIrd Drekkana	-	Death by smoke, aquatic creatures.

Scorpio Ist Drekkana	- Death by poison, arms, women or by taking excessive corn and betel leaves.
Scorpio IInd Drekkana	- Death by cloth or by weight.
Scorpio IIIrd Drekkana	- Death by hurt from stone, brick or by fracture of thigh.
Sagittarius Ist Drekkana	- Death by disease of arms, wind.
Sagittarius IInd Drekkana	- Death by poison or taking food corn, etc. or by windy diseases.
Sagittarius IIIrd Drekkana	- Death by drowning or by aquatic animals or by stomach diseases.
Capricorn Ist Drekkana	- Death by king, lion, or by fracture of thigh, aquatic creatures, poison, horse, snake.
Capricorn IInd Drekkana	- Death by fire, arms, thieves, fever etc.
Capricorn IIIrd Drekkana	- Death on account of woman.
Aquarius Ist Drekkana	- Death by woman, water, disease of stomach, by wild animals in forests and mountains.
Aquarius IInd Drekkana	- Death by woman, secret diseases.
Aquarius IInd Drekkana	- Death by disease of mouth or by animal.
Pisces Ist Drekkana	- By tumour, sprue, gonorrhoea, by diseases in thigh or stomach.
Pisces IInd Drekkana	- Death by drowning or by boat in water.
Pisces IIIrd Drekkana	- Death by worst diseases.

These are the results found and experienced by our great *rishis* for general human welfare and are the subject of research for astrologers and those who are interested in the progress of astrology.

PART II
REMEDIAL MEASURES

6

Yoga and Ayurveda

After knowing the possibility of disease from the horoscope precautionary measures are necessary so that the attack of the diseases may not disturb health. As the saying goes if health is disturbed then everything is disturbed. All the glands found in our body must be active and balanced so that our health may not be disturbed. There are so many remedial measures for proper treatment of the diseases. Some of them are being described here for the benefit of the readers.

Ayurveda means the knowledge of life. Whatever experienced by the *rishis, munis* and *yogis* is kept secured and is now available in the form of *Vedas*, *Upanishadas*, *Puranas*, Philosophy, *Ramayana*, *Mahabharata*, *Shrimad Bhagwad Gita*, *Guru Granth Sahib*, *Jinvani*, etc. In Europe and Islamic countries this knowledge is preserved in the *Bible* and the *Quran*.

Yoga is the vast ocean of knowledge which India gave to the world. It is said about yoga in *Patanjal Yoga Shastra*, "योगश्चित्तवृत्ति निरोध: means *yoga* is the combination of all our capacity—inner and outer—for controlling our inner mental or intellectual tendencies. Control over our senses leads to control over mind and control over mind leads to control over intellect. This is called "Samyam". After that our soul combines with the Lord of the Cosmos which means *Atma* meets *Parmatma* that is called *yoga*. Then only we can have divine experiences of "*Parmanand*" or the supreme bliss.

Knowledge is of two kinds—*Para* (परा) and *Apra* (अपरा). *Para* is the spiritual knowledge which leads to combine the human soul to God.

Apra means the materialistic knowledge of things that fulfil our physical necessities such as wholesome food, gocd house, good vehicles and all the essential things. In *Bhagwad Gita* it is called *Ashtadha Prakriti*. Hence in yoga there are eight ways to receive and conquer the world. We have to accept the challenge and start yoga from eight parts as follows: *Yama* (यम), *Niyama* (नियम), *Assan* (आसन), *Pranayama* (प्राणायम) *Prtyahar* (प्रत्याहार), *Dhyan* or attention (ध्यान), *Dharna* (धारणा) and *Samadhi* (समाधि). We have to follow some rules and regulations for the purification of body, mind, intellect, etc.

This knowledge of yoga leads us to Ayurveda which teaches us how to live healthy, and happily. Purity of heart is the essential thing for a happy life and healthy mind.

In the *Upanishadas* the knowledge given is called *Vedanta* (वेदांत) which leads to our goal of life. We are comprised not only of body, senses or mind but also have *Atma* (आत्मा) or soul. Our motto should be the realisation of self for then only we can meet the *Parmatma* (God). This divine knowledge is the key to all happiness. Hence, to know Ayurveda, the knowledge of "Yoga" is essential.

It is said about the philosophy of India, that spiritualism begins where materialism ends. Hence yoga is the greatest and most powerful knowledge of the world. It is the science of all the sciences.

Socrates had said, "Know thyself". This is the real knowledge that can be gained through *yogabhyasa* (योगाभ्यास) and not by reading of books only.

Our body is the residence of the senses, mind, intellect, life (Prana). There is power beyond bounds hidden in our body and mind. What we see, hear, smell and taste is the result of nature. Nature is within and outside of our body and mind. So, to know the natural forces astrology shows the way to commune with nature, which can be realised by knowledge of yoga only.

Our energy is stored at the base of the spine which is called *Mooladhar Chakra* (मूलाधारचक्र). It is light without fire is the abode of *Shankhini* (शंखिणी) with four leaves of lotus. When yogis open it by *sadhna* (साधना) then there is dazzle of light. Above this is the *swadhishtan chakra* (स्वाधिष्ठान चक्र). The spine, which we call backbone, has below the abode of *Kundalini* power, which is like a serpant whose mouth is underneath and that is in 3½ circle lying slept. It is the store of all the knowledge kept reserved. *Ida, pingla, sushuma nadis* are right, left and middle. *Apan Vayu* (अपान वायु) is found here also *Udan Vayu* (उदान वायु) where 12 suns are found (denoting the twelve months). On the navel area is the seat of fire, water and wind—the three elements of life. This *Kundalini* power is awakened by grace of *Guru* (God) when we exercise by means of *yama, niyam, asan, Sukhasan* or *Padmasan* and consequently through *Pranayam* (प्राणायाम) the knowledge of *Rechaka* by chanting ten times (ॐ) *Om, Kumbhak* by chanting 16 times *Om* (ॐ) and then *Rechaka* by chanting 12 times (ॐ). The long breathing is called *Poorak*, and stoppage of breathing is called *Kumbhak* and then leaving long breathing. These three main elements of Pranayam are attained by means of breathing.

By the exercise of *Pranayam* attention is gained and the *Kundalini* rises above awakening on *Manipur Chakra* where the second lotus of 6 leaves is situated on third lotus on *Anahat chakra* (Heart), then on 5th *chakra*, i.e., *Vishudha chakra* in throat, neck and then *Agyachakra* between eyebrows and lastly *Sahasrarchakra* which is above the head in the brain. The wind *Apan*, *Udan*, *Saman*, *Vayan* and *Pran* are the five kinds of winds residing in our body and are representative of five elements—fire, water, wind, earth and sky in our body.

After attention (ध्यान), the grasping power (धारणा) is gained and then occurs *Samadhi* (समाधि) or the meeting of the soul with God.

In our body bile and phelgm are due to the element of water. Muscle and marrow are the earthen elements, respiration is wind element. In our blood there are seven metals and twelve salts. These are called seven seas.

Kundalini power is below *Mooladhar chakra* while *Apan Vayu* is near intestines. It is awakened by *Mool Bandhasan* or *Vajrasan* (between arms and scrotum). Then on *Padmasan* it is aspected on the nose. This will be attained by chanting Om repeatedly.

Our head has three parts—the upper part is cerebrum—the lower (left) cerebellum and on the end of neck is the medulla. The life force is in medulla oblongata. In our body every part is operational but not the medulla. Due to this store of energy our heart and lungs move and the collar (left) heater (right) currents by breathing through nostrils meets at the spine.

When life force ends in medulla, death ensues. The nervous system works as a machine in our body automatically as the stars and planets move in the solar system.

Hence daily meditation by sitting in *Padmasan* is essential and concentration on the lower base of the spine should be undertaken. Thus practice makes a man perfect. Hence it is very essential to awaken the energy stored in the body and mind so that we can live healthily and happily in communion with nature.

In Ayurveda all the remedies are derived from trees and herbs grown in natural wind and the water in rivers and mountains forests, etc. Hence our *rishis* preferred to live in forests, on the banks of rivers and on mountains to keep coordination with nature.

Trees and Health. All the Ayurvedic medicines are useful and there is no expiry date on them. They are cheaper than Allopathic drugs, injections, chemicals, syrups, etc. According to *Narad Samhita* each tree is attached with each *Nakshatras* as each *Nakshatra* is attached with a god (Devta). Following is list of Devta and trees attached to each *Nakshatra*:

	Nakshatra and letters	*Devta*	*Tree*
1.	Ashwini Chu Che Cho La	*Ashwini Kumar*	*Bans*
2.	Bharni Lee, Lu, Le, Lo	*Yama*	*Falsa*
3.	Kritika Aa, Ee, U, E	Fire (*Agni*)	*Gooler*

	Nakshatra and letters	*Devta*	*Tree*
4.	Rohini O, Va, Vee, Voo	*Brahma*	*Jamun, Tulsi*
5.	Mrigsira VE, Vo, Ka, Kee	Moon	*Khair*
6.	Aridra Ku, Gha, Rda, Chha	*Shiv*	*Vaheda*
7.	Punarvasu Ke, Ko, Ha, Hee	*Aditi*	*Bans*
8.	Pushya Hoo, He, Ho, Da	*Guru*	*Peepal*
9.	Ashlesha Dee, Du, De, Do	*Sarpa*	*Gangeran*
10.	Magha Mee, Ma, Moo, Me	*Pitra*	*Bargad*
11.	Poorva Phalguna Ma, Ta, Ti, too	*Bhaga*	*Dhak*
12.	Uttra Phalguna Te, To, Pa, Pee	*Aryma*	*Rudraksha*
13.	Hasta Poo, Sha, Na, Tha	*Ravi*	*Reetha*
14.	Chitra Pe, Po, Ra, Ree	*Twasta, Vishwakarma*	Coconut
15.	Swati Ra, Re, Ro, Ta	*Vayu*	*Arjuna*

	Nakshatra and letters	*Devta*	*Tree*
16.	Vishakha Tee, Too, Te, To	*Agni, Indra*	*Pah*
17.	Anuradha Na, Nee, Nu, Ne	*Mitra*	*Vakul*
18.	Jyeshtha No, Ya, Yee, Yu	*Indra*	*Devdaru*
19.	Mool Ye, Yo, Bha, Bhee	*Niritiraksha*	*Ral*
20.	Poorvashada Bhoo, Dha, Fa, Dha	*Jal* (water)	*Ashoka*
21.	Uttrashada Bhe, Bho, Ja, Jee	*Vishwa Deva*	*Falsa*
22.	Sravana Khee, Khoo, Khe, Kho	*Vishnu*	*Aak*
23.	Dhanishtha Ga, Gee, Gu, Ge	*Vasu*	*Shami*
24.	Shatbhisha Go, Sa, See, Soo	*Varuna*	*Kadamba*
25.	Poorva Bhadrapada Se, So, Da, Di	*Ajaik*	Mango
26.	Uttra Bhadrapada Doo, Tha, Jna Gya	*Ahir budhnya*	*Neem*
27.	Revti De, Do, Cha, Chee	*Poosha*	*Mahua*

Now analyse your birth *nakshatra*. If your birth *nakshatra* is not known to you then by your current name see in which *nakshatra* the first letter falls, then the tree of that *nakshatra* may be planted on the day the *nakshatra* of your birth falls in. By doing this your health for the whole year will be safe and prosperity and happiness will come automatically.

The tree must be planted in the rainy season. If you cannot plant your tree (the tree of your birth *nakshatra*) then it may also be planted on the day when your birth *nakshatra* falls in.

It is written many useful things about trees in our holy books like *Veda, Upanishadas, Puranas,* etc. In *Shrimad Bhagwat Geeta* Lord Shri Krishna said to Arjuna that I am *Ashwattha* in tree, i.e., *Peepal.* Hence *Peepal* tree is worshipped. In the same way *Tulsi* is worshipped everyday in Hindu households and lighted at night with a deepak of *ghee* or oil. *Amla* is worshipped in the month of *Kartika* by Hindu ladies on *Navmi tithi* on moonless nights. I am giving some particulars about trees and plants which are useful for health below:

Tulsi. Tulsi is a very useful plant.Its leaves are used for cold, cough and fever by boiling with tea. In Hindu temples *charnamrit* is given to devotees by putting *Tulsi* leaf in bath water of Lord Shaligram.

Neem. Neem is an antiseptic plant. Its leaves are taken with black *veepal, sendha namak* for purifying blood to keep safeguard from itches, eczema, malaria, etc.

Ajwayan. Taking Ajwayan with black salt for pain of stomach or in the case of constipation is beneficial. I have experienced the benefit of this plant many times.

Shoutha. It is useful in body pain, cold, cough, etc. It can also be used in tea.

Mooly. It is very useful in jaundice. It also helps in gas troubles and digestion.

Amla. It is useful in many diseases, as lowering blood pressure, gas, stomach trouble eye, blood or skin diseases. Chavyanprash is made of *Amla*.

Sarpagandha. Take it with Ashwagandha. It is antiseptic and controls blood pressure.

Rudraksha. It is very helpful in heart troubles. It controls blood pressure by wearing its garland. A single rudraksha can also be worn.

Puaal. It is very useful in rheumatic troubles. It is used as vegetable. Its powdered seeds may be used with tea. It is available everywhere during the rainy season.

Sahjan. It is very useful in gas trouble. Vegetable is made from its fruits pods and is useful in gas trouble (*Vata Roga*).

Gajar. It is sweet in taste. It is full of iron. Its use as fruit after food helps in digestion and eyesight. It is also used as juice and halwa is prepared in winter season. It should be taken daily after meals.

Siras. Its juice is useful for eyesight. If somebody is suffering from night blindness (*Rataundhi*), the juice of the leaves of Siras is given. It can also be used by preparing *Batis* or bread and taking with milk.

Gurwel. Its juice is very useful in fever. Generally it is available on the trees of neem.

Adrakh (Ginger). Very useful in cold and cough. It is taken with tea, vegetables, etc.

Black pepper. It is useful in sufferings of throat, cold, cough, etc.

Nutmeg. It is useful in cold. It is also useful in epilepsy.

Senna. It is useful in digestion and as emetic to clear the motion.

Lahsun (Garlic). It is very useful in gastric troubles.

Bilwa. *Bilwa patra* is used in worshipping Lord Shiva by its leaves.

Its fruit (ripe) is very useful in dysentery. Its *murabba* is available in the market.

Aak or *Akanaa*. It is very useful in destroying pain of nerves or swelling. Its leaves are heated and put on the injury or swelling. Swelling and pain will be no more. Its milk is useful in cough. Prepare a *Bati* in milk of *Aak* and in a small mudpot that *Bati* must be kept surround by fire of dried cowdung and the ash will be prepared. It may be used with honey twice a day and cough will be cured.

Adusa. Its flower and leaves both are useful. Flower may be chewed for ulcers in mouth (*chhale*) and leaves applied on wounds or swelling.

Gwarpata. It is useful in pain and swelling. By taking out its middle part by knife and warming it with *haldi* (turmeric), and onion and applied on the affected part with cloth will keep away the pain.

Ayurvedic Medicines and their Importance

In olden days when necessities for life were less, man had control over his senses, mind and body, hence diseases were limited and natural treatment was easily available by means of residing in open air or caves, exercise, *Asanas, Pranayam*, vegetarian food, walking, etc. But nowadays due to scientific inventions our necessities are increasing day by day and we have become habituated towards materialism to have better tasting but less wholesome food, comfortable residence and clothing, and luxurious facilities, hence new diseases are also increasing day by day.

Allopathic medicines although are used by middle and affluent class people but they are to much costly and poor people cannot avail of them easily. But our great *rishis, munis* who lived in open air, in huts, and cottages and prayed to God, meditated and did many other things useful to health. They used herbs for medicines which were available at free of cost from forests and gardens.

Nowadays, Ayurvedic medicines are increasingly using in many countries like Sri Lanka, Japan, China, Mayanmar Mauritius, etc. In our country too, especially in the southern states like Kerala, Karnataka, Tamil Nadu, and Andhra Pradesh Ayurvedic medicines are very popular. These medicines are cheap and do not produce allergies or any side effect in the body. The system is very simple and benefits the patients permanently. Patients and their family members can prepare them easily by consulting Ayurvedic doctors. Due to more materialistic tendency everybody is more busy in earning more and more money and collecting materialistic facilities anyhow to maintain their standard of living. Due to the influence of western culture over eastern countries men have no time to think over the more important thing like health, many new diseases are producing illusion, sickness, melancholy in families.

Blood pressure has become a common disease as also diabetes, AIDS, heart attack, brain haemorrhage, cancer, etc. which are increasing due to strenuous labour in earning money (even whole family members are found busy in earning money consequently neglecting health) and these diseases are not commonly in control of Allopathic treatment. Diseases of children, women too are increasing rapidly due to improper education. Education has become dear and the luggage of books and educational materials are harming the health of children. They carry on their backs 5 to 10 kilos' weight materials and suffering from *Bastasur* (बस्तासुर) causing many diseases. Even then after education there is no guarantee of employment due to the policy of reservation increasing day by day and other factors General public is not happy with the present arrangement of education, medicines, courts, etc.

Hence it has become necessary that we must know about Ayurveda and its cheap price, better treatment for the happiness of the masses.

Given below are some names of medicines which are cheaper and easily available under the control of the pocket of the common man.

Fever. Bhairav Ras, Jwarankush Ras, Sanjeevani Vati, Tribhuwan Keerti Ras, Jwaramsak.

Prolonged Fever. Vasant Malti, Praval Bhasma, Godamti Mukta Shukti, Sringa Bhasma, Peepal Choorna, Maha Sudarshan Choorna, Sitopaladi Choorna, Amritarishta, Lohasava.

Typhus. Praval Bhasma, Sitopaladi Churna, Kappad Bhasma.

Dysentery. Ajmodadi Choorna, Triphala, Isabgol.

Constipation. Chitrakadivati, Gulkand, Kumari Asav, Narayan Choorna, Lavan Bhaskar Choorna.

Stomach trouble. Ajwayan with black salt, Hingastaka Choorna, Lahsun with honey.

Vomiting. Take castor oil with milk according to age.

Liver. Liv 52 tablets, *Chitrakadi vati.*

Acidity. Triphala 2 times after meals.

Headache. *Mahadosamool* oil, Amritdhara, Amritanjan, Vicks Vaporub.

Nervous pain. *Godaantih Bhasma, Mukta pishti, Ashwagandharist.*

Blood Pressure. Abana tablets.

Cough, cold. Take tea with *Tulsi* leaves, *black pepper, Adrak Sitopaladi* with honey.

Paralysis. *Yogaraj guggal basi* with milk 2 tablets daily with cow milk for 3 months. (Experienced).

Tuberculosis. *Chyavanaprash, Draksharist, Ashwagandharist, Punarnavasava.*

Stone. *Chandraprabha vati, Chandanasava.*

Hydrocele. *Mahayogaraj guggal.*

Fatness. *Loh Rasayan, Mukta Bhasma* with cow milk.

Epilepsy. Take *Lahsun* with dal or vegetables. *Bach choorna* with honey 2 or 3 times daily.

Hysteria. *Abhrak Bhasma, Sringa Bhasma, Godanti Bhasma, Shankha Pushpi.*

Diabetes. *Anand Bhairav Ras, Vasant Kusuma Ras, Chandra Prabha vati, Chandrodaya Ras, Kaith Choorna* with honey, twice daily.

Heart disease. *Ashwagandharist, Arjunarist, Vasant Kusumakar Ras, Swarna Bhasma, Mrig Sring Bhasma.*

There are many Ayurvedic medicines which are more useful, cheaper than Allopathic drugs, injections, syrups etc., and are easily available. Hence consult an Ayurvedic practitioner and prevent the disease forever by Ayurvedic medicines. In Ayurvedic medicines, some *pathya* (medically prescribed or salubrious diet) or *parhef* (abstinence) is necessary for different diseases and medicines. But generally they are as following:

1. Do not smoke or use *pathya* (medically prescribed or salubrious diet) or *parhef* (abstinence).

2. Do not take excessive tea or coffee.

3. Do not take eggs, meat, fish, wine as they produce toxins in our body system.

7

Yogasans

Yogasan is also a simple way of keeping good health and it strengthens our digestive system, makes the backbone flexible and gives strength to our nervous system. It also gives strength to our muscles and keeps free from mental tension and fatigue.

Yogasan refreshes our mind, gives strength to brain, memory, attention, lungs and heart and makes regulates life in action, diet, sleep. Hundreds of diseases are cured by yogasans. I am giving here some kinds of rules which are simple but very much helpful in our daily life for keeping good health and an alert mind.

Asan is the third element of *yoga* which is related to *Annamaya Kosha*. By practising *Asan Annamaya Kosha* develops in a way so that it is helpful in digestion of food an *Annams* is *Pran* or life, because our life depends on what we take in food. It is said that whatever, you take in food has full influence on our mind. "जैसा खाओ अन्न वैसा होय मन" Hence for choosing good quality of food, we have to think about *Yama* the first part of yoga. Five things are essential for *Yama*: (1) Non-violence (अहिंसा), (2) Truth (सत्य), (3) Non-stealing habit (अस्तेय), (4) Celibacy (ब्रह्मचर्य) and (5) Non-collection (अपरिग्रह).

The maintenance of these five qualities in man is very necessary for healthy and wealthy social life. Man is a social animal, hence he should follow these things in his life.

1. *Non-violence*. It means do not hurt any living being in any way by means of speech, action, hearing, sight, etc. Keep sympathy and harmony to all beings. This will help you in keeping good thoughts in mind and you will feel happy.

2. *Truth*. Truth is venerated as godliness. Always speak the truth. Do not lie. Be truthful in all your actions. Thus by remembering God who is in our souls, you will be away from bad things and habits which affect our mind. The person who follows the way of rightness is virtuous, pious and healthy.

3. *Non-stealing*. Do not try to take away anything secretly. This is the root of corruption. As we see corruption has spread everywhere nowadays, because we want to utilize everything without any labour, by means of stealing. This makes our heart pure, fearless. So we should not take anything secretly by means of stealing. This is sin and bad for health, society, etc. Corruption leads to stealing and many diseases are spread in society as it contaminates the conscience or the heart and heart is the abode of God. Non-stealing habit makes our heart strong and pure and give way to self-realisation.

4. *Celibacy*. *Brahmacharya* does not mean unmarried life and should not be understood so. If all the persons in the society will remain unmarried then how can humanity proliferate. In olden days, our *rishi*, *munis*, *yogis* married and even then they followed the path of Brahmacharya. Though this position is essential for students up to the age of 25 and is called as Brahmacharyashram. It means the security of semen, which is the essence of our blood and its security is essential to have good health. Control over unnecessary sexual action is stressed. Semen is the root of human life. The man who misuse semen by means of daily sexual intercourse weaken the health of himself and her spouse. Hence for this maintenance "Prayer" is essential to keep the thoughts away from sexual activities. Sexual action should be performed only when you want a child. Conserve semen and do not use it only for sexual pleasure. If you do not secure semen, definitely you will come in the grip of many diseases and the chances of premature death will increase. Nowadays open and suggestive sexual actions are shown on electronic media. These programmes and moves poisoning the minds of young generation.

5. *Non-collection*. In Upanishadas it is said:

'तेन त्यक्तेन भुंजीथा मा ग्रधः कस्य स्वद्यनम्'

which means God has left all the things for man. Hence use them but do not collect only for yourself. Air, sky, earth, water and fire are the five elements by which grain is produced and metal is taken out of earth. Hence these things are for all to be used. Hence it should not be hoarded. But let all the persons use them. This does not mean that you spend all the collected things at one time. But think of the happiness of others too to make you happy. Some people are greedy and have collected earning ill-gotten wealth instead make it available at reasonable rates to be distributed to all the persons who want it. This habit will make you satisfied both physically and mentally.

After following these five *yamas* the other five rules called *Niyam* (नियम) are also very essential for healthy life. These are: (1) Purity (शौच), (2) Satisfaction (संतोष), (3) *Tapa*, i.e., Labour (तप), (4) Self-study (स्वाध्याय), (5) Meditation (प्रणिधान) praying to God.

1. The first niyam is purity or *shauch*. For this purpose "Early to bed and early to rise, makes a man healthy, wealthy and wise." After early rising clean your body after taking at least two glasses of water, go to lavatory, wash the mouth, hands, take bath, be free and read some holy books like *Geeta, Ramayan, Quran, Bible,* etc. Do your duty being pure hearted and free of mind. Morning walk, exercise, *asan*, etc. are necessary for healthy life.

2. The second thing is satisfaction. Be satisfied with your progress of health, body, mind, monetary position. Do not have greed or lust and do not think of luxurious life. Be luxurious not in collecting money, property, and material things but in health, heart and mind. It is called संतोषी सदा सुखी which means that a person who is satisfied is always happy. Happiness comes from the mental state and not from money only. The materialistic view leads to sorrow, melancholy, false pride and other bad qualities unfavourable for happy human life. Hence do your duty and do not think of the reward. Because reward is in the hands of God. Then why do you think over the fruit only? If you are self-reliant, good reward will come automatically. Think of duty only and so it is wisely said, "Work is Worship." "Duty is God." Really luxurious life materially leads to

dissatisfaction and vicious life. We should try to be luxurious in health and mind only for materialist luxury is the root of all the vices.

3. *Tapa*. Means not only to go to the forest leaving the world. *Tapa* also means to accepting the challenges of troubles coming our way to progress. *Tapa* means physical and mental labour to reach to god, goal or aim of our life. For this purpose you will have to determine the state of your mind to withstand adversities, leaving the worldly happiness and doing good to others. उस हाल में जीना लाजिम है जिस हाल में जीना मुश्किल है। You have to pass your time in that period in which living is difficult. If you could stand in difficulties, then you can overcome your troubles in this world. Life is struggle and in struggle we have to face the enemies of our body, health, mind and prosperity. By *tapa* many good qualities will come to you and will bring happiness in life by courageous standing in spite of sorrow. It is all your mental state which depresses you so by means of endeavour and labour win the struggle of life.

4. Self-study or *Swadhyay*. This is very necessary to keep gooc health and sound mind. In *Shrimad Bhagwad Geeta* Lord Krishna has said, स्वाध्याय तपः means self-study is also a kind of *tapa*. We have vast knowledge of experiences of great writers in store. Hence a man is always a student in his life where he learns many things from these books. Self-study leads to mental and physical happiness, peace and satisfaction in life. Books arc our best friends. Hence, we should extract time for two or three hours daily to read books, think over them and apply them in our daily life.

(5) Meditation **(प्रणिधान)** - The fifth *niyam* is *Pranidhan* or praying the God through worshipping deity, reading holy books, chanting of *mantras*, meditation, etc. Some persons do not believe in the existence of God, some say it is a falsehood while some say it is superstition. Whatever the fact may be, it is certain that there is some power beyond this nature and cosmos who controls and regularises the elements of nature, human behaviour, etc. By means of praying to God concentration will be your friend and your inner soul will be full of virtues, courage, fearlessness and many other good qualities. Regular meditation at the feet of God will make pure hearted brainy and your intellect will automatically be balanced, worship, praying must be part and parcel of our life so that our body and mind both be trained to be healthy. Believe in God and you will get

success in every field of life. Tennyson, the great English poet has rightly said, "Trust in God and do the right." What a wonderful thing is that we spend thousands of rupees in curing diseases with medicines but we cannot afford some time to see the God in the form of poor, handicapped who are the living gods. Human body is the most wonderful creation of God. Mind or *Mana* is the greatest power of human body. Not only this (mind) but also there is a heart in the body. Lord Shri Krishna has said to Arjun in *Geeta*:

ईश्वरः सर्वभूतानां हृद्देशेऽर्जुन तिष्ठति।
भ्रामयन्सर्वभूतानि यंत्रारूढानि मायया।।

Oh Arjun! God lives in the heart of all creatures of the cosmos and by His *maya* (illusive power) makes them to walk illusively like a machine (according to their previous life's action). So heart is the main centre of all the sensation, perception, learning and knowledge. Mind is the chief informative head of all the actions. Mind is the root of all the actions done by man—virtuous or vicious. Mind cannot be seen but its activities are felt by us by the eyes, nose, tongue, skin, ear and palpitation of heart.

Mind's movement is very fast. It is always active even while sleeping in every field of cosmos by means of dreams. Mind's attention is not permanent on any one subject. It is changeable in every second. Light moves 285000 km per second but the movement of mind *(mana)* cannot be measured.

The arteries carry blood to the various parts of the body from the heart and blood returns to the heart through nevous system. In the nervous system brain and ''*sushmna nadi*'' (सुषुम्ना नाड़ी) are included. *Sushmna nadi* the minds goes through bones of the spine surrounded by *Ida* and *Pingla nadies* to the right and left of it. Through this *sushmna nadi* the mind's main power is awakened by means of concentration of mind. *Yogasans* help in attentive condition of mind. This attentive power helps in concentration on the aim of life, the realisation of self or combination of soul with God. Hence after maintaining *yama* and *niyama* (यम-नियम) by purifying body and mind the heart is clear and everything functions correctly. These *yogasans* help in curing diseases. The main *Asan* is *Siddhasan* or *Padmasan*. Sitting straight like lotus by bending the knees and putting right foot on left and left on right and concentrating on the tip of nose makes us achieve this *asan*.

The mind has close relation with life force—*Pran* (प्राण), by means of *pranayam* (respiratory system) through right and left nostrils to have command over passion. This is very necessary for the right path, otherwise passions produce many difficulties in focusing attention of mind. Respiration is the sign of life and its stoppage is death.

Benefits of *Yogasans*

1. It is the simple and natural way to exercise which is available at any place, at any time, without spending money and is common for the rich and the poor. Your body is the only thing required for *yogasans.*
2. The mind gets freshness, and the body is of tension due to coordination of body and mind through respiration.
3. *Yogasan* helps in regaining the lost power of body and mind.
4. It helps in securing semen and functioning of the inner glands of the body.
5. It improves our digestive system and clears the stomach.
6. It gives strength to the backbone and rejuvenentes the nervous system.
7. It helps in lessening fatness, weakness of body and mind.
8. It helps ladies in keeping and maintaining their health.
9. It increases intellectual power and enhances concentration of mind.
10. It regularises the respiratory system, and gives strength to lungs and heart.
11. It cures diseases and makes the body healthy and mind sound.
12. It improves eyesight.
13. Every part of body the gets exercise.
14. Harmonious development of body and mind is effected.
15. All-round success starts when you start *yogasans*.
16. From student life the practice of *yogasan* should be done so that in the long run it will enable the person to get victory over passions, lust and anxieties and success will be in his hands.
17. *Yogasans* not only increase our spiritual power but all the worldly progress is also gained through them. When the body and mind

are strengthened through *yogasans* then there is nothing impossible which we cannot gain.

Some Rules for *Yogasans*

It is very essential that *yogasans* should be performed under some rules to get fullest advantages, e.g.

1. The best time for *yogasan* is early in the morning, i.e., *Brahma Muhurta* (ब्रह्ममुहूर्त).
2. At one time only one *asan* should be performed.
3. After *yogasans* some rest is essential.
4. Do not take anything as breakfast or drink before *yogasans*.
5. When you feel fatigue, then *yogasan* should be stopped.
6. *Yogasan* can be performed before and after taking bath.
7. *Yogasans* are open to all ladies, gents, young and old.
8. Breakfast or milk can be taken after 45 minutes of *yogasans*.
9. Always do *yogasans* in the open air, near temple, or river, where there is no dirt.
10. Your diet should be neither heavy nor sparse but in proportion to age.

Hence *yogasan* is necessary to enjoy full pleasure of life because medicines can give little strength, not full.

Yogasans and Ladies. *Yogasan* is not only necessary and helpful to gents but is also helpful to ladies. It has been generally seen that most of the ladies do not properly maintain their health. The reason is that most of the ladies are illiterate, believe in superstition, have no fresh air to breath as they live 24 hours in their houses.

Though literacy is increasing in women, nevertheless they are still found ill. Most of the ladies are found ill due to leucomhoea in which white fluids comes out from vagina due to menstrual disorder. This is a dangerous disease which, if not taken care of at the time of delivery it becomes disease for ever. If at the time of delivery full attention is paid towards the health of ladies, this dangerous disease may not have the chance to strike.

Secondly, ladies generally are found suffering from stomach or gas troubles. This is due to the fact that their digestive system is not in order owing to lack of fresh air, sunlight, clean water, etc. In olden days, ladies had to grind the grain at home with stone *chakki,* fetch water from the wells, serve the domestic animals, e.g. to milk cows or buffaloes, make *uple* (कंडे) of *gobar,* to prepare ghee from curd. But nowadays all those activities are not done. In those activities ladies used to get physical exercise. But nowadays, due to inventions of science, ladies do not have to do all those things. Grain is ground by flourmills, water comes from pipes or hand pumps, milk from the market or milk dairies. Now they use gas or stove instead of wood (fuel) in preparing food. Spices are grounded in market. Everything is available readymade in the market. Hence ladies of today are devoid of physical activities. Hence nowadays they are suffering from mental diseases more than physical diseases. More care for children, unnecessary pressure on mind in father-in-law's house, misbehaviour of husband, mother-in-law, sister-in-law, brother-in-law and new demands of her husbands from her parents also causes many diseases among ladies. Due to these problems, waist pain, brain haemorrhage, heart attack, jaundice, blood pressure, hysteria, etc. are common diseases found even in educated ladies.

For these problems happy environment is essential, fresh air, sympathetic behaviour are necessary to get rid of diseases in ladies. Besides some *yogasans* are very useful and helpful in curing diseases for ladies.

For headache. Headache is found commonly in ladies. For this *Sarvangasan, Bhujangasan, Pawanmukti asan* are very useful. These *asans* should be performed under the guidance of any specialist in *asans.*

For hysteria. The cause of this disease is lack of physical strength. Fear of unnecessary cough and wind, dissatisfaction in sexual intercourse, marriage in late age, unnecessary heat in the body are the main causes for hysteria. Hence mental depression, giddiness, semi-unconsciousness, etc. are noticed. Ladies are generally seen suffering from this disease either when there is delay in marriage or after marriage in husband's house when they have to adjust to a new environment with new family. Hence lack of love, negligence by husband's mother, sister, sister-in-law, pressure for more dowry, etc. are the main causes of these diseases among ladies. For these diseases first of all love and sympathy with the patient is necessary, secondly, keeping the patient away from environment of depression, sorrow, fear. No excessive sexual activity is required. Hence the natural treatment of this disease is to exercise *Sarvagasan, Bhujangasan, Pawanmuktasan, Vajrasan* and use of *Trifala* made of *Harad, Baheda, Amla, Chandra Prabha Vati* and to partake use green vegetables, fruits so that there is no acidity, constipation, indigestion, gas trouble, etc.

For leucomhoea too *Sarvangasan, Bhujangasan, Dhanurasan,* etc. are helpful. *Ashokarishta* is the best Ayurvedic medicine prescribed for this disease. If care is not taken, at the time of delivery, this disease becomes lifelong disease. The *Banda* of *Peepal* tree which is red rosy in colour found on the fat branches is also given by grinding it with water and cow milk to patients.

Weak eyesight. Generally Indian ladies are very faithful and laborious and devoted to the family. Hence sometimes their eyesight is weak due to much pressure on eyesight while cleaning the grains, pulse, vegetables, and preparing food late at night. For this *Sarvangasan,* and *Bhujangasan,* is recommended when waking up early in the morning to wash the eyes with water kept overnight in a copper vessel, and to walk barefoot early in the morning on the green grass wet with dew.

For eyesight rose water should be applied in eyes, and food like cucumber, carrot, onion, blackberry, papaya, spinach, mint, mulberry, *karonda* fruits with milk are very useful to increase eyesight. Taking daily carrot after food is very useful for eyesight as also eating of *amla.*

Nourishment of hair. Smooth, black hair make ladies attractive and beautiful, but the maintenance of health of hair is very important. For this purpose ladies must wash the hair with *amla*, curd, lemon and put the oil of *amla,* Bhring Raj, walk in the morning in the fresh air, doing *Padmasan, Siddhasan, Sukhasan, Shavasan,* etc. is also recommended.

Insomnia. Slothful ladies who sleep in daytime can be victims of this disease. This disease is generally found among ladies of rich and aristocratic families who depend on servants for every small or big work, and sit or lie idly. To get rid of this disease physical exercise, work and walking are necessary. Before sleeping hands and feet should be thoroughly washed. *Sarvangasan, Vajrasan, Bhujangasan* should be performed daily. Use of *Badam* oil for massage, and drinking almonds with milk as also Shankh Pushpi, Brahmi, etc. is required.

Obesity. It can be with reduced sugar intake taking *Isabgol* or fleaseed husk, if you start morning walk. *Surya Namaskar, gymnastics,* hanging on bars, *Bhujangasan, Vajrasan* are good *asans* for controlling obesity. Control over your food. *Chandra Prabhavati*, slow running in the morning, etc. also diminishes fatness in the body.

For mental peace and light feeling in the body, practice the *Shavasan*. This is very simple *asan*. There is no possibility of harm in this *asan*. Lie straight on the back like a dead body keeping hands fixed at the sides of the body. Think that you are not inside the body. Freeness will come and its daily practice will keep you free from mental depression, uneasiness, fatigue, etc.

Constipation. Constipation is the worst enemy of health. This disease though seemingly mild but when not cared in due course causes other diseases. Hence to be free from constipation, proper digestion is very necessary. If you take food in proportion to age, season and climate then you may not be victim of this disease. To keep away this disease:

1. Rise early in the morning as far as possible.
2. Take two glasses of water kept overnight in a copper vessel.
3. Take bath daily.
4. Morning walk is a beneficial alternative. So go for a morning walk daily.
5. Keep your mind away from worries.
6. Do your work without feeling unnecessary burden of any kind. Always feel satisfied and happy.
7. "*Abhyarishta*" may be taken as Ayurvedic medicine.
8. *Vajrasan* is useful in constipation.

Rheumatism. It is the disease caused mainly by gas (air) and results in pain in knees and joints. For this digestion should be clear. *Vajrasan, Sarvangasan, Bhujangasan* are useful in this disease. Do not take much sour. *Surya Namaskar* is useful. *Chyavanprash, Chandra Prabha Vati, Yogaraj Guggal* are very useful. Use of ginger, black pepper, *amla, tulsi, maithy,* papaya, guava, spinach, etc. is recommended.

General Diseases Common in Men and Women

Heart trouble. Nowadays both gents or ladies are found more busy in their day-to-day works. Daily routine in every family is like a machine.

If there is some disturbance due to advent of guests, festival, ceremonies then daily routine work is affected. Hence there is tension in every family. There is a heavy load on children in the name of education. They are burdened with heavy schoolbags, then in adults, due to unemployment thousands of educated and talented persons are dissatisfied by their jobs, in old persons due to cares of their service, disturbance in the family due to maladjustment, dissatisfaction among students after completing studies and wandering for employment leads to sadness and heart stroke.

Heart is the centre of all activities and functions in human body. In body too heart is at the centre. According to Ayurveda excessive physical labour, hot, sour and acute things in food, irregularities in food, wrong medicines, fear, anger, etc. are the main causes of heart disease. Hence due to these things palpitation of heart goes above the normal 72 times per minute to 80-85 or 90 per minute. From weakness of heart other diseases like gas problem, hysteria, leucomhea in ladies, piles, etc. attack the human body.

In heart disease first of all palpitation of heart increases due to sudden sadness, anxiety, melancholy, rapid pulse movement constipation lack of appetite, tiredness, sloth, etc. are the symptoms seen in the patient.

Due to these factors pain starts in heart and heart attack ensues. The patient feels most uneasiness and heavyness in the heart. Vomiting, darkness before eyes and sweat exudes from the body hence all the body becomes flexible and it looks lifeless.

Those who are aged and are the victim of high blood pressure feel pain in heart and when blood pressure is above 160-100 or 160-100 the treatment should be started. No physical labour, rest is necessary. The following treatment should be given to heart patients:

1. Keep the patient in open air. The environment should be calm and quiet.
2. Proper food in moderated amounts should be taken.
3. Adequate rest will relieve the patient.
4. Going up and down stairs should be avoided.
5. Mental peace should be foremost.
6. Do not speak loudly where the patient is taking rest.

Medicines. According to Ayurveda, *Arjunarishta* and *Ashwagandharista* should be given. Use of garlic will also help. *Shringa Bhasma* should be given with honey. *Abhrak Bhasma* can be given. *Siddha Makaradhwaja* when palpitation increases should be given. *Sarpagandha* for high blood pressure is helpful. Physical and mental rest is very essential for heart patients.

Shavasan is the best *asan* for heart patients. It will calm them and mental pressure will be less. Rudraksha should be worn on neck so that it may touch the heart. Keep the patient away from worries of all kinds.

Diabetes. Most of the people nowadays are in the grip of this dangerous disease. This is mainly due to metabolic disorders. When sugar is not fully metabolised and is excreted in urine the urine is white and freezes soon. In this disease the patient suffers from headache, giddiness, swelling on jaws, pain and destruction of teeth, bad smell in teeth, defect in lungs, inflammation, itches on the body, constipation, uneasiness, coma, etc. are the main symptoms of this disease.

In Hindi this disease is called *Madhumeh*. In Ayurveda the cause of this disease is shown the weakness of fire glands. These glands are the liver, spleen and *agnasaya*. Due to lack of insulin the patient drinks much water and urinates frequently. Sometimes by injection of insulin the palpitation of heart increases and danger of death increases. In serious condition glucose is administered to the patient. For some persons this disease is hereditary while for others it ensues by irregularities in dietary habits and routine.

Treatment. This dangerous disease readily attacks those persons who have irregular dietary patterns. Mental pressure, carelessness, anger, fear, etc., increase this disease. Excessive sexual activity also leads to this disease. Keep your digestion clear and walk in open air in the morning. Do some *yogasans* as *Sarvangasan, Dhanarasan, Bhujangasan,* etc. Bitter gourd (*karela*) is very useful in diabetes. After *asans* take juice of bitter gourd in the morning or take in food cooked vegetable of bitter gourd. Do not eat much sweet food. Physical exercise is necessary. Use juice of *amla* and lemon in the ratio 50-50 with honey 2-3 times daily. In summer season *tericot*, terylene, nylon clothes should not be worn. *Giloy Gurvel, Gwarpatha* with *Ajwain* (a kind of aromatic seed) a spoonful, *saunf* (aniseed) a spoonful, 10 black pepper, 10 neem leaves, 10 neem stick should be ground with water and taken on empty stomach for 10-15 days with waist wash and early morning walk is necessary.

Liver trouble. If you want to live healthy keep the liver healthy. Do not take excessive butter, cream and ghee and take only as much as you may digest. Bread, rice, sugar should be used in limit. Use fresh vegetables and fruits such as carrot papaya. You can take juice of sweet fruits such as mausambi, apples, etc. Keep your mind always happy. Do not worry excessively but be happy. *Pranayam* is very helpful in liver trouble. If you feel uneasiness, headache, vomiting, tastelessness in mouth then it indicates that when liver is not working well.

Waist bath, *Pranayam, Sarvangasan, Vajrasan* are very useful for giving strength to the liver.

Cheap Treatments for some Minor Ailments

Inflammation in stomach. Take the juice of melon, cucumber or *kumbra* for 3 days continuously. Take *Ajwain* with powdered black salt with little hot water twice a day to ease the stomach pain.

Blood from nose or unconsciousness. Take the juice of onion and have the patient smell it.

Piles. Give *Dhunee* or smoke to the patient of *Dhatura* leaves for 2 or 3 times daily for 2 or 3 days.

Jaundice, anemia, lack of blood. Take a cupful of juice of bitter gourd in the morning while stomach is empty for 3-4 days.

Cold. Take 1 glass water, 2 *tola* joggery, 2 lemons a small piece of ginger, a spoonful of *Ajwain* and boil all these covered in a pot. After boiling, cut the lemon and mix the juice in the boiled water. Also mix a little black salt and drink it somewhat hot and then go to sleep for two hours. This juice also helps in dengue fever, malaria, typhoid, brain fever, etc.

Rheumatism (Gathiya or wind disease). Take *Gwarpatha* 50 gms, peel and cut into little pieces in a cup of water. In every 2-3 minutes take these pieces without chewing and gulp them into the stomach.

Cancer, blood cancer. Take a glass of carrot juice per day four times. Do not take food but take only the juice of carrot. This is cheap and the best medicine for cancer or blood cancer.

Remember life is more valuable than any other things of the world. Hence first of all control your desire to eat. Do not eat for taste only but eat for sustenance of life. You are not born to eat and take taste only.

Those who control their desire to eat are always healthy and happy and thus successful in life.

Chart of Diseases Treatable by medicines and Yogasans

Disease	*Medicine*	*Yogasans*
Headache	*Sankha churna* with milk, Rub sandal oil	*Sarvangasan, Sheershasan*
Brain weakness	*Shankh Pushpi*	*Sheershasan*
Diseases of mouth (Teeth)	Vicco Vajradanti, toothpowder is best for teeth	*Pranayam*
Eye disease	Onion juice with honey	*Sheershasan*
Ear disease	Put little warm onion juice in ears	*Pranayam*
Bronchitis	Clean by salted warm water	*Sarvangasan*
Goitre	Take *kachnar* chhal or the bark of tree of any species of *Bauhinia* mixing with water of rice	*Surya Namaskar*
Heart disease	*Arjunarishta, Makaradhwayj; Muktashukti pishti*	*Surya Namaskar, Padmasan*
Lung trouble	Walk in open air, take juice of fruits, honey.	*Surya Namaskar, Vajrasan*
Stomach disease	*Trifala* with warm water and ajwain with black salt	*Padmasan, Sukhasan*
Fever	*Dashmool Kadha* with *peepal*	Change the *Swar* from nostril soon
Jaundice	*Lohasava, Punarnavadi* churna	*Vajrasan*
Dyspepsia	*Hingashtak, Lavan Bhaskar Churna*	*Vajrasan*
Constipation	Castor oil with milk	*Vajrasan*
Piles	Juice of *bitter gourd* with sugar, onion juice with ghee and sugar	*Sarvangasan, Vajrasan*
Swelling	Take urine of cow for 3 days or 7 days as diagnosed	*Surya Namaskar* Sheershasan
Hydrocele	Take castor oil with warm milk for a month	*Surya Namaskar*
Impotency	*Chyavanprash vasant kusumakar ras*	*Sheershasan, Bhujangasan*
Syphilis	Wash the wounds with *trifala* or *neem* leaf water.	*Dhanurasan*
Diabetes	Stop salt and sugar immediately Take papaya, bitter gourd in large quantities	*Surya Namaskar, Dhanurasan*

Disease	*Medicine*	*Yogasans*
Gonorrhoea	Take juice of sugarcane and coconut	*Dhanurasan, Sheershasan*
Stone	*Varunadi churna, varna chhal* with jaggery	*Pranayam*
Kidney trouble	Use of carrot will check in the beginning	*Ushtrasan,* Bhujangasan
Epilepsy	Black *peepal churna* in the nose *Lobham dhumi, buch*	*Padmasan, Sukhasan*
Blood pressure	*Abana* tablets, 2, 2 daily	*Vajrasan*
Vomiting	Ash of *peepal chhal* with water	*Vajrasan*
Asthma	*Vilvapatra, Adusa ras* with mustard oil	*Shavasan, Sarvangasan*
Tuberculosis	Full rest, *ashwagandhadi Sitopiladi,* fresh air	*Pranayam*
Hysteria	Lohasara, *Swarna bhasma* Makradhwaj.	*Padmasan*

There are so many kinds of diseases, as also medicines. *Asans* are also of many kinds but useful for various ailments. Rules and regulations are many but their application is necessary.

Ayurveda consists of a vast store of knowledge gained by men like Danvantari, Charak, Sushrut, Vag Bhatta, etc. The most famous books of Ayurveda are *Charak Samhita, Sushrat, Vag Bhatta, Bangsen, Bhaishaj Ratnavali, Madhav Nidan, Rasraj Mahodadhi,* etc.

In the above chart in short the diseases and their common medicines, *yogasanas,* etc. are indicated. Only hints are given here. There are hundreds of medicines given for a disease in books. But those that are simply available and mostly common in use are given here. The main thing is that the *asans* are to be performed daily so that the diseases cannot attack the human body. *Surya namaskar, Padmasan, Sukhasan, Vajrasan, Sheershasan* are very easy to perform but in the beginning they must be learnt thoroughly. As it is said correctly that a little knowledge is a dangerous thing. So for *yogasans* and Ayurvedic medicines consulting an Ayurvedacharya Vaidya is necessary. It is said that the writer of *Madhav Nidan* devoted 12 years to deity Gayatri and chanted the Gayatri Mantra innumerable times. Then only could he write the great book *Madhav Nidan*. So mantras are also helpful in healthy life.

Yoga Leads to Meditation

India is the land of great saints who emphasized on the purity of heart, the base of all the purities, the basis of all the success and good health. What you want to be shown in outwardly, should be first of all shown unwardly. So, from the heart emanates health, wealth and wisdom.

According to our sages, praying and meditation of God keeps away us from all the vices, diseases, troubles, anxieties, melancholy, sorrows and unhappy life. They live in forest, on mountains, near nature to get fresh air which is difficult to get in the polluted environment of crowded cities. The dust, carbon, omake and other substances of vehicles make us unhealthy. Although nowadays villagers are migrating to the cities. Cities are only attractive places of material and luxury goods. Outer beauty is the curse to humanity which tricks human beings in many ways. The real beauty lies inside the conscience in virtues, not in shapes, faces, colour or fashionable things. So many of the diseases in modern civilization are due to the fact that we are running blindly towards the outward beauty. The inner beauty is the nectar of life described in *Upanishads, Vedas, Puranas, Geeta, Ramayana* and *Mahabharata*. It is also available in the teachings of the holy *Quran, Bible, Jinwani, Guruvani,* etc.

Science has developed new ways to facilitate ease and material comforts in our lives. Still there is no peace in our lives. What is the reason? The reason behind this is that we are running blindly after materialism without thinking about the good or bad results of it. Materialistic view can give us money, property, wealth, modern facilities but not mental peace or mental satisfaction which is very necessary. So for gain this we have to adhere to the path of wisdom, truth, non-violence etc. Spiritualism leads to self- realisation which is the real goal of life, i.e. to know ourselves, what are we? what we do? for what we are born? Are we born only to eat, drink and be merry? A life without virtues, purity and truth is baneful. So for living a virtuous life praying regularly to god and daily meditation is necessary.

Yogis awaken the serpentine power (*Kundalini jagran*) and combine their soul with God. This is a way of self-realisation to express the self. Besides there are *mantras,* means of donation and piety, *japa, tapa* and many other things but without purity of heart nothing is possible. So our *rishis* had prescribed *Yama, Niyama, Asan, Pranayam, Prtyohar, Dhyan,*

Dharna, Samadhi as the eight parts of yoga. This leads to good health and *amima garima,* etc. eight *Siddhi,* and nine *Nidhis* are under the feet of the *yogi.* They can change their body *(Kaya kalp),* can fly in the sky, can walk on water, can be short or tall as they desire. Hence in Indian mythology and philosophy great attention is paid on spiritualism. There are means to decrease the power of planets which are the cause of sufferings to man. Now we shall discuss the methods of reducing the malinfluence of each planet so that we can minimise sufferings and diseases.

8

Tress and Health

Herbs and Planets for Peaceful Life

If Sun is the cause of disease put the root of *belpatra* in rosy coloured thread on your body on Sunday.

If Moon is the cause of disease keep root of *khinni* in white thread on Monday.

If Mars is the cause of disease keep root of *Anantmool* in red thread on Tuesday.

If Mercury is the cause of disease keep root of *Bidhara* in green thread on Wednesday.

If Jupiter is the cause of disease keep root of *orange* or *plantain* in yellow thread on Thursday.

If Venus is the cause of disease keep root of *Sarpoukha* in white thread on Friday.

If Saturn is the cause of disease keep root of *Bichehoo* in blue thread on Saturday.

If *Rahu* is the cause of disease put root of white *sandal* in blue or black thread on Saturday.

If *Ketu* is the cause of disease keep root of *ashwagandha* in sky coloured thread on Tuesday.

Wear clothes from the point of keeping good health and not from the point of fashion. Put on loose clothes, and refrain from tight fitting clothes to the body because tight clothes will affect on nerves and body and may cause diseases. Hence wearing clothes save your health and life in the long run.

If you do not have horoscope then according to the *Rasi* name wear on clothes as follows :

Rasi	*Lord of Rasi*	*Favourable colours according to Astrology*	*Unfavourable colours*
Aries	Mars	Red, Yellow, White	Green, Blue
Taurus	Venus	White, Yellow	Deep Green, Red
Gemini	Mercury	Green, Blue, Sky	Red
Cancer	Moon	White, Yellow	Blue, Black
Leo	Sun	White, Red, Yellow	Black, Blue
Virgo	Mercury	Green, Blue, Sky	Red
Libra	Venus	White, Yellow	Deep Green, Red
Scorpio	Mars	Red, Yellow, White	Green, Blue
Sagittarius	Jupiter	Yellow, Pink, White	Green, Blue
Capricorn	Saturn	Blue, Yellow	White, Red
Aquarius	Saturn	Blue, Yellow	White, Red
Pisces	Jupiter	Yellow, Pink, White	Green, Blue

Herbal therapy

In olden days when there were less means of treatment as today most of the diseases were treated by herbs. They are useful today too. Herbal therapy is cheaper than modern medicine system.

For sleeping in fever. Put the root of *Kak jangha* on head bound by cloth.

For night fever. Keep the root of *Makoy* near ear bound with cloth.

In acute fever (Visham jwar). On Sunday the root of white *Dhatoora* should be bound on the right hand.

Fever of spirit's fear. Root of *Sahsevi* in white thread bound by a little girl in the right hand of the patient.

Fever by epilepsy. Keep the full *jayphal* enclosed in a cloth on the throat of the patient.

On increasing spleen. In black thread bind red onion on the throat of the patient.

On increasing the palpitation of heart. Make a garland of *palash* leaves and put on the throat of the patient. When the garland is dried then leave it on the crossroads.

In goitre. Wear the garland of leaves of *Apamarg*.

In elephantiasis. 11 seeds of *jiyapate* bound with 11 black thread should be bound on the swelling in feet.

In sunstroke. Keep red onion on the body of the patient after cutting it.

In pain of joints. Grind *Rai (Sarson)* and keep on paining joints.

Inflammation or blood in urine. Consume 2.5 grams leaves of sunflower daily.

Eczema. Milk of *Aak* destroys eczema.

In hydrocele. Keep flowers of *Tesu (Palash)* on the affected part. The patient will feel relief with in two days.

For happy delivery. (1) Root of *chidchida* ground in water and 3 or 4 drops applied on the navel of pregnant lady while suffering from pain due to delivery. The child will be delivered with ease.

(2) Root of *neem* tree bound at the waist of the lady and should be removed after the delivery.

In stone disease. Take milky grass and leaves of evergreen in equal quantity and grind them with black pepper with water and give to the patient to drink. It will be beneficial soon.

Guheri in eyes. Put your spit at the place where *guheri* is near the eyelid early in the morning.

Skin diseases. Mix *Bhimsemi kapoor* in *vanaspati* and apply on the skin where itches, eczema, scabies are seen.

To increase eyesight. Take *sounf* with *mishri* right at the time of sleeping.

Headache. Put *buch* ground in water on head.

Burning. Put honey at burnt portion.

In epilepsy, madness, giddiness. Take 5-10 rattie honey and the ground *churna* of *Buch*.

In skin diseases . Take the syrup prepared from the following things; *Chirayta* 180 gms, *Seharta* 150 gms, *Gorbkh mundi* 75 gms and Sounf 75 gms grind all these things and boil in the water for about 2 hours slowly. When it reduces to one-fourth then cool it and drink a cup or half cup as the case may be.

9

Gems Therapy

Our *rishis* and *munis* were aquainted with all the gems favourable to different signs and *nakshatra.* Each planet has been allotted a gem. Such gem and other allied cheap gems, e.g., ruby for Sun, pearl for Moon, coral for Mars, emerald for Mercury, topaz for Jupiter, diamond for Venus, neelam for Saturn, gomed for *Rahu* and lahsamia for *Ketu* are some of them.

Ruby. In Sanskrit it is called *manikyam.* Ruby is a combination of aluminium and oxygen. Traces of iron and chromium too are found. Thus ruby is of two kinds. Ruby is favourable in headache, skin diseases and heart trouble. It also helps in calming anxiety in mind, disappointment, lack in executive power, losing friendship. It is of red colour like red lotus flower. Ruby should be worn in golden ring in first finger of right hand. It should be above 3 rattie. It is to be worn on Sunday–*Pushya Nakshatra, Good ghatis*, after worshipping, should be prepared on Sunday between 6.00 a.m. to 12.00 noon. If *Ravi–Pushya* is not near and you want to wear urgently then should be worn on Sunday, but *nakshatra* should be of Sun as *kritika, uttrashad, uttraphalgun.*

In Sanskrit it is said that ruby helps in making blood. Constipation, cough and wind and all the troubles due to sins, ghost, etc. of previous lives are destroyed. If Ruby is not easily available or is dear then *Lalmani, Garnet, Padanrag, Neelgaanthi* and *Upratna* may be worn. While worshipping Ruby, Sun worship is also essential. *Surya Sahasranam* or *Gayatri japa* is essential daily to make the Ruby influencial. Chanting of *"Aditya Hridayam"* (आदित्य हृदयं) daily after wearing Ruby should be undertaken.

Pearl. Pearl is white in colour like curd, smooth and generally round in shape. It helps in treatment of diseases caused by weak position of Moon in horoscope. Specially goitre, cough disturbance, T.B., dropsy, heart disease, dysentery, fever, poor blood circulation, mental disturbance, urinary diseases, etc. are treated with pearl.

Pearl fulfils the lack of calcium in the body. In typhoid the ash of pearl is beneficial. The persons who are always in grip of cold should wear pearl in silver ring in little finger in right hand.

The best period to wear the ring of pearl is the half month of bright moon, i.e., *Shuklapaksha*. Weak moon's patient should worship lord Shiva daily with *Shiva Mahima Strotra*. After worshipping the *mantra* of Moon "Om Som Somay Namah" ॐ सों सोमाय नमः should be chanted for 7,000 times.

Sub gems of Moon. Moon's *upratna* is *Moonstone*. It is of milky colour. It helps to strengthen mental power and blood pressure.

Opal. This is also the subgem of Moon. It is a stone of milky colour. It is mysterious and beneficial and has the influence of Moon and Venus both. It increases spiritual power, mental peace and renunciation of worldly goods.

As Moon is planet of imagination, so Moon subject should always build castles in the air with flexible mind and heart broken. Before one work is fulfilled, the other work is begun hence mind is not at ease. Hence such people should wear the pearl of *Basra*. It is mythologically said that rain of *swati nakshatra* when falls on oyster shell (seep) the *seep* closes and pearl is formed inside it. Such pearl is the real pearl but it is difficult and hard to find.

Coral. Coral or *Moonga* is the gem of Mars. It increases self-strength, helps in troublesome period in enemity. Courage, and believe in yourself are all these qualities found through in coral. In blood pressure it is a sure remedy. Those who have Mars in 4th, 6th 8th, 11th, 12th houses in their horoscope should wear coral. It is always useful to wear in golden ring. Those who have Mars-Moon combination in a sign should wear in silver ring. Tuesday is the best day to wear coral. It should be worn in 3rd finger in right hand. Some propose to wear in left too. Position of Mars should be judged in horoscope. If Mars position is already strong, then it is not necessary to wear.

Coral sets right the palpitation of heart and lessens the heat of the body. It is useful in piles too and by immersing in water pot can be used for drinking water.

Corals are of many red hues. Blood-like coloured coral is harmful. By wearing it accidents may happen hence less dark colour like vermillion (*sindoor*) is useful. The astrologer should be consulted before wearing coral. He will advise you through your horoscope according to the position of Mars because the deep red coral increases irritation, fear, etc. It is formed in sea by aquatic creatures.

In place of coral red *Akik* can also be worn. Coral also controls blood circulation like *rudraksha* and thus helps in strengthening the heart too.

Emerald (Panna). Emerald is the gem prescribed for Mercury. When memory is weak, with idleness, nervousness, unhappiness on face, impotency, and intolerance then emerald should be worn in gold.

Emerald is of green colour and has the power to absorb heat. It is inspiring and destroys many diseases. Those whose Mercury is weak or with malefics or aspected by them or Mercury be in 6th, 8th, 12th houses then wearing of emerald is essential. It is also useful in, accounts work, business matters, family adjustment, and removal of evil spirits. If worn by pregnant lady the delivery pain is less. It is also helpful in blood purification and urinary, diseases to some extent.

Emerald should be worn on Wednesday. The Nakshatra should be of Mercury such as *Hasta, Revti, Jyestha*. The procedure should be as of other jewels like ruby, pearl, coral, etc.

The substitute of Emerald is *peridot* or in Persian *Jawarjad*. The other substitute is *Vairaj*. Emerald is very useful for mental peace. It should be worn in little finger of Mercury in gold.

Topaz. Topaz is the valuable gem of Jupiter. It is very useful for making social adjustments of life. It helps in making friends, increasing intelligence and popularity. When the person is afraid of envy of officers and has the ideas of doing ill to others, idleness, anxiety, undoing tendency increasing, mental disturbance, sorrow, paralysis, etc. are troublesome then Topaz should be worn in golden ring in first finger of the right hand.

Topaz gives relief in fatigue, diminishes bad habits such as gambling, wine, conflict, enmity, loss of money, etc. When there is obstacle in education, promotion, suffering from many diseases as asthma, T.B., cough, not getting success in writing, editorship, publication, etc. then wear topaz.

Topaz is the indicator of happiness, luck, prosperity. Ladies may wear topaz to get happiness from their husbands. Topaz purifies the mental, spiritual and intellectual faculties. It is fit for heart and wind troubles. It is also helpful in nasal diseases and jaundice.

Topaz should be worn on Thursday, *Pushya Nakshatra* specially in bright moon fortnight or *Shuklapaksha*. Jupiter is divine planet hence Topaz is powerful in attracting the person towards *satwic* (virtuous, rightous) views in life.

Topaz is substituted by *Sunela*. When ring is made worship it like deity and recite *japa* of Jupiter 16,000 times.

Diamond. Diamond is the most glittering and costly gem. If Venus is weak in the horoscope then diseases of secret parts of the body are common in the patient. He becomes weak due to lack of semen. Weak Venus gives attraction towards opposite sex. If in male Venus is weak or excessively powerful in both positions the person desires to have sexual intercourse with many ladies. Likewise is the case with ladies. Due to this generally family life is disturbed and the subject has excessive sexual desire in his mind all the time.

Diamond should be worn when Venus is in transit in her own sign Taurus or Libra or in exalted sign Pisces. The auspicious day should be Friday, the *nakshatras* should be of Venus, e.g., *Bharni, Poorvashada, Poorva Phalguna*, and worn in golden ring.

Diamond destroys all the diseases concerning sexual senses. It is also useful in constipation, weakness, lack of blood, wind and cough troubles, dysentery, poison, hydrocele, ghost and spirits, paralysis and epilepsy. Diamond should be worn in the morning after worshipping it fixed in the ring with japa of "Om Shum Shukray namah" (ॐ शुं शुक्राय नमः). The total *japa* of Venus is 20,000 times which should be performed before the wearing of the ring.

Venus is a materialistic plus spiritualistic planet. It is known as female planet hence all the prosperity of the world may be gained by the grace of the planet Venus. It is materialistic too. So strong Venus gives the subject all the comforts of the world. It is also *karaka* for vehicles and accidents may happen. Venus gives success in the field of love, materialistic prosperity, art, music, film, painting, etc.

The substitute gem of diamond is Turmali. It is light blue and influencing but only gents can wear it.

Sapphire (Neelam). Sapphire is also powerful just like diamond. Sapphire is the indicator of courage, consistence and horror. It diminishes the difficulties and diseases produced by weak position of Saturn in horoscope. It is worn on Saturday in *Dhanishtha, Sravana, Uttrashada, Swati, Vishakha* and *Chitra nakshatras* in golden five metal or iron ring as the case may be. It indicates favour or opposition in dream on the wearing day. If in dream the indication is not favourable then should not be worn further.

Sapphire is beneficial in fever, hiccups, weakness of brain and nervous system, coma, T.B., melancholy, bronchitis, and disturbance of bilious, memory and mind.

The substitute of sapphire is *Jamuniya* of blue colour like sapphire. It ensures victory over enemies, and is killer of diseases. It should be worn in iron or steel ring in third finger, the finger of Saturn.

Saturn is the disease giving planet. Hence when Saturn is weak in 6th, 8th, 12th houses or with their lords the diseases are born and in *mahadasa, antardasa, prtyantardasa* or *Sadesati* and *Dhaiya* of Saturn sapphire should be worn. For those who are unable to purchase it the ring of iron of horse shoe should be worn in third finger.

Before wearing the gem, worship it and *japa* the *mantra* of Saturn "Om Sham Shanye Namah" 19,000 times. Then after wearing *japa* for 108 times daily ॐ शंशान्ये नमः. Sapphire should be worn after consultation with an expert astrologer who has full knowledge about gems.

Zircon (Gomed). Zircon is soft and transparent, without leaves and is somewhat heavy. Clarity of the best zircon is like the urine of cow. It should be somewhat yellow, orange and transparent. Small, not clear, with dots or lines, shadowless, dried, unlighted, torn should not be weared.

By wearing zircon success in getting love and happiness from spouse, victory in litigation, freedom from diseases, etc., is achieved. As we know zircon is concerned with *Rahu,* the most strong malefic. So zircon clears the way of success in difficulties suddenly produced by *Rahu.*

The ash of zircon is useful in many diseases such as epilepsy, melancholy, madness, wind trouble, eye disease, piles, weakness, syphilis, fever and physical or mental weakness. When *Rahu* is harmful according to horoscope in transit or *mahadasa, antardasa* of *Rahu* is in order, then wear zircon in five metal made ring in third finger in *Shatbhisha, Swati, Aridra,* nakshatras with the *japa* of "Om Ram Rahwe Namah" (ॐ रां राहवे नमः) 18,000 to 1,25,000 times.

Cat's eye (Lahsuniya). When *Ketu's* position is weak in the horoscope then cat's eye is worn. It is beneficial and killer of diseases of secret parts, hydrocele, cough, cold, diabetes, impotency, eye disease, obesity, constipation, pregnancy pain, mysterious diseases which are out of the grip of doctors and also eliminates ghosts and spirits.

Like zircon it is also worn in five metal ring gold and iron too in *Ashwini, Magha, Mool nakshatras* or when Moon is in Sagittarius or Pisces signs in transit.

Colour Therapy

Sunlight is the laboratory of nature. There are seven basic colours found in the sunlight. Red, white, blue, green, yellow, orange, red-yellow, etc. These colours inspire us in many ways. Sunlight is beneficial to our body. Each colour has its special characteristics as following :

Blue and yellow colours when are mixed they make green colour. Green colour gives light sleeping, keeps away from mental tension. It is helpful in fever, wounds, injury, cold, cold fever, sexual diseases, cancer, etc., and helps in increasing eyesight. It is the colour of peace and control. It helps in reducing filling of wounds and pains in dysentery, asthma, breathing, high blood pressure, skin diseases.

Red colour. It is hot in nature. Deep red gives excess irritation and anger. It is irritating and increases blood circulation.

It gives heat to calm persons. It helps in treatment of blood circulation, irritation, low blood pressure, rheumatism, paralysis, anaemia and T.B.

Blue colour. Blue colour is helpful in keeping mind quiet. It is the colour of persistence, thought, and is the colour of Saturn.

Rosy colour. It is the colour of pure love and attracts peacefully.

Dust colour (Matmaila). It is the colour of passion and attachment.

Yellow like lemon. It is the colour of higher intellect and is the colour of Jupiter.

Orange colour. It is the colour of selfishness.

Almond colour. It is the colour of dislike and disinterest.

Green colour. It is the colour of sympathy, religious devotion, spiritualism and mysticism and awakening. Deep green colour sometimes is cheating and envy awakening colour of Mercury.

Yellow colour. It is helpful in controlling the senses, and treatment of brain, liver, backbone, kidney, spleen, stone, hernia, appendicitis, etc.

Deep yellow. It is helpful in T.B., hydrocele, leucohoea, eye disease, skin diseases.

Purple colour. It is helpful in nervous diseases, mental disturbance and melancholy, insomnia, T.B., etc.

Treatment by Coloured Bottle's Water

Fill bottles with water and different colours and keep them in sunlight for three or four hours (Colour not water but use bottles of different colours). Then that water may be drunk as medicine for different diseases. It may also be used in washing ulcers, wounds or with a clothed cover. Water from red coloured bottle is useful in swelling of skin. It may be used in drinking and washing the skin. Water from yellow coloured bottle is helpful in constipation, breathing, urinary disease. Water from blue bottle is helpful in skin diseases, comfortable in sleeping. Water of orange coloured bottle is helpful in old rheumatism disease. Water of green coloured bottle is helpful in cold, eye disease, syphilis. Water of purple coloured bottle is useful in nervous diseases.

Treatment by Coloured Fruits and Vegetables

Red coloured fruits and vegetables. Watermelon, cherry, red berries, carrot.

Orange coloured fruits. Mango, *mausami,* orange, etc.

Yellow coloured fruits. Lemon, grapes, papaya, plantain, pumpkin.

Green coloured vegetables and fruits. Green vegetables like, spinach, bhindi, beans, *Toroi*. cabbage, lettuce, bitter gourd and green mango.

Purple coloured fruits and vegetables. Black berries, grapes, brinjal purple carrot.

Clothes should be used of your name's colour sign.

Those born on Sunday, on 1-10-19-28 , 4-13-22-31 dates and Leo sign should wear white clothes. It will help in keeping good health.

Those born on Monday on 2-11-20-29, 7-16-25 dates and Cancer sign should also wear white clothes.

Those born on Tuesday on 9-18-27 dates and Aries and Scorpio signs should wear light red coloured clothes.

Those born on Wednesday on 5-14-23 dates and Gemini and Virgo signs should wear light green coloured clothes.

Those born on Thursday on 3-12-21-30 dates and Sagittarius and Pisces signs should put on light yellow coloured clothes.

Those born on Friday on 6-15-24 dates and Taurus and Libra signs should wear white or yellow coloured clothes. Friendly colours as yellow, black and blue can also be used.

Those born on Saturday on 8-17-26 dates and Capricorn, Aquarius signs should wear slightly black-blue clothes. Friendly colours are yellow and green can also be used.

In this way make the environment favourable by colour therapy by colouring walls of the house, wearing clothes, having screen on gate, windows, bedsheets, etc. we can make ourselves healthy, wealthy, wise and comfortable.

Urine Therapy

Urine therapy is the old system of remedies found in Ayurvedic text *Bhava Prakash* where it is explained "Vishaghna Rasayan" for urine. It is a part of Damar Tantra explained by Lord Shiva to Mother Parvati known as "Shivambu Kalpa Vidhi".

"Vishagna Rasayan" means destroyer of poisons when used as a remedial measure with some herbs. As a remedy our urine is like a chemical syrup which destroys all the poisons produced in our bodies while eating, drinking and taking so many other harmful things into our bodies.

Urine is the best remedy for many chronic diseases as eczema, dysentery, cholera, ulcers in mouth, lips, feet, tumours in any part of the body and even cancer and AIDS.

In urine, urea, sodium, potassium, calcium, vitamins, enzymes and hormones are found which are of great importance for vitality in our bodies.

It contains antibiotics and antigens which help in containing virus, bacteria and other diseases. Medical experts and scientists found many valuable elements in urine. Urine is not a waste product in our bodies but a valuable remedy free of charge given to each individual by nature. Our *yogis* and *rishis* used urine as medicine for thousands of years but this therapy remained kept hidden.

Urine may be taken as medicine against all infectious diseases as preventive cure.

How to Take Urine as Remedy?

In minor illnesses like cough, cold, gas, fever, indigestion, enema should be given with warm water fifty per cent and urine fifty per cent. This procedure should go for 2-3 days and no food should be taken. Only water can be taken. After breaking the fast, juice of fruits, milk or water of *moong dal* should be taken.

For diseases like cancer, tuberculosis, asthma, heart and kidney, diabetes, skin diseases the above-mentioned method is applicable. In treatment period all the urine should be stored. In these diseases the stored urine should be rubbed on the skin of the body from head to foot for one hour for seven days.

Old urine is the most useful remedy for all the skin diseases.

Besides urine may be used as lotion in shaving, eye and ear troubles, pimples on face, mouth wash for dental trouble, sinus trouble, rheumatic, muscular pain, burns, piles, fistula, snake bite and scorpion poison.

Ladies can use it in leuocorrhoea and menstrual disorder. Mouth washing should be done before sleeping in the night.

While treatment of skin diseases or the other diseases some kind of reaction may take place but this should not be of worry. At this time no other medicine should be taken. In skin diseases old urine should be rubbed on affected places.

During urine treatment only simple light food should be taken. Fruits, salads, raw vegetables are necessary and bread, biscuits, jams, fried and spicy foods be avoided. Wine and tobacco must be stopped.

Wynhousen of the U.S.A. declared, "Urine therapy is the quickest way to cure any disease."

Our former Prime Minister, the late Mr. Morarji Desai who used to take urine as remedy declared this fact in 1978, in U.S.A. when he went on a visit there. He accepted the fact that secret of his health and long life was the drinking of his own urine as a free gift to man.

For further guidance readers may contact Water of Life Foundation India, 377-B.J Shankarshet Road, Mumbai - 400002 founded by Dr. G.K. Thakkar, an expert in urine therapy.

Therapy of Acupressure

Therapy of acupressure is the oldest system of self-treatment in India. This is very simple and you can control your disease yourself. Our palm is the mirror of our body where our soul or *pran* works according to the nervous system. In the palm there are certain fixed places which work like a switch of burning light connected to our body nerves. We feel sometimes that there is pain in certain parts of the palm but due to lack of knowledge of acupressure we are unable to comprehend the diseases striking and progressing in our bodies. For each disease striking numbers are given. For that disease's treatment press your other hand's thumb on that part of palm for one to two minutes daily for three-four times continuously for two weeks. You will see that there is relief from that disease. No doctor is needed for this. For cold, tonsils, cough, sinus 1 to 7, 34 and tips of all fingers.

Cold fever—Bronchitis 1 to 7, 30, 34

Malaria —1 to 7, 37

Headache—1 to 7, 22, 23, 25, 27, 34

Gas trouble, Stomach pain, loose motion, vomiting—19 to 23 (all) i.e. 19, 20, 22, 23

Jaundice—22, 23, 26, 27

Acidity, Hypertension—22, 23, 25

Constipation - Press on chin 3 to 4 times

Appendix/Allergy—21.

Menstrual disorder —9 to 16

Stone, urinary disease—11, 18, 26

Asthma, sneezing, T.B.—1 to 7, 30-34

Fatigue—37

Diabetes—25-26

Epilepsy—Fits - 37

Anaemia—10

Piles—Rub 8 nails of 4 fingers on to each other

Hernia—Rub 8 nails of 4 fingers on to each other

Hair loss—Rub 8 nails of 4 fingers on to each other

B.P. High—3-4-8- 25 - 28

B.P. Low—3-4-8 - 22-23-25-28

Heart Attack—All points + 36 twice a day

Eye trouble—35

Ear trouble—31

Rheumatism/Arthiritis/Paralysis/Polio—Both palms and toes.

The best way is to press the palm daily evening + morning for 1 or 2 minutes.

Sinus point at the top of fingers and thumb

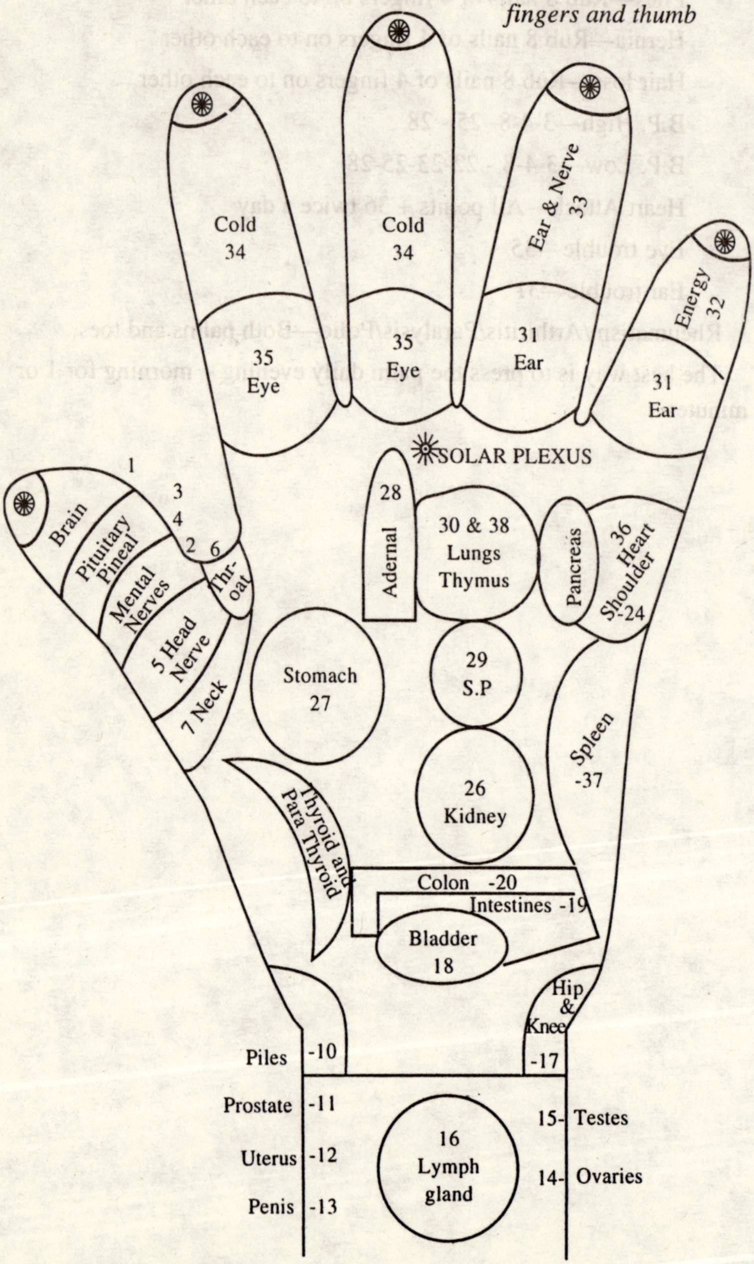

As palm is the mirror of the body so is the soles of both feet. In body in which part is pain or disease rub in sole on right or left as the case may be.

Sinsm Head & Brain Area

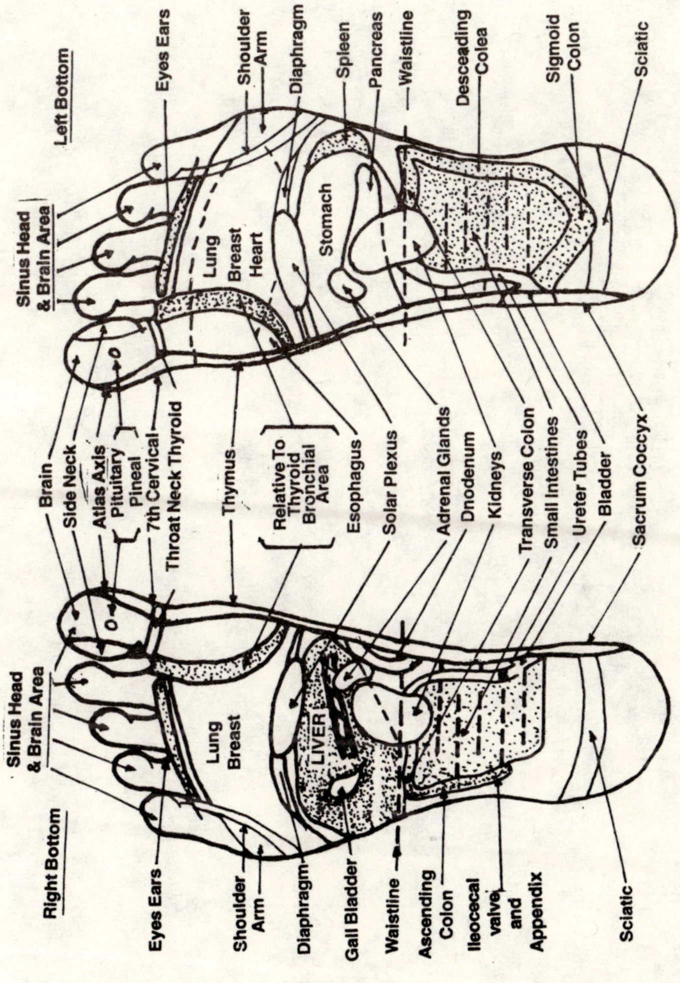

10

Mantra, Yantra

We have described earlier the facts of sufferings due to our sins or the bad actions of previous lives. By the study of horoscope we can know due to which planet we are in the grip of sufferings and diseases.

Sun. If the Sun is responsible of our sufferings and diseases it is known by the position of Sun in the horoscope through *Mahadasa, antardasa, prtyantardasa, sookshma dasa* or in transit. Thereafter wear ruby in golden ring in first finger. Donate *jaggery*, red cloth, red sandal, gold, copper, saffron, coral, and recite the *Mantra "Om ghrini suryay namah"* (ॐ घृणि सूर्याय नमः) 7000 times for peace of Sun in *Home Samidha* (wood) of *Ark (Akanda)* to reduce its effect. Sun is the head of all planets and lord of the solar system. *Gayatri mantra* is the *mantra* of the Sun. One lakh twenty-five thousand *japa* of *Gayatri mantra* destroys the bad influence not only of Sun but also of all planets. For *japa* of *Gayatri mantra Deeksha* is necessary. *Gayatri mantra* is as following:

"Om Bhoor Bhuwah Swa Tatsaviturvarenyam Bhargo Devasya Dheemahi Dhiyo Yonah Prachodyat."

ॐ भूर्भुवः स्वः तत्सवितुर्वरेण्यं

भर्गो देवस्य धीमहि धियो योनः प्रचोदयात्

Daily reading of *Suryashtaka Strotra, Surya Sahasranam,* fasting on Sunday and reading *Surya Puran* and abstaining from salt in food will help in decreasing diseases caused by Sun as bile, fever, stomach trouble, heart palpitation, epilepsy, skin diseases, etc.

Surya Yantra

6	1	8
7	5	3
2	9	4

Surya Yantra. Write *Surya Yantra* in the night of Diwali, Holi or during Sun or Moon's eclipse on *Bhoja patra* by *astagandha* (अष्टगंध) or red sandal by making pen of pomegranate Wood. Worship this yantra daily with *Surya Mantra* for 108 times daily but purity of heart is most essential.

Rahu. *Rahu* is the most powerful of planets (though *chhayagraha*). *Rahu* is famous for accidental changes in the lives of human beings. He is the most malefic and an enemy of Sun and Moon. All kinds of sudden loss, harm, and accidents are attributable to it as epilepsy, wind troubles, troubles from evil spirits, small pox, blood disturbances, secret conspiracies, disbelief, sudden attack, etc. If *Rahu* is troublesome, getting sufferings from *Rahu* according to his position in horoscope in his *Mahadasa, antardasa, prtyantardasa,* etc. or in transit is harmful to you then donate seven maize grains mixing, blue clothes, black flowers, *til* oil, iron, *soop,* rugs, *til* in copper pot, horse, jewels. Wear *gomed* (zircon) of 3, 6, 9 *rattie,* weight mixing five metals on middle ring.

Japa 18000 times *Rahu Mantra* "Om Ram Rahwe Namah" (ॐ राँराहवे नमः). Reading the story of *Gajendra Moksha* daily *(Shrimad Bhagwad)* or *Shri Gajendra Mokshawali* written by the author in simple Hindi language in verse form (श्री गजेन्द्रमोक्षावली) will help you in diminishing the bad effects of *Rahu*.

Rahu Yantra

13	8	15
14	12	10
9	16	11

Rahu Yantra. For worship *Rahu* prepare *yantra* on *Bhoja-patra* of pen of pomegranate wood. *Rahu* acts as Saturn in giving troubles and diseases to man. Hence *japa, tapa, hawan, hom, japa* of *Vishnu Sahasranam* or *Gopal Sahasranam* or *Ram Raksha Strotra* is very helpful in *Rahu's Mahadasa*, *antardasa,* etc.

Moon. When diseases are caused by Moon such as cold and cough, lungs trouble, nose diseases, eye and blood diseases, dysentery, mental disturbance, disturbance in daily occupation, family troubles, anxieties and worries then understand that either there is Moon

Mahadasa, antardasa or *prtyantardasa* of Moon is continuing or the *dasa* of lord of that house where Moon is posited in the natal horoscope. Donation of articles such as *bans,* white rice, white cloth, white sandal, white flower, sugar, silver, ox, ghee, curd, conch, pearl, kapoor, etc. is undertaken. The *japa* of Moon 11000 times of the Moon Mantra "Om Som Somay Namah" (ॐ सों सोमाय नमः) should be done. Pearl should be worn in the little finger in silver ring of 4-5 *rattie* in weight. Undertake fast on Monday, worship Lord Shiva, *Japa* of Om Namah Shivay "ॐ नमः शिवाय" should be done daily 108 times without fail. Moon is the lord of Cancer.

Moon Yantra

7	2	3
8	6	4
3	10	5

Moon Yantra. Prepare *Moon Yantra* on Monday on Bhojpatra with pomegranate wood pen. Worship the yantra daily. Yantra also can be engraved on silver plate. Preparation and worship should be when the subject is pure by heart and mind both. Worship of this yantra should be after bath so that in *japa* the mind and body should feel happiness.

If you are a theist then after taking bath daily performing the *japa* of Moon is very necessary.

Ketu. Like *Rahu, Ketu* is also a malefic planet *(Chhayagrah).* It is also called dragon's tail, because *Rahu* is called dragon's head. Diseases which are out of the grip of doctors are caused by *Ketu. Ketu* is *karaka* of hidden, sudden and mysterious diseases, though *Ketu* is also the planet of *Moksha*. Divine power and divine curse too are caused by *Ketu*. Smallpox, skin diseases and many other mysterious diseases are caused by this planet. It shows the conspiracy performed by other hidden methods. Secrecy is the base of this planet. Hence, from whence and when any disease may attack nothing can be said. This planet is the mysterious elements of the solar system.

For propitiating and consoling *Ketu* black flowers, white and black clothes, black sesamum, oil, iron, flowers and clothes of mixed colours may be donated.

Japa of *Ketu Mantra* "Om *Ketu* Ketuwe Namah" (ॐ कें केतवे नमः) 18000 is prescribed.

Ketu Yantra

14	9	16
15	13	11
10	17	12

Wear the cat's eye in five mixed metals ring of 5, 7, 9 rattie.

White flag may be submitted at places of *Siddha*, *Jinda* on Thursday with *prasad* of coconut and *rewdi*.

Ketu is the enemy of Sun and Moon. Hence, when and where disease will attack and the manner in which attack will affect the patient is not known, in the same way secrets of divine God power cannot be known. So for the peace of *Ketu* daily chanting of religious books, fasting, offering meats to little girls will increase the divine power. *Japa* of *Gayatri* and *Maha Mrityunjay mantra* may disclose the mystical secrets of *Ketu*. *Ketu* acts like Mars according to astrology.

Mars. Mars is known as the chief of the army of planets. Fear of enemy, lack of courage, fear of accidents, fractures, wounds, cuts, blood diseases, high or low blood pressure, struggle in life, useless discussion, fights, mental or brain haemorrhage, surgery, all these come within the influence of Mars. Mars is the killer of enemies as also of diseases and enforces ill-effects too.

Mars is called the son of earth (भूमिपुत्र). Hence all the diseases having materialistic origin are the result of the influence of Mars.

For propitiating Mars donate coral, land, wheat, red flower, red cloth, red sandal, gold, copper, saffron, musk, *jaggery* or red colour sweets.

Feed bread with *gud* (jaggery) to red dogs, specially on Tuesday. Read *Hanuman Chalisa, Sundar Kand, Bajrang Van, Shri Hanumant Kavacha, Rahu Raksha Strotra*. Worship Hanumanji with red *sindoor* and light lamp with ghee on Tuesday in Hanuman temple.

Wear coral in golden ring in 4th finger *Anamika* (ring finger) of 3, 4, 5 or 7 rattie weight. Chanting should be done of Mars *Mantra* on *rudraksha mala* "Om am angarkay namah" (ॐ अं अंगारकाय नमः), or

Dharni garbhsambhootam vidhyutkanti samprabham
Kumaram shakti hastam tam mangalam pranamamyham"

धरणी गर्भसंभूतं विद्युत्कांति समप्रभम्

कुमारम् शक्ति हस्तं तं मंगलम् प्रणमाम्यहम्

Mars Yantra

8	3	10
9	7	5
4	11	6

Prepare Mars *yantra* on copper plate and worship it daily like deity. This will diminish diseases and imnrove health.

Mercury. Mercury is the controller of the nervous system in our body. It is very sensitive and polite by nature. Hence when Mercury is in weak position or with malefics or in evil houses or in evil signs the whole of the nervous system is affected and nervousness, obstacles in daily life, opposition with friends, loss in business, diseases of skin, loss of memory, epilepsy, giddiness, failure in examination occur.

For strengthening Mercury donate green clothes, ghee, elephant's teeth, coral, emerald, sapphire, papers and books with green colours, fruits (mostly green in colour) flowers and feed little girls and give them green ribbons.

Worship Lord Ganesh daily with green *durba* (दुर्वा). Read *Ganesh strotra* daily. Have fast on *Ganesh Chathurthi* and Wednesday because nervousness affects memory and weakness in memory affects our intellect. So far bodily as well as intellectual development are concerned do all these acts without delay. Wear emerald in gold in little finger.

Mercury *mantra* is "Om Bum Bhudhay Namah" (ॐ बुं बुधाय नमः) 17000 *japa* should be done daily 108 times this *mantra* must be chanted by you. Mercury is the lord of three *mool nakshatras*. These are *Jyestha*, *Mool* and *Rewati*. *Jyeshtha's* 4th *charan* is not said to be good, *Rewati's* 4th *charan* only and *Mool's* first, second and third *charanas* are not said to be good. *Rewati's* first, second, third *charanas* are good while *Asheesha's* fourth *charan* is good. Those born in *nakshatras* of Mercury should chart *japa mantra* of Mercury daily.

Mercury Yantra

9	4	11
10	8	6
5	12	7

Mercury Yantra. Prepare this *yantra* on *Bhojpatra* or engrave on bell metal or bronze plate and worship it. Read *Vishnu Sahasranama* daily *which running* Mercury *Mahadasa* or *antardasa* is in progress. It will give inspiration.

Jupiter. Jupiter is the most benefic and blessing planet filled with divine powers. It gives courage to the subject. It produces many good *yagas* in the horoscope as with more or in quadrants from *Moon gaja keshri yoga*. In quadrants in our signs Sagittarius or Pisces or in his exalted sign Cancer produces *Hamsa yoga* which is called *Pancha Maha Purusha Yoga*. It is also said about Jupiter than when Jupiter in quadrants is powerful then other planets even combined can do no harm to the subject.

"किं कुर्वन्ति ग्रहास्सर्वे यस्य केन्द्रे बृहस्पतिः"

Sufferings from diabetes, liver, fever, cough, brain, heart, disturbance in service, business, occupation, break in service or promotion, degradation or suspension, delay in marriage, progeny, prosperity, litigations in money matters all are due to weak position of Jupiter.

For peace of Jupiter in his *mahadasa, antardasa* or weak in transit donate yellow corn, yellow flowers, fruits, clothes, Pukhraj, haldi, horse, honey, books, salt, sugar, land, umbrella. Undertake fast on Thursday. Read religious books like *Geeta, Ramayana, Vishnu Sahasranama,* daily. Wear Pukhraj in gold ring of 4, 5, 9 rattie in first finger on *Guru Pushya Yoga's* day, i.e. on Thursday when there is *pushya nakshatra*.

10,000 *japa* of Jupiter mantra should be recited "Om Brim Brihaspatye Namah"

(ॐ बृं बृहस्पतये नमः)

Jupiter Yantra

10	5	12
11	9	7
6	13	8

Jupiter Yantra. Prepare this yantra on Bhojpatra or engrave on gold or silver plate and worship it with yellow flowers, fruits. It should be prepared on Diwali, Holi, Sun, Moon's eclipse period or on Guru Pushya day.

Venus. Venus is the lord of Taurus and Libra signs. Pisces is her exalted sign. When sufferings and diseases like sexual in hidden parts of the body, hydrocele, gonorrhoea, loss of wife, diseases to wife occur they are due to the influence of Venus.

Venus is also *karaka* for vehicles. Accidental hurt from vehicles such as bus, train, motorcycle or from other vehicles are due to Venus in relation with other planets.

For placating of Venus planet donate white sandal, rice, white cloth, flowers, fruits, silver, ghee, gold, curd, scent, scented clothes, papers, sugar, cow, land, feeding of cows and little girls with sweets.

Wear diamond 2, 7 rattie in middle finger (finger of Saturn as Saturn is the friend of Venus). Red coloured diamond is very dear and rarely available. Hence in place of red diamond American diamond may be used.

The *mantra* of Venus is "Om Shum Shukray Namah" (ॐ शुं शुक्राय नमः). It should be chanted 20,000 times accompanied with hawan, donation and feeding of girls. Fast of Venus on Friday may be undertaken. Worshipping of Santoshi Mata (deity) has also been prescribed to minimise the bad effect of Venus on man.

Venus Yantra

11	6	13
12	10	8
7	14	9

Venus Yantra. This yantra of Venus should be prepared on silver plate as yantras of other planets are prepared. Venus gives all kinds of materialistic facilities property, happiness from vehicles. Love in arts, music, painting, etc. Thus having performed above-mentioned activities sufferings and diseases caused by Venus may be minimised.

Saturn. Saturn the son of Sun and brother of Yamraj, is the most malefic planet. It is the *karaka* of diseases. He is like the magistrate who punishes people according to their previous deeds through suffering and diseases of many kinds. Saturn is the lord of Capricorn, Sagittarius, Libra exalted and Aries debilitated signs of Saturn. In *Sade Satee* or *Dhaiya, Mahadasa, antardasa* or in transiting over the birth *nakshatra,* birth *rasi*, it causes troubles of many kinds.

For placating of Saturn wear ring of black iron of horseshoe.

Melancholy, loss of dignity, wealth, health, anxieties, rheumatism, mental troubles, fever, paralysis, dyspepsia, disturbance due to wind trouble in feet, gastric troubles, indigestion, loss of appetite, etc. are due to Saturn. Either 19,000 or 23,000 *japa* of Saturn (ॐ शं शन्ये नमः) "Om Sham Shanye Namah" should be recited.

Donate blue, black things as iron, black clothes, oil, umbrella, fruits and sesamum, *urad*, black shoes, woollen clothes.

Wear blue saphire, *Neelam* either in gold or silver ring in middle finger of 1, 2, 5, 10, 11 rattie and care should be taken before wearing ring. Hence wear ring of black horse's shoe.

Saturn Yantra

12	7	14
13	11	9
8	15	10

Prepare this yantra on Bhojpatra worship it then wear in right elbow with black cloth or engrave on five metal plate and worship with *mantra* of Saturn.

Other Disease Destroying Mantras and Yantras

Goswami Tulsidas in *Ramcharit Manas* said, मंत्रमहामणि विषय ब्याल के मेटत कठिन कुअंक भाल के means remembering name of God (Rams') is just like a great lighting jewel for serpent of passion and the bad sign written on the head by Bramha destroys itself. There are so many famous mantras, e.g. the poison of snake bite can be dismissed by *mantra*. There are many stories of such type when a man by reading and chanting *mantra* sweeps the poison of snake bite hearing on phone and the snake bit person gets alright. What is this power? This is the power of *mantra* not superstition as some modern educated persons would think.

For happy delivery of pregnant woman. The following *mantra* should be read or chanted 8 times and then the reader should blow his breath on the pregnant lady. The delivery will be happy:

"Om mukta Pasha Vipashashcha Mukta Suryenraimpah
Mukta Sarvam Bhavat Garbhah Ehyehi Marachi Swaha"

(ॐ मुक्त पाशा विपाशाश्च मुक्ता सूर्येणरईमापः
मुक्तर्भ सर्वं भवात् गर्भः एहयेहि मारचि स्वाहा)

In Dysentery when blood exudes. This *mantra* should be chanted 8 times *abhimantrit* and then blown on the patient.

"Kali janni Mahakali Namostute Han Han Dah Dah Shoolam Trishoolen Hun Phat Swaha"

काली जननी महाकाली नमोऽस्तुते
हन हन दह दह शूलं त्रिशूलेन् हुँफट स्वाहा

Disease Destroyer. This mantra is from *Srimad Bhagwad Gita*

"Kutastwo Kashmalmidam Vishyen Samupasthitah
Anarjushtam Aswargam Akeerti Karam Arjun"

कुतस्त्वा कश्मलमिदं विषमे समुपस्थितम्
अनार्यजुष्टमस्वर्ग्यमकीर्तिकरमर्जुन

This mantra will be chanted 25,000 *japam* in 11 days.

To get rid of ghosts and spirits. This has been proven now that there are some mysterious souls who capture the bodies of human beings rather than diseases. To get rid of them *Shrimad Bhagwad Gita's* following *sloka* should be chanted for 15 days daily at least a thousand *Japam*.

"Vayuryamognir Varanah Shashankah Prjapahistwam Namo Namastute

Namoastu Sahasra Kritwah Punashch Bhooyoapi Namo Namastey."

वायुर्यमोऽग्निर्वरूणः शशांकः प्रजापतिस्त्वं नमो नमस्ते

नमोऽस्तु सहस्र कृत्वः पुनश्च भूयोऽपि नमो नमस्ते

To get rid of ghosts and spirits write this yantra on white paper at noon before the patient and speak before him so that he may hear and thereafter burn it before the patient. The use of this yantra can also be done before the patient whose disease is out of the grip of doctors or when doctors are not successful in diagnosing the disease.

Yantra

1	15	14	4
12	6	7	9
8	10	11	5
13	3	2	16

Read this mantra:

"Bhoot Pishach Nikat Nahi Awe

Mahavir Jab Nam Sunawe

Nashe Rog Harae Sab Peera

Japat Nirantar Hanumat Veera"

भूतपिशाच निकट नहीं आवे महावीर जब नाम सुनावे

नाशै रोग हरै सब पीरा जपत निरन्तर हनुमत वीरा

Yantra of Adhashishi (migraine). Given below is the *yantra* of *Adhashishi*. This *yantra* and *mantra* is very *useful*. After preparing the *yantra* read this *mantra* 21 times and keep the *yantra* on the limb of the patient within the clothes.

Mantra: "Om namo phalsavo (ॐ नमो फालसावौ).

Yantra

21	41
81	181

1	15	14	4
12	6	7	9
8	10	11	5
13	3	2	16

Yantra of Tijari (Fever repeating after 3 days)

Write this *yantra* on the leaf of *Nagbel* and after worshipping with scent *(dhoop)* of *gugal* light *(deepak)* and keep bound to limb.

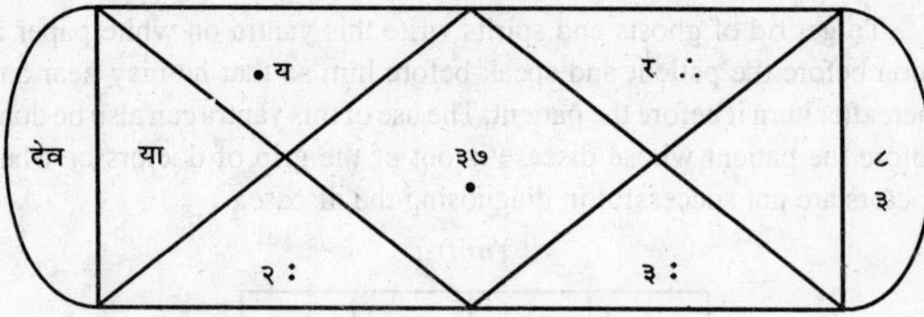

Yantra of epilepsy. After taking bath on Sunday or Wednesday write this yantra with the ink of *gugal,* jaggery and vermilion then worship with *dhoop* of *gugal.* All these acts should be performed before the patient and kept on the limb of the patient. The patient shall be able to gain control over himself. The *yantra* is as follows:

Mantra for piles relief : On Sunday or Tuesday read this *mantra* for 108 times before water and give the water to drink to the patient and to clear the stools too. After 7 times on 7 days, use piles will be treated. *Mantra* is "Om Chhai Chhui Chhalak Chhalai Ahum Ahum Kleem Kleem Kleem Hoon" (ॐ छाई छुई छलक छलाई आहुम आहुम क्लीं क्लीं क्लीं हूं)

Mantra for Small pox : *Sheetla Mata* or *Chechak* is the disease which highly contagious. The small pox turns into big pox or *Badi Mata.* The *mantra's* exercise is for 3 days by reading the *mantra* and placing the hand on the body of the patient. "Om ghat ghat baithee sheetla ferat awe hath Om shreem shreem shreem shabda sancha furo wach"

(ॐ घट घट बैठी शीतला फेरत आवे हाथ
ॐ श्री श्री श्री शब्द सांचा फुरो वाच)

Science of Respiration (Breathing) (*Swara Vigyan*)

Through the knowledge of respiration or *swara vigyan* many diseases can be cured without medicines in a very simple way. This is the natural simple method of maintaining one's good health by proper respiration or breathing.

We all know that we respire through nostrils, sometimes through right nostril and vice versa. When we respire through right nostril it is called Sun respiration *(Surya swara)* and when we respire through left nostril it is called Moon respiration *(Chandra swara)*. Sun respiration comes through *Pingla Nadi*. Moon respiration comes through *Ida Nadi* and when we breathe from both nostrils it is called *Sushumna Nadi*.

The twelve signs of the Zodiac correlated with science of respiration. For example, Taurus, Cancer, Scorpio, Capricorn, Pisces, Virgo are Moon respiration signs *(Chandra swara rasis)* and Aries, Leo, Aquarius, Libra, Gemini, Sagittarius are Sun respiration sign *(Surya Swara Rasis)*. For the success of work, treatment taken in hand should be followed according to the principle of respiration in which *tithi* (Hindi date) on which day in which transit of Sun, which respiration—right or left should be in order, that should be known to the practitioner of respiration.

Principle of Respiration

1. On Monday, Wednesday, Thursday, Friday left respiration should be in order to get success in all work. This means that the respiration should be from left nostril, i.e. *(Moon swara)*. If it is bright Moon fortnight on these days that will be better.

2. On Sunday, Tuesday, Saturday right respiration should be in order *(Surya swara)* then success in moving actions *(Char Karya)* is sure. If dark Moon fortnight falls on these days that will be better for moving action, i.e., temporary works.

3. Some scholars of science of respiration tell that if both nostrils are in order in respiration on Wednesday that is too good.

4. On bright Moon days *(Shukla Paksha)* the respiration should be as follows:

Tithi	*Respiration at Sunrise*
Prtipada - 1	Moon respiration (Left *Swara*) *Ida Nadi*
Dwitiya - 2	——do——

Tritiya - 3	——do——
Chaturthi - 4	Sun respiration (Right *Swara*) *Pingla Nadi*
Panchmi - 5	——do——
Shasthi - 6	——do——
Saptmi - 7	Moon respiration (Left *Swara*) *Ida Nadi*
Ashtami - 8	——do——
Navami - 9	——do——
Dasami - 10	Sun respiration (Right *Swara*) *Pingla Nadi*
Ekadasi - 11	——do——
Dwadasi - 12	——do——
Triyodashi - 13	Moon respiration (Left *Swara*) *Ida Nadi*
Chaturdasi - 14	——do——
Poornima - 15	——do——

5. On dark Moon days *(Krishna Paksha)* the respiration should be as follows:

Tithi	***Respiration at Sunrising time***
Prtipada - 1	Sun respiration *(Surya Swara) Pingla Nadi*
Dwitiya - 2	——do——
Tritiya - 3	——do——
Chaturthi - 4	Moon respiration *(Chandra Swara) Ida Nadi*
Panchmi - 5	——do——
Shasthi - 6	——do——
Saptmi - 7	Sun respiration *(Surya Swara) Pingla Nadi*
Ashtami - 8	——do——
Navami - 9	——do——
Dasami - 10	Moon respiration *(Chandra Swara) Ida Nadi*
Ekadasi - 11	——do——
Dwadasi - 12	——do——
Triyodashi - 13	Sun respiration *(Surya Swara) Pingla Nadi*
Chaturdasi - 14	——do——
Amavasya - 30	——do——

In this way from Sunrise on bright Moon and dark Moon days the respiration right or left as written above in the charts should be kept in mind. It should be done for one hour according to the chart.

(दिन मै स्वर चन्दा चले रात चले स्वर सूर

तो निश्चय ही जानिये मौत बहुत है दूर)

It means if in daytime mostly moon respiration is in order and in night sun respiration is in order then it is sure that the person will live long. His death is far from him. During sexual intercourse man's Sun respiration and woman's Moon respiration make them healthy and beloved to each other.

Son Birth. Fifth day from menstrual period husband and wife should engage in sexual intercourse when husband's right nostril respiration and wife's left nostril respiration is in order. Then birth of a son is sure.

This system is very easy and you can check it any time in 24 hours which respiration *(swara)* is in order. The nostril from which long breathing is flowing the same *swara* (respirations) is in order. It may be right or left.

Check in fever. When you are suffering from fever see which respiration is flowing? If right is flowing thenclose it by putting your first finger's tip on the nostril from which long breathing is coming out and try to breathe from the other nostril. In this way fever will be lessened. If in fever left nostril is expiring then there is cold fever and if right nostril is expiring then there is hot fever. When left respiration *(Chandra swara)* is running then do auspicious and permanent work and when right respiration is in order then ominous job should be done. And when both nostrils are expiring from *Sushumna Nadi* then be done nothing except devotion to God. This is ominous and curse can be given in this position, otherwise, man may get success in spiritual fields.

In left respiration do. Permanent job as to purchase ornaments, go to far-off lands, house construction, well digging, *Rath yatra,* pilgrimages, etc.

In right respiration do. To meet with your boss or officer, gambling, selling of animals, *mantra, tantra, yantra* preparation, exercises, etc.

Walk in interview or meeting with boss. In these cases when you go from your home then from which nostril long breathing is running then the feet of that side should be come in first then the other and when your right respiration is in order then stand by the right side and when left respiration is in order stand by the left side of the person taking your interview. In this way success can be achieved easily.

In fire. When anywhere by chance of heat or fire is raging then on the side of fire in which side the nose breathing long on that side put inside the breath by drawing it from outside and then taking a little water in a small pot read the *Mantra*:

उत्तरस्याग्चदिगभागे मारीचः नाम राक्षसः

तस्य पुत्र पुरीराभ्यां हुतः वह्नि स्तम्भं स्वाहा

seven times on water and put the water on fire by throwing respiration. In this way fire will stop and loss will not take place.

In travelling. When right *swara* (respiration from nostril) is in order do not go to west and south and when left *swara* is in order do not go to east and north. In this way troubles and loss in travelling may be minimised or cancelled.

In Moon *swara* go on long journey and in Sun *swara* go on short journey.

Signal of death. If for 30 days continuously the Moon *swara* (left nostril respiration) is in order then the persons respirating thus will die within a month. If for 18 days continuously the Sun *swara* (right nostril respiration) is in order the person will die within a month.

In this way by experiencing the right and left nostrils you can be benefited by changing or using the above said methods and can get success and victory over enemies. Check your *swara* according to this and act accordingly. Remember the following:

(1) Take food when right respiration is in order. Drink water when left respiration is in order. Sleep while right respiration is in order.

(2) The knowledge of respiration leads to super knowledge of the five elements—Earth, Water, Fire, Sky and Wind. The earth element is in *mooladhar chakra* and causes elephantiasis and jaundice. Water element is in *swadhisthan chakra* and causes diseases through excess feeling of relations, dropsy, diabetes, etc. Fire element is over the water and causes constipation, fever, etc. Wind element is near *Anahat chakra* and causes bronchities, influenza, etc. Sky element is in *vishuddha chakra* above of the four elements. Hence *yogasans* and science of respiration are deeply correlated to each other and help in keeping our health good.

PART III
MISCELLANEOUS

11

Horoscope of Doctors

It is true that in the world there are many persons who teach or tell us to do this or that thing but they do not act according to what they say or teach others. Tulsidas has said in *Ram Charit Manas*—

पर उद्देश कुथल बहुतेरे
जे आचरहिं ते नर न घनेरे

The meaning is clear as mentioned above. Example is better than precept. First apply rules in your life then ask others to do. It will have influence over others as Mahatma Gandhi said whatever he did and felt in his life.

Friends! Stand and go ahead. Success is in your hands. There is a saying in Hindi -

भोजन आधा पेट कर दुगुना पानी पीव
तिगुना श्रम चौगुन हंसी वर्ष सवा सौ जीव

It means eat till your stomach is half and drink double the water of the food's weight and you undertake three times labour and four times laughter is necessary. In this way you can live for 125 years. If you can't smile you can do nothing. Be positive in ideas and actions. Leave negative thinking. Smiling and patience are more valuable than medicines as the saying goes·

Early to bed and early to rise
Makes a man healthy, wealthy and wise.

Tumour in uterus. I am giving below the example of an operation of tumour in uterus in January 1998 of a lady born on 27-8-1964 in Gemini ascendant with planetary position as following Day : Wednesday; birth time : 1.30 a.m.; Nakshatra : Third quarter of *Revti*.

Ascendant	S	0	1	*Nakshatra*	*Charan*
Gemini	02	13	23	*Aridra*	3rd
Sun	04	09	56	*Magha*	3rd
Moon	11	24	03	*Revti*	3rd
Mars	02	24	10	*Punarvasu*	2nd
Mercury	04	14	21	*Poorva Phalguna*	1st
Jupiter	01	02	38	*Kritika*	2nd
Venus	02	25	02	*Punarvasu*	2nd
Saturn	10	03	56	*(R) Dhanishtha*	2nd
Rahu	02	05	19	*Mrigsira*	4th
Ketu	08	05	19	*Mool*	2nd

Birth Ascendant

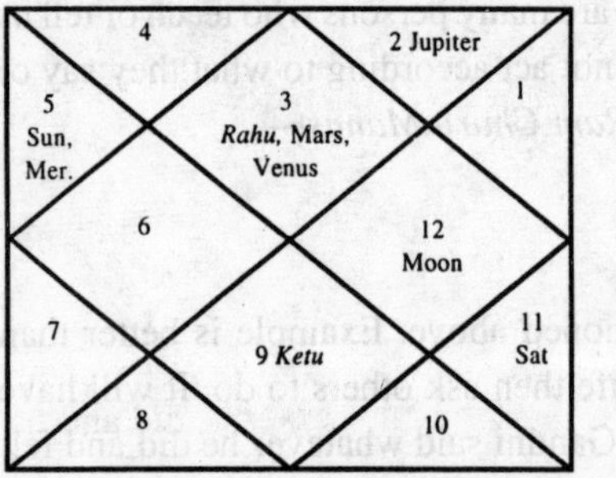

Navamsa

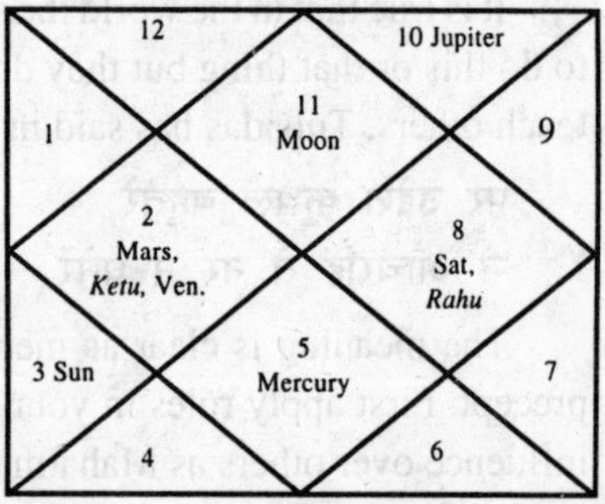

Balance of Mercury : 7 years, 5 months and 23 days according to *Vimshottari Mahadasa* system. The operation of tumour in uterus was held in Venus *mahadasa, Ketu antardasa* which was 20-12-1997 to 20-2-1999. The *prtyantar dasa* was of, *Ketu* in January 1998 when the operation was held in January 1998. It has been already mentioned about *Ketu* "All secret diseases which are incurable are caused by *Ketu*". Really the tumour in uterus increased slowly and could not be diagnosed easily. When the pain increased, the tumour was increased more and doctors could hardly know about it.

See that *Ketu* is in *Mool Nakshatra* the 2nd *charan* of *Mool Nakshatra* represents womb (कुरक्षे, कौख) which is inside the uterus of ladies. Mars, *Rahu,* Venus aspect *Ketu*. Mars is the lord of 6th house (house of diseases) showing the indication of operation being in 1st house (body) and aspecting the 4th house (house of belly, stomach). The lord of 4th house is being aspected by *Ketu* and Saturn (*karaka* for diseases). Mars aspects the 8th house too where there is the sign of Saturn and Capricorn. Leo represents belly and Mercury nerves so Sun too is under the aspect of Saturn.

See that the Mars as lord of 6th house (an evil house), Saturn as the lord of 8th house (an evil house) and Venus as lord of 12th house (an evil house) thus the ascendant is under the malinfluence of 6th, 8th, 12th house lords. Because Mars and Venus are in ascendant and Saturn aspects the lord of ascendant, from Moon there is Leo in 6th house which also indicates the disease in belly aspected by Saturn. From Moon in 4th house are *Rahu*, Mars and Saturn. Jupiter's aspect on 4th house could save the body. See in *Navamsa* chart Jupiter and Mercury are in *Vargottama Navamsa*.

In *navamsa* chart too Saturn and *Rahu* are in Scorpio (the 6th house of birth ascendant) aspecting the 4th house where Mars, *Ketu* and Venus are present. In *navamsa* too Jupiter is in 12th house and aspects the 4th house as in birth chart. In January 1998 Saturn was in Pisces (in Moon sign of birth ascendant) and Mars in Aquarius both aspecting the 4th house (belly). Saturn was also aspecting the lord of ascendant Mercury in Sagittarius in January, 1998. Hence operation was inevitable. Besides *Rahu* in Leo in transit in January 1998 made the operation accidentally necessary. In January 1998 all planets were in between *Rahu* and *Ketu* producing *Kalasarpayoga* too. Jupiter in Aquarius in January 1998 could save the person's life as operation was successful, though, about 2 lacs of rupees spent on the operation.

Generally I have seen in the horoscopes of doctors that their 6th house (disease) is connected with lord of *lagna,* 2nd 10th and 11th houses. The argument is that when 6th lord has any relation with 2nd and 11th lords it is proved that the subject earns money through curing diseases. Some doctors have consulted me hence I am giving some horoscopes for readers to study medical astrology.

1. This is the horoscope of Dr. S.K. Sharma, M.S., an expert in surgery of the T. Choith Ram Hospital, Indore (M.P.).

Date of birth of the subject 15-10-1951, *Ishta* 3 *ghatis,* 57 *palas*, Tuesday, first quarter of the *Ashwini nakshatra.*

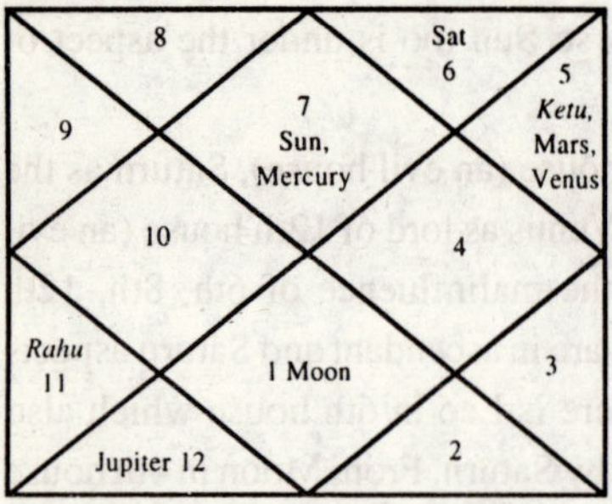

In Ayurveda it has been mentioned that doctor's Mercury should be strong. It should be either in *lagna* or be related with 6th house or its lord. Here Mercury is in *lagna* being lord of 9th and 12th houses lord of 6th Jupiter aspects the 10th house which is its exalted sign Cancer. From Moon the 6th house has been occupied by the disease giving Saturn aspected by 6th lord of *lagna* Jupiter. Lord of *lagna* Venus is with Mars lord of 2nd house which is telling that the subject earns money in surgical operations (Mars being lord of money's house in 11th house of income). Sun-Mercury combination in *lagna* makes subject expert in his work. It is called *Budhaditya yoga* equal to *Rajyoga*. From Moon 11th house is occupied by *Rahu* aspected by *lagna* lord Venus and Mars (Surgeon). I regard Mars as *karaka* for surgery and Saturn as disease giver. Both of these should be connected with 6th house, *lagna* and with their lords.

2. Dr. (Mrs.) Madhu Sharma, M.S., (gynaecologist), wife of Dr. S.K. Sharma, Indore, (female diseases expert) born on Thursday 2-7-1953 at 3.30 a.m., in the third quarter of *Shatbhisha nakshatra*.

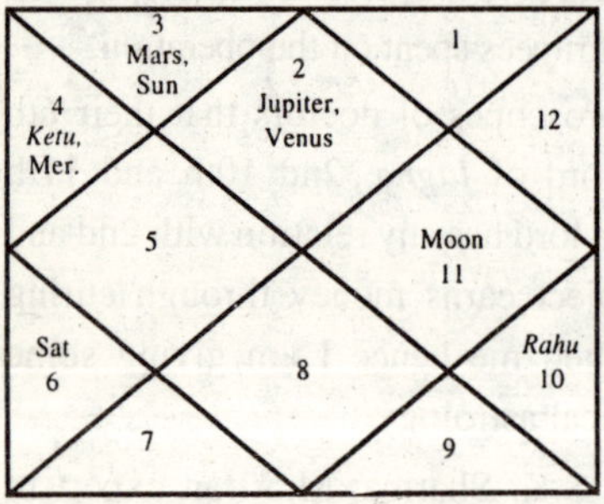

This is the horoscope of a very successful lady doctor. Venus in *lagna* with Jupiter from Moon in 4th house producing *Gaja Kesari Yoga*. Venus in Taurus in *lagna* producing *Malavya yoga (Panch Mahapurusha yoga)*. The lord of 6th Venus in *lagna* is the lord of 11th Jupiter, promising income from curing diseases of ladies. Mars in 2nd house (house of money) also promising coming money from surgical operations. Saturn (causes of diseases) aspecting the 2nd and 11th houses of income and money again promising benefit and income from curing diseases. From Moon in 6th house there is Mercury with *Ketu*. See the Mercury's relation with 6th house either from *lagna* or Moon. Hence it has been proved that the subject is a doctor.

3. Horoscope of a Unani doctor Mohammed Haider who was born on 9-1-1955 at 5.00 a.m.

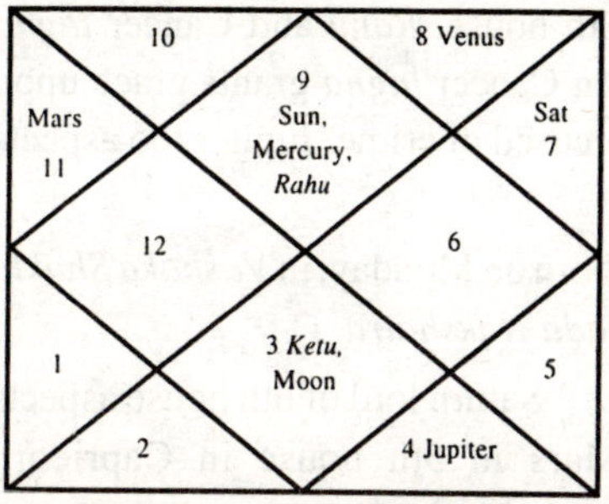

Mercury is in *lagna.* Lord of 6th house aspecting the 6th house. Saturn as lord of 2nd house of money in 11th (house of income) promising to give income from curing diseases. Summary combination in quadrant from birth *lagna* and Moon is important.

4. An expert Ayurvedic Vaidya, Om Prakash Sharma, Ashok Nagar (M.P.) born on 4-2-1953, *Ishta* 8 *ghatis* 01 *pala*, Wednesday, in the third quarter of *Hasta Nakshatra.*

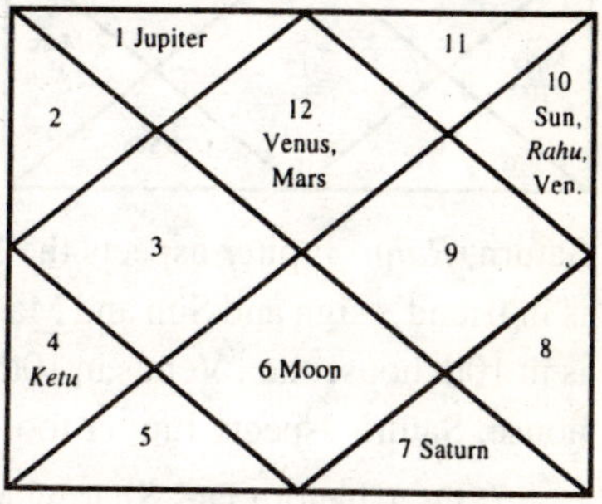

Here see the Sun-Mercury combination is in 11th house. Jupiter lord of *lagna* is in 2nd house of money aspected by Saturn, promising for giving money from curing diseases. Lord of 6th Sun in 11th house too proves incomes from diseases. Jupiter and Saturn both aspect the 10th house. Both are *karakas* for Ayurvedic medicines.

5. Dr. S.M. Tiwari, M.S., J.A. Hospital, Gwalior (M.P.) born on Sunday 26-12-43 at 8.00 p.m. in the first quarter of *Mool Nakshatra.*

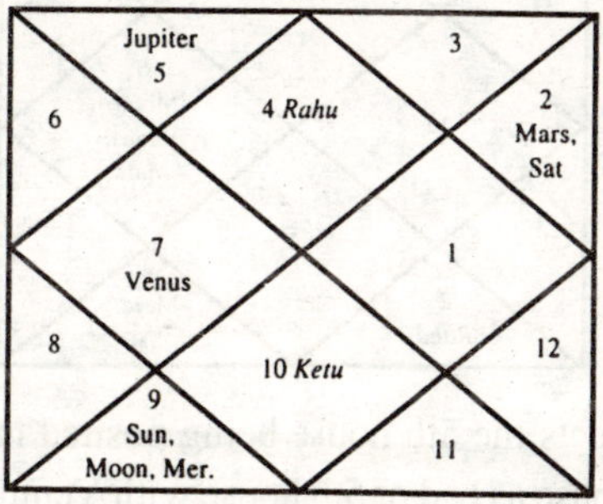

Here Sun-Mercury combination is in 6th house (house of diseases). Lord of 6th house Jupiter is in 2nd house of money aspects the 10th house of profession promising money from curing diseases. Saturn (disease) and Mars (Surgeon) both are combined in 11th house of income again proving an expert surgeon. Venus in 4th in quadrant producing *Malavya yoga (Pancha Maha Purusha yoga).* Lord of *lagna* Moon in 6th house also promises an expert doctor. Mars aspects the 6th house and Saturn aspects *lagna* and 8th house both aspect the 5th house. Mars also aspects the 2nd house. Ninth lord Jupiter thus has been related with 10th lord Mars aspected by Mars and aspecting Mars sign Aries in 10th house. *Rahu* and Cancer *lagna* became *karake* (beneficial) as *Rahu* in Cancer *lagna* grants grace upon the subjects as a king pleased on an accused of crime. Jupiter too aspects Moon in 6th house.

6. Dr. Naresh Jain, M.S., Bhopal born on Monday, in *Vashaka Shukla* 5, in the second quarter of *Poorvashada Nakshatra*.

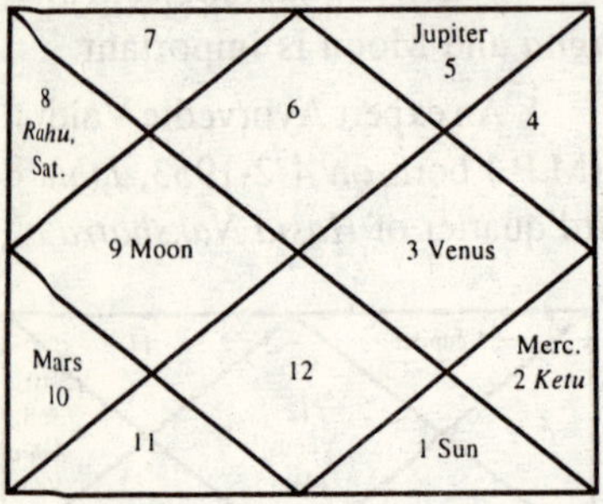

Saturn lord of 6th house aspects Mars in 5th house in Capricorn aspecting the 11th house thus proving curing diseases by surgery and income from medicines. From Moon 5th house is that of sign of Mars in Aries where Sun is posited in exaltation. In 6th house from moon there are Mercury-*Ketu* aspected by Saturn, *Rahu*. Jupiter aspects the Moon and the 6th house. Here Jupiter is in friend's sign and Sun and Mars both are exalted. The 2nd house lord is in 10th house, i.e., Venus in 10th house aspected by Moon lord of 11th house. Saturn aspects Jupiter too.

7. Dr. Chandra Das Sharma M.D., Child Specialist, Bhopal.

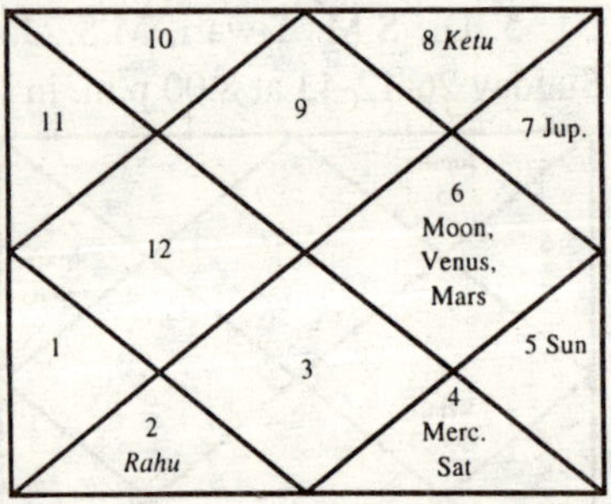

Born in Sagittarius *lagna* Moon sign Virgo. In horoscope the 5th house denotes children. Here Mars as lord of 5th house is posited in 10th house with Moon and lord of 6th house Venus aspecting the 5th house lord of 2nd house. Saturn also aspects the Mars (lord of 5th house), 2nd and 5th houses.

Jupiter as lord of ascendant aspects the 5th house being posited in 11th house. Sitting of Mars in 10th house as bad of 5th house with Venus lord of 6th house is proving as a doctor of children by aspecting *lagna* and 5th house. 10th house denotes profession.

armful and

wels from
Ianthan",
edicine or
drink like
s curse to
, factory
troys not
l prey to
diseases
iibited.
) health.
garettes,
s. Hence

ugs are
secretly
ften are

nds of
an any

tion of
e good

by the
them
ighly
ty.

s that
al to

12

Simple Methods of Keeping Good Health

ter taking dinner or meal and comb your hair
method headache, wind pain will go forever
good.

eason you have to go somewhere at noon in hot
n or handkerchief on both ears or take onion with
unstroke will be certain.

all ill if you put your tongue in the roof of mouth
or half an hour daily early in the morning or at

n constipation, dysentery, stomach pain sit daily
dmasan, sukhasan or *siddhasan,* keep on looking
closing eyelids. In this way you will feel greater
ealthy.

ve the bed at morning see which nostril is having
1) then the palm of that side should be kept on mouth
d. The whatever you will desire, success will be at

ternal fever smell the leaves of the lemon tree early
afternoon from 12 to 3 p.m.Definitely you will be out
within a week.

h and long life walking before sunrise and after sun set
for all the persons. Do not eat anything if you are not
ter after taking good, not in the midst of taking food.

Keep Yourself Away from Any Kind of Intoxication

Nowadays the habit of drinking is increasing like tea. This is h injurious to health.

Wine. Though wine is jewel because it was born with 14 j sea when Devas and Rakshasas were busy in "*Samudra M* according to Hindu mythology, hence when wine is used as m with other medicines it works as nectar. But when the people a fish it destroys lungs and bronchitis, digestion and proves a human beings. Mostly lower class people such as labourer workers, drivers, etc. drink lower type of wine daily which de only their health but also money. They are short lived and fa many diseases. Lungs troubles, heart troubles, T.B. are such which are caused by heavy drinkings. It should be strictly pro

Tambacoo (Tobacco). Use of tobacco is also harmful t Persons mostly take tobacco with betel leaves, in form of bidis, ci hukka, chilam, etc. It gives birth to cancer and many fatal disease smoking, chewking of tobacco should be strictly prohibited.

Bhang, Ganja, Charas, Heroin, etc. All these narcotic d harmful to health. Government has prohibited but these are taken from one place to another by smugglers and drug traffickers and c sold at exorbitant rates.

Human life is a boon. So for keeping good health all k intoxication should be strictly prohibited. Life is more valuable th other thing of the world.

Hence to keep good health and high status in society, intoxica any kind to human beings is not good. It deprives the person of th qualities and economically also makes him poor.

Drinkers and drug addicts should be psychologically treated society. They are also our friends and brothers and we should bring in the mainstream. Most of these persons are tallented and h educated and their talents and qualities will be beneficial for socie

Take Vegetarian Food and Get Healthy Life

Nowadays all the countries of the world are well-known with the fact in spite of non-vegetarian food only vegetarian food is most benefic human health.

Scientists have proved that vegetarian food is nourishment providing food. The facts are as following:

An egg has 13.3 per cent protein while in green gram it is 24 per cent, in ground nut 31.5 per cent, in soyabean 43.2 per cent protein is found. Hence green gram, groundnut, soyabean are more nutritious than egg. Egg eating is harmful to health. It makes a man more sexy than healthy. In the same way egg has 85 per cent calory while wheat has 76.5 per cent calory. Hence wheat is more calorific than egg.

Spinach has 25 times more iron and vitamin A than egg. Hence stop egg eating and take in your food green vegetables, fruits such as onion, cauliflower, cabbage, mint, potatoes, bean, tomatoes, carrot, garlic, apple, mulberry, banana papaya, orange, blackberry. Carrot has much iron and is useful to eyesight.

Heart attack is increasing among non-vegetarians. Hence vegetarian food helps in increasing heart strength. With vegetables, corn, take milk, curd, butter and ghee. Cashewnut, almond, cucumber, grapes, pineapple, chestnut, mango, sugarcane, etc. are more nutritious than eggs, meat, chicken, etc. Non-vegetarian food is for animals like lion, dog and not suitable and nutritious for men.

Vegetarian food is natural food for mankind. Man is lover of nature since birth and nature has given man pure air, water, fruits, flowers, trees to make environment happy and healthy. Vegetarian food balances the body and mind and is cheaper than non-vegetarian food.

For food and nutrition if we kill animals it is violent and against the laws of nature.

Famous Ayurvedic Medicines Useful to Health

Name of the Medicine	*Useful in*
Bhairav Ras	Wind fever, constipation, swelling, bile, pain. To be taken with ginger juice.
Tribhuwan Keerti Ras	Cough and wind fever, pneumonia, influenza, cold fever. To be taken with honey.
Makradhwaj	In cold, bronchitis, old fever, useful for physically weak persons. Very suitable to strengthen heart.
Vasant Malti	It controls old fever with cough. *Vasant malti* with gold ash is more useful.
Praval Bhasma (Coral ash)	Useful in all types of fever.

Name of the Medicine	Useful in
Godanti	It is also useful in cold, cough, headache, flu, malaria, etc.
Loha sav	Useful in strengthening physical and mental powers.
Drakshav	Very useful medicine to be taken specially in winter season for improving health.
Ashwagandharishta	Very useful in heart troubles, weakness.
Arjunarishta	Very useful in balancing blood pressure.
Dashmoolarishta (for ladies)	After delivery of 2 or 3 days ladies generally suffer from fever. For such ladies this medicine is very useful.
Sitopaladi Churna	For cold, cough, fevers and in T.B.
Sudarshan Vati, Amritarishta	For persons suffering from old fevers.
Abhayarishta	In long constipation and piles.
Brahmi Rasayan	For improvement of health.
Yoga Raj guggal, Mahayogaraj, guggal	In gout and paralysis, spleen and liver troubles.
Amlant Vati	In acidity.
Live 52 tablets	In liver troubles and indigestion.

And so on there are many useful ayurvedic medicines which are prepared by Vaidyanath Pharmacy, Dabur, Jhandu, Unjha, Charak, Hamdard, Himalaya Drug Companies, etc.

It is better to take ayurvedic medicines than allopathic medicines. Ayurvedic medicines are not harmful and these drugs have no serious side-effects.

Index